AF323601

MARGARET LAURENCE
AN APPRECIATION

EDITED BY CHRISTL VERDUYN

JOURNAL OF CANADIAN STUDIES
BROADVIEW PRESS

Canadian Cataloguing in Publication Data

Main entry under title:

Margaret Laurence: an appreciation

"A journal of Canadian studies book."
ISBN 0-921149-18-2 (bound) ISBN 0-921149-20-4 (pbk.)

1. Laurence, Margaret, 1926- – Criticism and interpretation. I. Verduyn, Christl, 1953-

PS8523.A86Z75 1988 C813'.54 C88-093515-4
PR9199.3.L33Z75 1988

Second printing August 1988

broadview press
P.O. Box 1243
Peterborough, Canada, K9J 7H5

in the U.S.: broadview press
421 Center St.
Lewiston, N.Y. 14092

Printed and bound in Canada by
Gagné Ltd.

Cover art: Harold Town
Cover design: Louis Taylor
Frontispiece: Harold Town

Table of Contents

Preface

Margaret Laurence had a long and close association with Trent University and the *Journal of Canadian Studies*. This volume is a reflection of the desire of both groups to commemorate and celebrate this association.

After her return to Canada in 1969, Margaret Laurence purchased a cottage on the Otonabee River near Peterborough where she spent summers writing substantial portions of *The Diviners*. A few years later she established permanent residency in Lakefield, a small town ten minutes drive from Trent University. She was awarded an honorary degree by Trent in 1972, and she joined the Editorial Board of the *Journal of Canadian Studies* the following year. Her active involvement in the *Journal* continued until the Fall of 1986, when her resignation was accepted with regret and understanding. In the intervening years, her association with Trent University deepened. She became Trent's first Writer-in-Residence in 1974. She participated generously in the life of the university, attending tutorials and seminars, delivering formal and informal talks, and counselling young writers. Her involvement with Trent culminated in her nomination as Chancellor in 1981.

A few months after Margaret Laurence's death in early 1987, some of her friends and admirers at Trent met to discuss ways of commemorating and celebrating her association with the university community. Many recalled the extraordinary "Margaret Laurence and Friends" weekend held in March 1974 at Trent, at which time over 1500 people attended a series of public readings by writers such as Robertson Davies, Al Purdy, Graeme Gibson, A.J.M. Smith and W.O. Mitchell. A similar tribute to Margaret has been organized for the weekend of March 10-12, 1988, with readings by Alice Munro, Miriam Waddington, Sylvia Fraser, Roo Borson, Robert Kroetsch, and Timothy Findley, among others. Adele Wiseman will deliver the inaugural "Margaret Laurence Lecture," an annual event which will deal with one of four of Margaret Laurence's major concerns: literature, feminism, the peace movement, and ecology. Numerous related events, such as a fund-raising dinner, are being organized to help establish an endowment in Margaret Laurence's name to support a writer in residence at Trent.

This volume is an integral part of the March 1988 celebration in honour of Margaret Laurence. It symbolizes the *Journal of Cana-*

dian Studies' appreciation of her considerable contribution to the work of the *Journal* and reflects readers' and critics' appreciation of her substantial literary *oeuvre.* The essays in the volume span a twelve year period from 1976 to 1988, and are witness to changing critical approaches and attitudes to Laurence's work. Ten of the essays first appeared in the Fall 1978 issue of the *Journal of Canadian Studies* on Margaret Laurence, which was edited by current *Journal* editor Michael Peterman and which quickly sold out. This present volume provides readers with access to most of the essays in that issue, as well as a number of essays on Laurence's work published in the *Journal* in subsequent years. It also includes two previously unpublished articles, by Michael Peterman and Christl Verduyn, and two texts presented by Margaret Laurence to Trent audiences. These are "Books That Mattered to Me," delivered to the Friends of the Bata Library, and the now-legendary "My Final Hour," which was read to the Trent Philosophical Society in March 1983.

Margaret Laurence: An Appreciation would not have been possible without the support of a number of people whose efforts have been greatly appreciated. Michael Peterman should be given double thanks, first for his earlier work in editing the Fall 1978 *Journal of Canadian Studies* issue on Margaret Laurence and, second, for following up the proposal to initiate a series of *Journal* publications on important Canadian topics, which this volume inaugurates. Robert Campbell, an Associate Editor of the *Journal,* provided invaluable advice and assistance both in devising the proposed *Journal* series and in the construction of this inaugural volume. Financial support for the new series of *Journal* book publications has been generously provided by the Samuel and Saidye Bronfman Family Foundation, Trent University, and the University's Canadian Studies Program. All of the contributors are warmly thanked for their cooperation. The Laurence family kindly permitted the use of "Books That Mattered to Me" and "My Final Hour," and the Engel estate gave permission to reprint Marian Engel's essay "Steps to the Mythic." Harold Town generously provided the cover, as a result of Orm Mitchell's initiative. Members of the committee organizing the March 1988 celebration have been supportive, particularly John Wadland. Finally, Don LePan gave early enthusiastic support to this volume and to the *Journal* series, and his cheerful and expert advice have made the *Journal*'s collaboration with Broadview Press productive and rewarding.

Final thanks rest, of course, with Margaret Laurence.

Christl Verduyn
Trent University
Peterborough, Ontario
December 1987

Introduction

The essays and texts in this volume are not arranged chronologically in order of their publication. Rather, they have been ordered so as to follow the evolution of Margaret Laurence's work.

Earlier Writings

The volume begins with "Margaret Laurence's Early Writing: 'a world in which Others have to be respected'" by Patricia Morley. In this essay Morley investigates those works by Laurence associated with her extended experience in Africa. These include *A Tree for Poverty: Somali Poetry and Prose* (1954), *This Side Jordan* (1960), *The Prophet's Camel Bell* (1963), *The Tomorrow-Tamer* (1963), and *Long Drums and Canons: Nigerian Dramatists and Novelists: 1952-1966* (1968). Morley suggests that Margaret Laurence's African writing and her Canadian-based fiction form a seamless fabric and represent together the evolution of a vision which was first shaped in Neepawa, Manitoba. Of Laurence's earlier works, *The Prophet's Camel Bell* is considered by George Woodcock, in his essay "Many Solitudes: The Travel Writings of Margaret Laurence," to be a key to understanding the author's writing as a whole. Like Laurence's *Heart of a Stranger, The Prophet's Camel Bell* reveals the state of mind out of which the author's novels and stories emerged. The third essay of the volume, "The Long Trek Home: Margaret Laurence's Stories" by Patricia Morley, turns attention to Laurence's short stories. Morley establishes a recurring theme both in the short stories and throughout Laurence's fiction: the search for spiritual freedom. W.H. New addresses Laurence's short stories in a precise way in his essay "Text and Subtext: Laurence's 'The Merchant of Heaven'," which explores one of the stories included in *The Tomorrow-Tamer.*

The Canadian Setting

The collection continues with the first of two essays by Clara Thomas. "Pilgrims' Progress: Margaret Laurence and Hagar Shipley" shifts the volume's focus to those novels set in Canada. Thomas's essay scrutinizes the memorable protagonist of *The Stone Angel* – Hagar Shipley. Thomas explores the possibilities of a parallel between author and character. Laurence's heroines –

notably Hagar Shipley – appear to mirror their author's sense of life as a gift and a pilgrimage. The essay also sets the stage for a number of subsequent comparisons between Laurence's work and that of other writers. In her essay, Thomas juxtaposes Laurence's novels with those of an author Laurence herself greatly admired – the British novelist Joyce Cary. Michael Peterman draws attention to the work of another writer Laurence admired – Tillie Olsen. In his essay "'All that happens, one must try to understand': The Kindredness of Tillie Olsen's "Tell Me a Riddle" and Margaret Laurence's *The Stone Angel*," Peterman establishes fascinating parallels between Olsen's novella and Laurence's novel and between the two authors' experiences as women writers, their politics, and their place in their countries' literature and culture.

Evelyn Hinz also considers *The Stone Angel,* this time in conjunction with Margaret Atwood's *Surfacing.* In "The Religious Roots of the Feminine Identity Issue: Margaret Laurence's *The Stone Angel* and Margaret Atwood's *Surfacing,*" Hinz draws upon feminist reconstruction of concepts of human identity and religion in demonstrating the extent to which Laurence and Atwood both concur and differ with feminist revisions. Hinz suggests that while *The Stone Angel* and *Surfacing* quarrel with "God the Father," both novels emphasize the need for religious support systems and locate the cause of contemporary sexism and alienation in the decadence of traditional religious symbolism and authority. Both works present the monotheism of the Judaeo-Christian tradition and the non-ritualistic aspects of Protestantism as problematic features for women. The essays by Hinz and Thomas both point to some of Laurence's lifelong concerns about human religious and spiritual aspirations.

Laurence's political dimension is evoked in Kenneth James Hughes's "Politics and *A Jest of God.*" Hughes draws out what he considers to be the powerful political essence underlying *A Jest of God*'s psychological and apparently apolitical surface. This digging below the surface is also undertaken in an essay by Christl Verduyn on *The Fire-Dwellers.* This novel, not highlighted in other essays included in the volume, has perhaps too readily been labelled Laurence's "somewhat dated housewife and mother" novel. "Language, Body and Identity in Margaret Laurence's *The Fire-Dwellers*" proposes that the novel marks the beginning of the author's exploration, from a distinctly female – not to suggest feminist – perspective, of language and of the reality and fictions of human identity and the female body. *The Fire-Dwellers* reveals Laurence as a forerunner in feminism's revision of language, reality and fiction.

The next three essays address aspects of the last in Laurence's Manawaka series: *The Diviners,* subject of numerous essays and debates. In both Clara Thomas's "The Chariot of Ossian: Myth and Manitoba in *The Diviners,*" and Marian Engel's "Steps to the Mythic: *The Diviners* and *A Bird in the House*," *The Diviners* is approached from the perspective of the mythic. Thomas writes of Laurence's belief in the close interweaving of history and myth in literature. For Engel, it is the streak of gritty realism in Morag Gunn that lifts *The Diviners* into the mythic. Morag is, moreover, "one of the few heroines who achieves the apocalypse of knowing what her life has been about not through the agency of a man, but through her own experience." In dealing with her world, Morag raises Laurence's work "to a higher level through her incorporation with myth, memory and dream." Sherrill Grace also turns attention to Laurence's Morag Gunn in her essay "A Portrait of the Artist as Laurence Hero," which examines the nature of the Laurence hero. As an artist creating out of the very centre of her experience, celebrating the richness of life, Morag exemplifies the Canadian hero who is neither a victim nor an Adam, but one of a long line of builders, working to forge the uncreated conscience of her race.

Overviews

The remaining essays provide overviews of Laurence's work or address overriding features of the body of her writing. In "The Unity of the Manawaka Cycle," David Blewett argues that the Manawaka cycle is unified not only by the centripetal pull of the home town itself, but by the development of a vision of the human condition. This vision reconciles the fragmented nature of ordinary life and a sense of design and purpose in the universe. John Lennox draws insights from the juxtaposition of Laurence's Manitoban world and Robertson Davies's world of Deptford in his essay "Manawaka and Deptford: Place and Voice." For Lennox it is ultimately the voices emanating from Laurence's Manawaka which most authentically articulate the accents and places of the Canadian imagination. For Robert Chambers, in the essay "The Women of Margaret Laurence," Laurence's heroines are particularly memorable among the many fictional characters who reflect religious experience in Canada, not only because of the liveliness with which they are dramatized but also because of the rich diversity of their religious responses. Through the women in her novels, Laurence allows us to begin to comprehend humanity's potential to redeem tragedies of human waste. Susan Warwick provides an invaluable resource in her chronology of selected events in Margaret Laurence's life as a writer. This essay includes an accounting of Laurence's book and periodical publications.

In Her Own Voice

It seemed inappropriate to construct a volume on Margaret Laurence without allowing her to speak for herself. The volume concludes with two splendid examples of Margaret Laurence engaging her friends and community in a direct way. "Books That Mattered to Me" and "My Final Hour" were addresses given at Trent University. It is perhaps fitting to allow Margaret Laurence herself to have the final word in our attempt to celebrate and commemorate her significant accomplishments and her much appreciated association with the *Journal of Canadian Studies* and Trent University. In "My Final Hour," she wrote:

> ... my entire life as a writer has been concerned with my belief that all individual human beings matter, that no one is ordinary... As a writer, therefore, I feel I have a responsibility to write as truthfully as I can, about human individuals and their dilemmas, to honour them as living, suffering and sometimes joyful people. My responsiblity also must extend into my life as a citizen of my own land and ultimately of the world.

Christl Verduyn

Margaret Laurence's Early Writing: "a world in which Others have to be respected"

PATRICIA MORLEY

Margaret Laurence's African writing and her Canadian-based fiction are very much of a piece. Together they represent a seamless fabric, a steady growth and maturation of a way of seeing which was first formed in Neepawa, Manitoba. The Canadian Prairie where her world began is both harsh and beautiful: a land of extremes, of testing, of pride in the face of defeat.[1] This environment, together with the fact that Canadians have never been an imperial power and have emerged relatively recently from their own experience of being colonized, helped to prepare for Laurence's sympathetic understanding of Somaliland and Ghana in the 1950s. At the same time, the prevailing liberalism of Canadian culture bred a naiveté in the young Laurence which the African experience cauterized. In Africa, exposed to puzzlingly different people and cultures, Laurence began to understand herself and her own culture. In Africa she was a stranger, subject to the alienation which she depicts as central to human experience everywhere. In Africa, her recurring themes of strangerhood, exile, bondage, freedom and human dignity took shape and were first expressed, as Laurence herself notes, in non-fiction: "I began to write out of my own background only after I had lived some years away."[2] Above all, Africa deepened her appreciation both of human differences and of shared universals in a world of people both different and similar to themselves. Africa was catalyst and crucible for much of Laurence's work.

In 1954 Laurence published *A Tree for Poverty: Somali Poetry and Prose,* which she called a labour of love.[3] Her translations are the first written expression of this ancient oral literature. Laurence had never experienced a foreign culture before Somaliland. She went there in 1950 with her husband, a civil engineer hired to construct reservoirs or earth dams. Laurence's "Preface" to the 1970 Canadian reprint apologizes for "unwitting

* First published in *Journal of Canadian Studies,* Vol. 13, No. 3 (Fall 1978).

condescending, in the manner of white liberals, out of pure ignorance." Both the 1952 "Introduction" and the later "Preface" stress the significance of human differences, cultural and individual. In commenting on the folk tales, Laurence writes of the pride, courage and humour of the ordinary Somali herdsman in a land where individualism and independence are necessary to survival.

Somali literature reminded Laurence of the deep divisions in human nature. In the folk tales, an individual is commonly both kind and cruel. She terms the paradox a superficial one: "The characteristics of guile and craftiness plus generosity and piety can exist here within the individual person with no lack of harmony. Life is hard.... One later comes to see an underlying realism – a realism that recognizes the presence of both good and evil in the world and in the individual."[4] Neepawa had prepared her for this realistic approach. All forms of human behaviour were to be found in a community such as her home town, which she calls "Belsen, writ small but with the same ink" (*HS* 216).

Many of the individual portraits in her travel memoir, such as the venerable old Somali who extended hospitality to the Laurences after they had been lost for several days, resemble characters in the folk tales. After being disappointed by the generous old man's sanctimonious pride, Laurence recognized the folly of her reaction: "He was not perfectly designed and lifeless like a cardboard cut-out figure" (*NW* 93).

The Prophet's Camel Bell (1963) is probably the most important work to come from Laurence's seven years in Africa. Her African writing includes a fine first novel and a magnificent collection of short stories. But the travel memoir, record of Laurence's two years in the Somali desert, is central because it spans more than a decade in the writer's development. It is based on diaries from the early fifties, but is written out of a later maturity which judges and frequently scorns the initial reactions.[5] It is thus both a spiritual autobiography of a critical decade in Laurence's life, and a portrait of a people. Many of the individual Somalis described in the memoir are not fully understood – Laurence freely acknowledges her deficiencies in this regard – but are nevertheless valued for their ability to endure incredible hardships with dignity and courage.

Laurence's reaction to Africa stems, first and foremost, from her hatred of imperialism, and indeed of any form of oppression, psychological or physical.[6] In this connection we should look briefly at Mannoni's *The Psychology of Colonization* before proceeding to the travel memoir. Laurence acknowledges Mannoni as the only theoretical influence on her work. She read his study in Vancouver in 1960 at the time of the crisis in the Belgian Congo and just before *This Side Jordan* was published.[7] She read with "the shock of recognition," since Mannoni clarified and confirmed her own African experience (*NW* 229). Moved by his book and by the Congo crisis, she wrote "The Voices of Adamo," a story of an African youth who is cut adrift from family and village, taken into an African regiment as a drummer, and suddenly discharged. Adamo's reaction to the 'freedom' which he sees as abandonment and betrayal helps to explain, as does Mannoni's study, the tragic violence which has often accompanied the passage of former colonies to independence.

Like *The Prophet's Camel Bell,* Mannoni's study stems from self-searching. Race relations in Madagascar in the 1940s provided the French ethnographer with parallels between the structure of society and the structure of individual personality. Using two complementary character types, Mannoni explains the 'ingratitude' and hostility of native peoples towards their former masters. Mannoni sees the dependence complex and the inferiority complex as present in everyone in rudimentary form, but most Europeans repress one and most colonized people, the other.[8] The colonial administrator acts paternally, thereby invoking the subconscious hostility that Freud associated with the father figure. When a native is detached from tribal life, secured to a new master, then abandoned, his Oedipal instincts issue in hostility and violence. Mannoni portrays the colonial European as someone secretly convinced of his own inferiority, needing the homage of dependents as ego reassurance, and projecting on those dependents his inner guilts and fears. This fits Laurence's portrait of expatriates in *This Side Jordan* and her African short stories, despite the fact that the novel and many of the stories were written before reading Mannoni. His influence is reflected in her later work, including *The Prophet's Camel Bell, The Diviners,* and "The Poem and the Spear." The latter piece is a long essay about a late-nineteenth-century Somali leader. It was written in 1964 but not published until 1976. In a recent prefatory note to the essay, Laurence links the Somali struggles with those of the Highland clans and the Canadian Métis. She sees all three groups as tribal societies facing imperialist oppressors who have superior weapons, not superior values. Mannoni's *The Psychology of Colonization* is included in the sources for the essay (*HS* 76).

Mannoni strikes another chord which is basic to Laurence's work: the validity of the Other, the difficulty yet the importance of understanding other individuals and cultures. Mannoni writes: "I saw that the problem for human beings, however much they differed from one another, was to acquire, not the ability but the *will* to understand each other. It is as difficult to see something of oneself in all men as it is to accept oneself completely as one is."[9] Laurence's African work reveals the advances in self-understanding and self-acceptance which were fostered by being a stranger on another continent. In her travel book she quotes Mannoni's reference to the colonial's lack of awareness of "the world of Others, a world in which Others have to be respected" (*NW* 277). Over and over, in analyzing incidents and characters, the memoir illustrates her sensitivity to other ways of seeing, to others' pain and joy, the kind of sensitivity whose lack defines the colonial mentality. To illustrate: why should Africans resent someone who feels friendly towards them? "But they looked at me from their own eyes, not mine" (*NW* 32). What does it feel like to offer a cup of water to a woman who may well be dead from thirst the next day? "What I felt, as I looked into her face, was undeniable and it was not pity. It was something entirely different, some sense of knowing in myself what her anguish had been and would be, as she watched her child's life seep away for lack of water to keep it alive" (*NW* 81). How should they deal with their servants' quarrels? "We felt ourselves to be misunderstood, and we knew that we had misunderstood both of them" (*NW* 202). Laurence's ability to write great fiction is due in part to her ability to comprehend imaginatively the Other, something that was nurtured by her African experience.

A verse from "Exodus" stands as epigraph to her most recent collection of essays and supplies its title: "Also, thou shalt not oppress a stranger, for ye know the heart of a stranger, seeing ye were strangers in the land of Egypt." The author's "Foreword" to the collection emphasizes the satisfaction of trying to understand other cultures, just as the writer struggles to understand his fictional characters and to respect them for themselves. A writer, she concludes, is a perpetual psychic traveller, an explorer of the strange lands of heart and spirit. The memoir cautions that "the strangest glimpses you may have of any creature in the distant lands will be those you catch of yourself." The same injunction from "Exodus" occupies a prominent place in the first chapter of *The Prophet's Camel Bell,* a book filled with metaphors of travel, exile, and the search for the Promised Land of fulfilled inner freedom. En route to Somaliland, where she would be a stranger in a strange land, Laurence read for the first time the five books of Moses. The themes and metaphors of the Pentateuch, which belong to desert experience, stayed with her in Somaliland, and thereafter.

The timeless desert with its sand and thorn trees taught Laurence quietness and caution. With that note of self-mockery which often belongs to her fictional narrators, she describes her efforts to arrange their new home; she contrasts her buzzing with the desert calm: "I might enter its quietness or not, just as I chose. Hesitantly at first, because it had been my pride to be as perpetually busy as an escalator, I entered" (*NW* 34). Local wildlife concealed unsuspected dangers. She began to see that the quiet hills required a person to tread carefully. Especially with people. Her initial brashness, a verdict Laurence later applied to her behaviour when she was new to Africa, often failed to elicit the desired information. Finally she perceived her mistake: "People are not oyster shells, to be pried at – I no longer questioned people in this glib fashion" (*NW* 50, 78).

The rigours of desert survival evoked a deep response in the woman from the Canadian Prairie who had been raised amid drought and depression. Laurence describes her grandparents' generation as people who had inhabited a wilderness and made it fruitful, people whom she loved and valued because they were great survivors (*HS* 16). Survival included human dignity, human warmth. Laurence also admired the Somali toughness, their ability to eke out life, their refusal to die easily (*NW* 173). She respected their places of worship, brushwood circles of thorn boughs. Faced with medical problems well beyond the range of her first aid chest,

Laurence found the courage to admit her helplessness rather than faking aid: "The searching sun of the Jilal exposed not only the land but the heart as well" (*NW* 77). Her descriptions of the harsh and exotic beauty of the desert are often very moving, but the most interesting portions of the memoir deal with her encounters with the Somali people – *and with herself.*

"The Very Best Intentions" describes a Ghanaian friend whose real identity is concealed under the name of Mensah. This 1964 essay reveals one of the ways in which Laurence's youthful naiveté was dispelled. Mensah was one of the first well-educated Africans she had met in the days when, by her own description, she wore "militant liberalism" like a heart on her sleeve (*HS* 34). Tense and introspective, Mensah's sardonic surface masked his real concern for his land. His conversation ran to shock tactics. When Laurence spoke reverently of African history, Mensah pretended that his people had no history, to emphasize silently that the possession of a history is basic to one's humanity and should be taken for granted. When Laurence praised the richness of tribal culture, Mensah spoke of fear, squalor, infection, death. Laurence realized that she could afford to be fascinated because she stood apart and beyond. Mensah and his people did not, and the time to move forward was long overdue. Mensah is doubtless the model for the London-educated journalist Victor Edusei in *This Side Jordan* and for the artist Danso in "The Merchant of Heaven." More importantly, the tension between these points of view *and the necessity of coming to terms with them both* underlie all of Laurence's African-based fiction. Characters who opt for one position and ignore the other are subjected to the author's gentle mockery, such as the amateur British anthropologist in "The Pure Diamond Man" who reveres ancient cultures until his own health is threatened by them.

The Laurences were in Ghana from 1952 to 1957. *This Side Jordan* and *The Tomorrow-Tamer* are set in Ghana in this period when the country hovered on the brink of independence from Britain. But only part of the novel and some of the short stories were actually written in Africa. The rest was assimilated and reworked later in Vancouver. Laurence has never published hurriedly.

The novel deals with the way in which people experience and

react to the cultural changes that inevitably accompany the passing of time. These changes have been especially rapid all over the world in the last generation or two. Laurence is concerned with how we experience time, with our relation to our ancestors, with the necessity for coming to terms with our personal and cultural past while continuing to grow and move towards fulfillment. Her most recent novel, *The Diviners,* contains the fullest working out of this theme. Its opening metaphoric statement, "The river flowed two ways," perfectly expresses the time continuum as we experience it.

A network of parallel situations and characters is the chief literary device in *This Side Jordan.* There are two communities, Ghanaian and expatriate British; two protagonists, Nathaniel Amegbe and Johnnie Kestoe; and two sets of cultural pasts which continue to influence the present and with which the characters must come to terms.

The expatriates' attitude of superiority, as we have seen in our discussion of Laurence's reaction to Mannoni's ideas about the structure of the colonial personality, are shown to cover feelings of inferiority and a deep insecurity. Despite her dislike of the type, Laurence treats these figures with the compassionate understanding that she extends to all her characters. In the memoir, she writes: "I did not appreciate then the really desperate boredom of some of these women, the sense of life being lived pointlessly and in a vacuum. Nor did I perceive the need many of them felt to create a small replica of England here in the desert and the enormous effort they put into a task that must inevitably fail" (*NW* 29). In the novel, the textile firm's British employees have "the grim humour of exile" in their eyes. In the sanctuary of their club they mourn their island home and a lost world of private schools and comfortable security. The mingled attraction and repulsion which Johnnie Kestoe feels for Africans ("a disgust that beckoned almost as much as it repelled") suggests that he is projecting his own guilt on them. In a traumatic encounter with an African girl, Johnnie, "wanting both to possess and destroy," symbolically re-enacts the rape of a continent. The girl's pain and humiliation bring Johnnie to the realization of both her uniqueness ("She was herself and no other") and their shared humanity. Nathaniel has a parallel experience when he is confronted with the pain and humiliation of Johnnie's wife in childbirth.

Nathaniel, product of two cultures, is more important to the novel than is Johnnie. The African schoolteacher, son of the drummer/priest in a chieftain's court and educated in a mission school, is pulled two ways. He is torn between past and future, bush and city; between ancient tribal culture and modern Western ways. He finally rejects the offer of a job as secretary to a chief in favour of remaining in Futura Academy in Accra, "in this city where you could feel tomorrow being reached for." His son Joshua, born in a city hospital instead of at home attended by relatives, symbolizes Nathaniel's hope that his people will "cross Jordan" and possess the Promised Land.

Nathaniel's struggle and confused despair are presented in a series of dramatic inner monologues. Some of these were criticized by the publisher and were revised by Laurence. Like Douglas Killam, however, I find the monologues convincing. Their formality suits their content, and while they derive from Nathaniel's boyhood experience of Akan religion, "they also derive from his own research into the history of his peoples."[10] Nathaniel feels that two gods have fought over him, and both have lost. He believes in both, and in neither. Except sometimes. He must come to terms with the emotional pull of the old ways, neither succumbing to them nor rejecting them outright: "There must be pride and roots, O my people." Nathaniel finally exorcizes his fear in a private meditation in church, after he has made the decision to stay in the city: "My God is the God of my own soul, and my own speech is in my mouth, and my home is here here here" (*TSJ* 275). He must possess his own land in his own way and in his own time.

The novel has been praised by African reviewers for giving "a highly informed insight into Africa today"[11] and for illuminating African problems and tensions "in a striking and memorable way."[12] African reviewers also note the richly *comic* treatment of the tragic predicament. Laurence's comic voice has not received as much critical attention as it deserves. Her sense of humour is an integral part of her way of seeing the world.

The nine stories collected in *The Tomorrow-Tamer* (1963) are all, like the novel, set in Ghana in the 1950s. All had been previously published, in periodicals of such a widely varying scope and content as to testify to the range of their appeal, as Clara Thomas notes in her Introduction.[13] The stories, like the rest of

Laurence's fiction, deal with problems of human alienation or exile, the struggle to incorporate the past into the present, the dignity and value of the individual, and the movement towards inner freedom.

"Godman's Master" is one of the most exceptional in a fine collection. Henry Kreisel called it "extraordinary."[14] The story is basically an analogue of human evolution, of the movement of the human spirit towards independence and maturity; on another level, it symbolizes women's emancipation from dependence on man; the author's humour is especially evident in this reading. Godman Piru is a dwarf, one of the *pirafo* whose ancestors were court jesters to Ashanti kings. Godman is rescued from the box in which he has been imprisoned, and taken to a city by an African chemist. He is happy to exchange slavery for household serfdom, but very unwilling to undertake freedom. Yet he aspires to be a man, and as Moses Adu instructs him, "that is what men do – they work." They earn money, they are responsible for their own lives; "There is more to freedom than not living in a box," and dependency is "a cord which could strangle" (*TT* 155). Knowing that no one is ever really ready for freedom, Moses evicts the frightened little man. A year later he finds the dwarf making his living with a travelling troupe of jugglers and magicians. Godman tells Moses something of his harrowing experiences during the early months of his freedom, and concludes: "'I have known the worst and the worst and the worst,' he said, 'and yet I live. I fear and fear, and yet I live.' 'No man,' Moses said gently, 'can do otherwise'" (*TT* 159).

The story illustrates Laurence's wit and her technical virtuosity in word play, mood, atmosphere. The tropical storm at the beginning evokes a mythic genesis of the world: "The sky cracked open like a broken bowl that held a sea-full." Egrets huddle "like flocks of sorcerers," suggesting the fears of man's ancient past. The dwarf is a "god-in-the-box. Like the up-jumping jacks," a "manforsaken little god" (*TT* 139, 143). Godman squeaks, scuttles, has a tiny cough "as though a butterfly had cleared its throat." In his final metamorphosis he is as "flamboyant as a canna lily in scarlet turban and green robe" (*TT* 157). His occupation picks up both the old metaphor of the world as a stage and the godman's dual nature as artist and con man, as in every man.

Laurence's other African book, *Long Drums and Cannons,* is a pioneering study of the work of Nigerian dramatists and novelists writing in English. Because she feels a sympathetic identification with many Africans, her comments on their work reveal her attitudes towards her own writing. In the "Preface" she speaks of the social and political engagement of Nigerian writers who are concerned with "the clash between generations, the social and individual disturbances brought about by a period of transition, the slow dying of the destructive aspects of tribalism, the anguish and inadequacy of uncompromising individualism as an alternative to tribalism."[15] She writes of the necessity for planting universal themes in some specific geographic and cultural soil. She writes of the need for self-knowledge, of human duality (creative and destructive, free yet dependent upon gods and ancestors), of dignity and responsibility, and of the significance that the past continues to exercise in the present. Of Wole Soyinka's fiction, she says: "Any process of going forward must also take into account the past" (*LD* 73).

Laurence's early work has been widely praised as the best expatriate writing on Africa. And justly so. Her Canadian experience of prairie drought and depression bred sympathies and intuitions which prepared for her receptiveness abroad. Her African experiences, in turn, nurtured her understanding of others and of herself. Her African writing is both valuable in itself and a necessary preparation for her Canadian fiction. And as we make our way through Laurence's work, the strangest glimpse we are likely to come across will be those we catch of ourselves.

NOTES

1. See Ken Mitchell, ed., *Horizon: Writings of the Canadian Prairie* (Toronto: Oxford University Press, 1977), Preface p. xi, where the editor links the attraction to Indian culture exhibited by many Prairie writers with the wider Prairie character. See also Margaret Laurence, *Heart of a Stranger* (Toronto: McClelland and Stewart, 1976), p. 213: "Because that settlement and that land ... remain my world, my way of viewing. My eyes were formed there."
2. Laurence, *Heart of a Stranger,* p. 11. Further page references are in the text as *HS.*
3. Margaret Laurence, *New Wind in a Dry Land* (New York: Alfred Knopf, 1964), p. 275. Further page references are in the text as *NW.*
4. *A Tree for Poverty: Somali Poetry and Prose,* Collected by Margaret Laurence (Hamilton: McMaster University Library Press, 1970), p. 25.

5. See Clara Thomas, *Margaret Laurence*, Canadian Writers Series (Toronto: McClelland and Stewart, 1969), p. 14. Professor Thomas quotes from a letter in which Laurence speaks of the diaries as being unusable in the form in which they had been written. Laurence writes that she had to "recreate the situation while also trying to understand it at a distance of ten years."
6. See *New Wind in a Dry Land*, p. 21: "My feeling about imperialism was very simple. I was against it.... Like most Canadians I took umbrage swiftly at a certain type of English who felt they had a divinely bestowed superiority over the lesser breeds without the law." Laurence dislikes the title of the American edition of *The Prophet's Camel Bell* (London: Macmillan, 1963), possibly because of its suggestion that Western technology is bringing a superior culture to a benighted land.
7. Conversations with Laurence at her home in Lakefield, July 25-26, 1976.
8. O. Mannoni, *Prospero and Caliban: The Psychology of Colonization*, trans. Pamela Powesland, Foreword Philip Mason (London: Methuen, 1956), p. 13.
9. *Ibid.*, p. 34.
10. Margaret Laurence, *This Side Jordan*, Introduction by G.D. Killam, NCL 126 (Toronto: McClelland and Stewart, 1969), p. xvii. Further page references are in the text as *TSJ*.
11. Anthony Babalow, Review of *This Side Jordan*, *British Columbia Library Quarterly*, 25 (July 1961), p. 34.
12. Richard Le Fanu, Review of *This Side Jordan*, *Transition* (Kampala), 2, 4 (June 1961), p. 28. See also Ibrahim Tahir, "Anthropological Curiosity?," *West Africa* (November 9, 1963), p. 1273.
13. Margaret Laurence, *The Tomorrow-Tamer*, Introduction by Clara Thomas, NCL 70 (Toronto: McClelland and Stewart, 1970), p. xi. Further page references are in the text as *TT*.
14. Henry Kreisel, "The African Stories of Margaret Laurence," *Canadian Forum* (April 1961), p. 8. See also Patricia Morley, "The long trek home: Margaret Laurence's stories," *Journal of Canadian Studies*, XI, 4 (November 1976), pp. 19-26, for a discussion of "Godman's Master" and Laurence's other stories, African and Canadian.
15. Margaret Laurence, *Long Drums and Cannons: Nigerian Dramatists and Novelists: 1952-1966* (London, Melbourne, Toronto: Macmillan, 1968), p. 9. Further page references are in the text as *L.D.*

Many Solitudes: The Travel Writings of Margaret Laurence

GEORGE WOODCOCK

Margaret Laurence has published only one travel narrative in the conventional sense, which is *The Prophet's Camel Bell,* and that book, produced a decade after the period of life in Somaliland which it narrates, she has described as the most difficult of all her works to write. The difficulty is not evident in the finished version, which is one of the finest and most evocative travel books ever written by a Canadian, and the existence of difficulty at any time in connection with this book in particular seems at first a little surprising, since the creation of a natural setting and the placing of human drama in that setting (which is the main content of *The Prophet's Camel Bell*) are prime constituents of all Laurence's writing. Her novels are all in a sense travel books, vividly descriptive in terms of environment, involving a great deal of journeying, both inner and outer, and coming at the end to those self-transforming realizations that are the destinations of all internal voyagings.

I suspect that a great deal of the difficulty incurred in the writing of *The Prophet's Camel Bell* arose from the fact that, while it is a narrative in which an inner journey and arrival at a personal destination run parallel, as in the novels, with a great deal of external and physical journeying through a dramatic landscape, in this case the inner journey is not that of a fictional persona; it is the journey of the author herself. *The Prophet's Camel Bell,* in other words, is much more than a mere narrative of exploration; it is an autobiographical document, a guide book to a large area of the mental world in which the novels, from *This Side Jordan* to *The Diviners,* were conceived.

The Prophet's Camel Bell is not the only piece of travel writing Margaret Laurence has done. The first book she ever published, *A Tree for Poverty,* is to all appearance a brief treatise on Somali oral literature, with selected translations of poems and stories, but even here the experience of a traveller is evident, as it is in

* First published in *Journal of Canadian Studies,* Vol. 13, No. 3 (Fall 1978); published subsequently in *A Place to Stand On,* ed. George Woodcock, NeWest Press, 1983.

Laurence's only book of literary criticism, *Long Drums and Cannons,* concerning the work of West African novelists who emerged during the 1950s and 1960s. More directly relevant, however, are the occasional pieces collected in her one volume of essays, *Heart of a Stranger*; these, as the title suggests, are largely concerned with the places that have been significant to Margaret Laurence in both her life and her writing. They cover the important periods of the life, from childhood in Manitoba, through the crucial experience of Africa, and on in later years to the Scotland she visited in search of her ancestry, and back to the Ontario where she now lives, in full consciousness that the land of her birth has more significance for her than the land of her forefathers, of which she has neither direct recollection nor even a vicarious memory transmitted through immediate relatives. Perhaps, indeed, one can describe the final effect of *Heart of a Stranger* as an arrangement of personal myths in their order of relevance.

It is, of course, possible to treat these various books as sources of clues to the content of Margaret Laurence's fiction. The essays in *Heart of a Stranger* lay out the physical background – that part of Manitoba where the prairie begins to roll in the direction of the northern forests – of the fictional town of Manawaka that figures in the four Canadian novels and also in the cycle of stories, *A Bird in the House,* which Laurence confesses in *Heart of a Stranger* is "semi-autobiographically" modelled on her own childhood in the actual town of Neepawa. There are people mentioned in these essays whose characteristics were obviously combined with those of others to make characters in the novels; a water diviner and an ageing boatman neighbour, two different people in real life, come together and form the nucleus of the wise old man Royland who provides a title and much of the plot for *The Diviners.* Margaret Laurence's early relationship with "Mensah," the Ghanaian, which she describes in the essay entitled "The Very Best Intentions," resembles Miranda Kestoe's with Nathaniel Amegbe in *This Side Jordan,* though "Mensah's" acerbic nature and his pessimism regarding the future of Ghana after freedom obviously contributed more to the character of Victor Edusei in the same novel than to that of Nathaniel.

One can similarly turn to *The Prophet's Camel Bell* – that narrative of fact so strange and so startling in its impact that Margaret Laurence never seems to have had any desire to turn it into fiction – and find touches that were later melded into the fiction of other places. The marble angels which Margaret Laurence saw with such astonishment in the Staglieno cemetery at Genoa on her way to Somaliland not only appear in the short story "The Perfumed Sea" in *The Tomorrow-Tamer,* but also, of course, provide the most commanding image in *The Stone Angel.* The child prostitute encountered in the Somali desert reappears in the West African child Ayesha in "The Rain Child." The double solitude of Indians in Somaliland, isolated from both the native people and the British overlords, is reflected in the predicament of the Italian hairdresser, Mr. Archipelago, in *The Tomorrow-Tamer.* Diligent readings can disinter many echoes and links of this kind without in the least detracting from the essential imaginative autonomy of Margaret Laurence's novels, and clearly the importance of *The Prophet's Camel Bell* and *Heart of a Stranger* lies in another direction, in what they reveal of the state of mind out of which Margaret Laurence's novels and stories emerged.

There is no question of the experience of Somaliland having started Margaret Laurence in the career of writing, though all her publications postdate it. Indeed, it may have beneficially delayed the maturing of a talent – and on this point there is no reason to doubt the autobiographical nature of *A Bird in the House* – which she had already begun to develop as an assiduous scribbler during her Manitoba childhood. Obviously the early experience of Somaliland, and particularly as member of a moving camp in the drought-ridden desert, produced the kind of culture shock which often makes it hard for a writer to say anything immediately about a country in which he has moved as "a stranger in a strange land," and forced Margaret Laurence into a salutary re-examination of her own character that prevented her writing more about the country at the time than the rather brief descriptive paragraphs which are part of the introductory material to *A Tree for Poverty.* Her literary activity in Somaliland was restricted to translating the poems and stories that appear in *A Tree,* and this was perhaps excellent work under the circumstances, since it brought her into contact with a number of Somalis through their own literature and traditions and so gave her an insight into the land and its people no merely external observation could have produced, as well as providing a temporary substitute for more originative writing.

In Somaliland Margaret Laurence also kept a diary, but she found that when she returned to the experience a decade later she had to begin anew, recreating and giving something of a literary structure to the phase of life which *The Prophet's Camel Bell* re-enacts. It is significant that when, in West Africa, she experienced another strange land and strange culture, her inhibitions about making fiction out of such material no longer existed, and the first version of *This Side Jordan* was actually written in Ghana, though even here – as Margaret Laurence remarked in "Ten Years' Sentences," an article published in *Canadian Literature* in 1969 – departure from Africa provided a new perspective, and much of the novel had to be rewritten to suit the more distanced view.

The Prophet's Camel Bell is in fact a much more complex work than the travel narrative it may appear at first sight to be. In the Laurence chronology it stands after *This Side Jordan* and *The Tomorrow-Tamer,* and we have to view it with this experience of fiction-writing in mind. While much of the basic content may indeed have been provided by the original diary, the shaping is that of an experienced novelist, and if we see *The Prophet's Camel Bell* as representing an intermediate genre between the novel and the ordinary travel narrative, we appreciate most fully what the book has to offer.

There are really three levels on which *The Prophet's Camel Bell* moves forward. A landscape is described, with the kind of vivid feeling for the surface of the earth that had already become evident in her West African fiction, and on that bizarre terrain – usually barren but at times bursting into fantastic blossomings – a people is observed which has created a way of life and an accompanying philosophy as specialized and as closely adapted to survival in an extreme environment as that of the Eskimo. Like so many Canadian writers, a generation or so away from the pioneers, Margaret Laurence was interested in the theme of survival long before Margaret Atwood made it the subject of a perhaps excessively celebrated book; in fact, in 1970, looking back over her career in the essay "A Place to Stand On" (*Heart of a Stranger*), she made some remarks that have an obvious bearing on her reaction to the Somalis and their existence:

> The theme of survival – not just physical survival, but the preservation of some human dignity and in the end some human warmth and ability to reach out and touch others – this is, I have come to think, an almost inevitable theme for a writer such as I, who came from a Scots-Irish background of stern values and hard work and puritanism, and who grew up during the drought and depression of the thirties and then the war.

At the second level, *The Prophet's Camel Bell* provides a series of rounded character vignettes, with four of the Somalis being given a chapter each, and chapters being devoted to the Italian workers with whom Margaret Laurence and her husband associated in the course of their dam-building project and also to "the imperialists," including many kinds of Englishmen in Somaliland. Finally, on the third level, it is a study of the author's own mental development, and of the transformation of her reactions to a strange world during the two years she lived in Somaliland; this process of unfolding self-revelation runs through the book from beginning to end, and is not only its profoundest theme but also its main structural connection.

The construction of the ballehs or earth dams which was entrusted to Jack Laurence took place in the Haud, the arid inland region of Somaliland that Margaret found "so seemingly remote that one almost doubted the existence of the rest of the world." It was a place of drought, broken by rare and violent periods of rain, of which there was only one during the Laurences' term of service; one was enough, for they only narrowly escaped disaster in the flash floods that tore down the dry watercourses. At the time of their arrival there, the Haud was in the grip of one of the great prolonged droughts known as *Jilal.* The Haud then

> seemed to be no place for any living thing. Even the thorny bushes, digging their roots in and finding nourishment in that inhospitable soil, appear to have a precarious hold on life, as though at any moment they might relax their grip, dry up entirely and be blown clear away.

But the thorn bushes did not blow away, any more than the people became extinct, no matter how many human beings and camels died during the *Jilal,* and Margaret Laurence was to see a resemblance between the men of the Haud and the vegetation they moved among:

> There was a toughness deep in these people, like the fibre of desert cactus, the ability to eke out life, the refusal to die easily.

The tough vegetation even provided a location and a symbol for the faith of the Somali herdsmen. Arriving at a tiny desert hamlet, Margaret Laurence saw an enclosure of thorn, and when she asked its purpose, she was told that this was the mosque:

> I looked again at the thorn boughs that formed the place of worship. It seemed to me that more genuine faith might reside in this brushwood circle than in the jewelled and carved magnificance of the Blue Mosque at Istanbul.

She saw the Somalis in the *Jilal* as "a dying people in a dying land. The dust filled their nostrils like a constant reminder of mortality." Yet as a people they did not die:

> They were not a passive people. They struggled against terrifying odds to get through to the wells. But always in their minds must have been the feeling that if Allah intended them to make it, nothing would prevail against them, and if he did not intend them to go on living no effort of theirs would be of any use. This fatalism did not weaken them. On the contrary, it prevented them from wasting themselves in fury and desperation.

Margaret Laurence finds herself as unable as Ivan Karamazov would have been to accept with Islamic calm the fate of the innocents in such a world, yet is forced to recognize the relevance of such a religious attitude to the realities from which it emerges:

> So the Qoran gives suffering a meaning and refuses the finality of death. I saw the necessity of this belief, without which life for these people would be intolerable. I would have shared such a faith, if it had been a matter of choice, but I could not. To me, it seemed that these children died pointlessly, and vanished as though they had never been, like pebbles thrown into a dark and infinite well.

With most of the Somalis who lived that hard life and professed that faith of resignation, Margaret Laurence's encounters were necessarily fleeting, and limited by the lack of a common language or anything in the way of a shared view of existence, yet often they had the epiphanic quality which only such brief encounters can acquire, and it is a measure of Margaret Laurence's artistry that she recognized their value as revelations. Encounters of this kind punctuate her book, and constantly strengthen its authenticity as an account of a strange and stark culture. One of the most striking of such vignettes describes an encounter with a woman at the height of the *Jilal,* and I quote the incident in full because it is an admirable example of the traveller's perceptiveness and narrative skill, deepened but never softened by the compassion that accompanies them, and not merely relates us empathically with the Somali woman but also takes us into the centre of Margaret Laurence's mind as she experiences and reflects in memory on the incident:

> Driving along the Awareh-Hargeisa road, we saw two burden camels laden with the crescent-shaped hut-frames and the bundled mats. They were halted by the roadside, and as we drew near, we saw one of the beasts slide to its knees, sunken in the apathy of thirst and exhaustion. Beside them, squatting in the sand, was a woman, a young woman, her black headscarf smeared with dust. She must have possessed, once, a tenderly beautiful face. Now her face was drawn and pinched. In her hands she held an empty tin cup. She did not move at all, or ask for water. Despair keeps its own silence. Her brown robe swayed in the wind. She carried a baby slung across one hip. The child's face was quiet, too, its head lolling in the heavy heat of the sun. We had a little water left in our spare tank, so we stopped. She did not say a word, but she did something then which I have never been able to forget.
>
> She held the cup for the child to drink first.
>
> She was careful not to spill a drop. Afterwards, she brushed a hand lightly across the child's mouth, then licked her palm so that no moisture would be wasted.
>
> To her I must have seemed meaningless, totally unrelated to herself. How could it have been otherwise? I had never had to coax the lagging camels on, when they would have preferred to stop and rest and die. But what I felt, as I looked into her face, was undeniable and it was not pity. It was something entirely different, some sense of knowing in myself what her anguish had been and would be, as she watched her

> child's life seep away for lack of water to keep it alive. For her, this was the worst the *Jilal* could bring. In all of life there was nothing worse than this.
>
> What we could do here was only slightly more than nothing. Maybe she would reach the wells. Maybe she would not. She might with good reason have looked at us with hatred as we began to speed easily away, but she did not. She was past all such emotions. She knew only that she must keep on or she would perish, and her child with her. As we drove away, we saw her rise slowly and call the burden camels. The beasts struggled up and began to follow her.

Other vignettes tell of communities, of the temporary halting places in the desert or the old and decaying towns on the coast, where only vestiges remain of the flamboyant past of Arab merchants and slave traders, of pearl divers and warring sheikhs whose exploits have been magnified in tribal legend. Such a place was Zeilah, where they stayed in a Residency haunted by the ghost of an English administrator who had killed his wife and then shot himself. There was something ghostly also about the people of Zeilah who, living in memories of their past as traders and pearl divers

> chanted songs whose meaning they had forgotten. The words were Galla, or Danakil, mixed with Arabic or archaic Somali, all so blended and changed that they were unrecognizable. They would chant them over and over, the mysterious words and phrases of a dead past, possibly imbued now with a magical significance.

The Somalis whom Margaret Laurence got to know reasonably well were already men between two worlds, the servants and tractor-drivers who retained some links with their tribes, but who had already been affected by their contacts with the modern world. There was Hersi – Hersi Half-tongue, the interpreter and teller of traditional tales who suffered a speech defect for which he compensated by a dramatic style of narration in which he acted out elaborately every role he recounted. There was Abdi, the tough old warrior whose loyalty turned to bitterness when he realized that the reward for faithful service would not be the automatic employment of all the fellow clansmen he cared to propose. Abdi was a man of immense courage and anger who "never knew –

and who probably could not have borne to know – that his truest and most terrible battle, like all men's, was with himself." And there was Mohamed their servant, the first and the last Somali whom Margaret Laurence ever saw, and whose relationship with her and her husband was a matter of satisfying his own code of service rather than of personal devotion, as she had first imagined:

> But only slowly did we come to see that Mohamed's identification of his own interests with those of his employer would have taken place whoever the employer happened to be. He acted not in response to what we were, but to what he himself was.

All these people come alive, not only in their actions, but also through Laurence's extraordinary ear for eccentricities of speech, so that she can convey a twist of Somali character in the very way a man speaks brokenly the alien tongue of English.

The gradual recognition of the complexity of Somali motives and the ambiguities of relationships with these people was as much part of Margaret Laurence's self-transforming education as the horrors and harshnesses of life in the Haud during the famine of the *Jilal.* She learnt how excessively simplified had been her assumptions about a nation of tribal peoples who nevertheless adhered to one of the world's great civilizing religious traditions.

Parallel with this humbling acquisition of knowledge about another people (accompanied as it was by the loss of the illusions created by that most foolish of all travellers' expectations – the wish to be liked), there was another process of adjustment to be made, towards the British in Somaliland. When she first reached the colony, Margaret Laurence tells us:

> I believed that the overwhelming majority of Englishmen in colonies could properly be classed as imperialists, and my feeling about imperialism was very simple – I was against it.

But from the beginning, when her first English acquaintance in the colony turned out to be a foreman mechanic with no pukka English airs who spent his life patiently instructing Somali drivers in the ways of a mechanized world, she found her attitude changing. Alongside the conventional imperialists (a pathetic lot of insecure people as she later realized), she encountered those who spent their lives doing what they could for the people, and sometimes earning the respect and even the reverence of the

Somalis, who normally hated the British as infidels. One such man was the Padre, a wispy Anglican clergyman who never made a convert among the Somalis, but who was universally accepted by them as a holy man and who would wander the desert confident that the poorest tribesman would protect, shelter and feed him if it were necessary.

> Because his faith illuminated him so, it was tempting to see him simply as a saintly man, some gentler John the Baptist. But how intricate must be the forces which make life seem possible to some men only in the wilderness.

What Margaret Laurence was encountering, as others of us have met them in the dwindling Empire, were representatives of that strange breed, more common in the British than in other empires, who were drawn towards the colonies not for the sake of money or a career or the opportunity of exercising domination, but because there was a need in them to live in some way as "strangers in a strange land":

> I had not really believed such people existed. Yet here they were, confounding every preconceived notion of old colonials or pukka sahibs, and defying any neat labelling. Each was unique, utterly unlike anyone else, and yet they had this in common – they were all intensely concerned with this land and with the work they were doing here, and they were all drawn to Africa, or some place far from home, deeply and irresistibly.

Margaret Laurence was drawn to these people, largely because she felt that her own attitude had become very much like theirs, as she indicates in analysing her own feelings on leaving Somaliland:

> It seemed to me that my feeling of regret arose from unwisely loving a land where I must always remain a stranger. But it was also possible that my real reason for loving it was simply because I was an outsider here. One can never be a stranger in one's own land – it is precisely this fact that makes it so difficult to live there.

And finally, she recognized the paradox that was latent in this situation so far as her own behaviour was concerned:

> This was something of an irony for me, to have started out in righteous disapproval of the empire builders, and to have

> been forced at last to recognize that I, too, had been of that company. For we had all been imperialists in a sense, but the empire we knowingly sought was that of Prester John, a mythical kingdom and a private world.

Essentially, it is the experiences of foreignness, of the special self-recognition that comes to exiles, of the difficulty of communicating over cultural barriers, that carry forward from Margaret Laurence's Somali experience into her later work and make *The Prophet's Camel Bell* so important as a key to understanding her writing. As late as 1976 she called her very personal book of essays *Heart of a Stranger,* and the phrase dates from the very beginning of her Somali experiences when, lacking reading matter on the voyage out, she read for the first time in her life the five books of Moses – in a Gideon Bible.

> Of all the books which I might have chosen to read just then, few would have been more to the point, for the Children of Israel were people of the desert, as the Somalis were, and fragments from those books were to return to me again and again. *And there was no water for the people to drink – and the people thirsted.* Or when we were to wonder how the tribesmen could possibly live and maintain hope through the season of drought – *In the wilderness, where thou hast seen how that the Lord thy God bare thee, as a man doth bear his son, in all the way that ye went.* Or the verse that remained with me most of all, when at last and for the first time I was myself a stranger in a strange land, and was sometimes given hostile words and was also given, once, food and shelter in a time of actual need, by tribesmen who had little enough for themselves – *Thou shalt not oppress a stranger, for ye know the heart of a stranger, seeing ye were strangers in the land of Egypt.*

The last sentence lingered on, echoing through Margaret Laurence's career, summarizing much of her experience as a stranger, and taking on a new relevance when she found that "my experience of other countries probably taught me more about myself and even my own land than it did about anything else." Certainly the Somali experience, as it affected Laurence herself and other Europeans, underlies the preoccupation with exile, from one's own land, from one's adopted land, even from a traditional way of life, that is so prominent a theme in *This Side Jordan* and *The Tomorrow-Tamer,* some of whose remarkable stories, like "The Rain Child" and "The Drummer of All the World," are about the complexities of being a stranger, as they affect Europeans for whom Africa has been a home and who will return to their nominal homes as melancholy exiles, or even Africans, like Ruth in "The Rain Child": the Ghanaian girl brought up in England and incapable of fitting in to the missionary school where she is placed when her father returns to his own country. Always behind these stories about exiles or misfits or people thrust out of their traditional ways by the forces of change, there looms a deeper strangeness, which comes from the difficulty of human communication of any kind, and it is perhaps appropriate that Margaret Laurence should have drawn out this point in her 1968 book on African writers, *Long Drums and Cannons.* It is obvious that among these writers she feels the greatest affinity with the Nigerian novelist, Chinua Achebe, and she might be talking about her own novels – including those set in Canada as well as the African fiction – when she stresses his preoccupation with communication between men, and ends her study of him in this way:

> Beyond Achebe's portrayal of the old Ibo society or his portrayal of a contemporary society in the throes of transition, there is one theme, which runs through everything he has written – human communication or the lack of it. He shows the impossibly complicated difficulties of one person speaking to another, attempting to hear – really to hear – what another is saying. In his novels we see man as a creature whose means of communication are both infinitely subtle and infinitely clumsy, a prey to invariable misunderstandings. Yet Achebe's writing conveys the feeling that we must attempt to communicate, however imperfectly, if we are not to succumb to despair or madness.

Surely the difficulty and yet the necessity of communication is not only the major theme of such novels as *The Stone Angel* and *A Jest of God* and *The Fire-Dwellers,* but is also a leading preoccupation of the principal characters in each of these works. In *The Diviners,* Morag Gunn's special gift and so her special reward is her capability of understanding – of divining – more than other people the hidden strangenesses of the human heart, including her own. And so we understand what Margaret Laurence means when she says at the beginning of *The Prophet's Camel Bell* that "the strangest glimpses you may have of any creature in the distant lands will be those you catch of yourself" and, at the end of the book, "and yet the voyage that began when we set out for Somaliland could never really be over, for it turned out to be so much more than a geographical journey."

As I hope I have shown, *The Prophet's Camel Bell* is a book that lies at the centre of Margaret Laurence's achievement, partaking of many of the characteristics of fiction (for the character sketches often read like stories and the book has a novelistic kind of structure), and many of the characteristics of autobiography, dealing with a key phase of the author's personal life, in the form of a travel book. It was, one now realizes, a difficult book to write, but one that demanded writing, for nobody returns to an experience after ten years unless there is some special inner reason to give it the permanence of recording it, and in so doing to understand its real significance.

Margaret Laurence's other travel writings, the essays which form the greater part of *Heart of a Stranger,* are largely occasional pieces, produced on commission, like the two sketches of the Valley of the Kings and of the Suez Canal written during a winter month in Egypt ten years ago, and "Sayonara, Agamemnon," written for *Holiday* magazine after a first visit to Greece. Like any tale of experiences, these narratives do tell us a certain amount about the writer and the way she sees her world. Other essays like "The Poem and the Spear," about Mahammad 'Abdille Hasan (the so-called Mad Mullah of Somaliland), and "The Epic Love of Elmii Bonderii" (about a Somali poet) must really be read as supplements to *The Prophet's Camel Bell* and *A Tree for Poverty,* deepening our view of the breadth of Margaret Laurence's sympathies, but not really telling us much that is new about her or her work. The same might perhaps be said of "Man of Our People," a generous essay on my own book on Gabriel Dumont which gives a non-fictional expression to the special feeling for the tragedy of the Métis that plays so large a part in *The Diviners* and indeed enters all but one of the Magaret Laurence's Manawaka books through the presence of the Métis family, the Tonnerres.

The geographical pieces in *Heart of a Stranger* that, in a more or less direct way, bear a relationship to Laurence's fiction similar to that of *The Prophet's Camel Bell* are two essays, "A Place to Stand On" and "Where the World Began," relating to her origins in Manitoba; "Road from the Iles," which tells how she came to terms with her Scottish ancestry and its mythical implications; and two pieces, "Down East" and "The Shack," which relate to the parts of Ontario, formerly associated with Catharine Parr Traill, where in recent years she has chosen to live.

Curiously, at first sight at least, Ontario seems to be the only place she has been able to set in fiction while she was experiencing it. She only wrote successfully of Africa when she had reached Vancouver, but, as she says in one of these essays, "I always knew that one day I would have to stop writing about Africa and go back to my own people, my own place of belonging." But going back is in the mind, and not a physical return, for as Margaret Laurence also says:

> Living away from home gives a new perspective on home. I began to write out of my background only after I had lived some years away.

And one can follow the removes by which Margaret Laurence makes sure, after she has finished writing of Africa in Vancouver, that she is still distant enough to write with fictional detachment about the worlds of her past. Going to England, she writes of Vancouver in *The Stone Angel, A Jest of God, The Fire-Dwellers,* and locates the present tense of two of the novels there. Even more in these novels and also in the stories of *A Bird in the House* she writes of the mythical small town of Manawaka, where the past of all the novels, and the present of *A Jest of God* and *A Bird in the House* are set. This is the country of which Margaret Laurence says, in "A Place to Stand On":

> I doubt if I will ever live there again, but those poplar bluffs and the blackness of that soil and the way in which the sky is open from one side of the horizon to the other – these are things I will carry inside my skull for as long as I live, with the vividness of recall that only our first home can have for us.

At another point in the same essay, she remarked that: "Writing, for me, has to be set firmly in some soil, some place, some other and inner territory which might be described in anthropological terms as 'cultural background'." In the Canadian novels as much as in the African novels, this sense of an outer territory every bit as sharply apprehended as the inner territory of the mind is vividly present; I know of no living novelist – and very few in the past – who have quite so marvellously balanced the two necessary landscapes of fiction.

I think the relationship of *The Diviners* to what Margaret Laurence has to say about the role of place in her novels is in some ways a major key to her work, certainly as it has been manifest during the past fifteen years. At the end of "Ten Years' Sentences," which Margaret Laurence wrote for *Canadian Literature* in 1969 but did not collect in *Heart of a Stranger,* she makes a distinction between the local character of her writing on Africa and the more universal applicability of her writing on Canada and Canadian life:

> A strange aspect of my so-called Canadian writing is that I haven't been much aware of its being Canadian, and this seems a good thing to me, for it suggests that one has been writing out of a background so closely known that no explanatory tags are necessary. I was always conscious that the novel and stories set in Ghana are *about Africa.* My last three novels just seem like novels.

One has the feeling at the same time that she regards her coming to literary maturity as being connected closely with her being able to express in convincing fictional and almost mythical form her perceptions of her own country, and this gives a profound significance to the shifting terrain of *The Diviners,* which she has told us (unwillingly as we may hear it) is her last novel. Morag Gunn's beginnings are in Manawaka, intimately linked through her scavenger guardian Christie Logan with the town dump, known, as in Margaret Laurence's native Neepawa as

> "the nuisance grounds," a phrase fraught with weird connotations, as though the effluvia of our lives was beneath contempt but at the same time was subtly threatening to the determined and sometimes hysterical propriety of our lives.

In Vancouver Morag has her child, Pique, sired by the Métis Jules Tonnerre, last of a line of descendants of Riel's warriors, whose presence long troubled the consciences of Manawaka people. And in Scotland, like Margaret Laurence, Morag comes face to face with the real meaning of her ancestry, and could have said, as her creator does in "Road from the Isles": "But this, my first view of Scotland, was in some strange way also my first true understanding of where I belonged, namely, the land where I was born," i.e. the Canadian prairie. Perhaps this experience is best summarized in Laurence's final reflections in the same essay on her trip to Scotland:

> I am inclined to think that one's real roots do not extend very far back in time, nor very far forward. I can imagine and care about my possible grandchildren, and even (although in a weakened way) about my great-grandchildren. Going back, no one past my great-grandparents has any personal reality for me. I care about the ancestral past very much, but in a kind of mythical way. The ancestors, in the end, become everyone's ancestors. But the history that one can feel personally encompasses only a very few generations.

The Diviners, as I have said, goes beyond any of Margaret Laurence's other books by including the region where she is actually writing and a simulacrum of the river she looks out on while she works. Experience and its transmutation, in other words, have drawn together in terms of time and place, and this is the kind of encounter one can understand a writer facing with awe, perhaps even regarding as creatively terminal. Yet though *The Diviners* contains the artistic transfiguration of all the experience that relates to Margaret Laurence's ancestry and youth – the memories that make her the kind of writer she is – Africa is dropped out. Unlike Laurence, Morag Gunn never goes to Africa, or anywhere outside Canada except to Britain. At this point, one has the feeling that Africa played in Margaret Laurence's writing the cathartic role, teaching her the necessary distance between experience and its imaginative reconstruction, teaching her the value of the stranger's role, preventing her – as she remarks – from writing an autobiographical first novel about her prairie youth that would have been "too prejudiced and distorted by closeness," and giving her the subject matter out of which she could write her early fiction (too fine to be classed as apprentice work) and the magnificent farewell of *The Prophet's Camel Bell.* After that she was liberated to attempt the great task of her life up to the present, the Manawaka tetralogy. Perhaps one can end a survey of the significance of her travel writing no better than with some sentences from the final pages of *Heart of a Stranger,* which for me express with a vividness I have rarely encountered elsewhere the importance, to novelists of Margaret Laurence's kind, of a link approaching the closeness of symbiosis between the creative sensibility and the living environment:

> The land still draws me more than other lands. I have lived in Africa and in England, but splendid as both can be, they do not have the power to move me in the same way as, for example, that part of southern Ontario where I spent four months last summer in a cedar cabin beside a river. 'Scratch a Canadian, and you find a phony pioneer,' I used to say to myself in warning. But all the same it is true, I think, that we are not yet totally alienated from physical earth, and let us only pray we do not become so....
>
> I am not very patriotic, in the usual meaning of that word. I cannot say 'My country right or wrong' in any political, social or literary context. But one thing is inalterable, for better or worse, for life.
>
> This is where my world began. A world which includes the ancestors – both my own and other people's ancestors who become mine. A world which formed me, and continues to do so, even while I fought it in some of its aspects, and continue to do so. A world which gave me my own lifework to do, because it was here that I learned the sight of my own particular eyes.

The long trek home: Margaret Laurence's stories

PATRICIA MORLEY

The vision which underlies Margaret Laurence's fiction is remarkably unified. Whether one considers her long fiction or her short, her African oeuvre or her work with a Canadian setting, Laurence's theme of themes remains the search for spiritual freedom, and the difficulties inherent in that search. This paper is concerned with this recurring theme in Laurence's short stories as seen through patterns of imagery, characterization, and narrative structure.

There is nothing sentimental about this vision. Man is rarely free, and no one knows this better than Laurence. The other side of the coin is bondage, entrapment, alienation. Some of the bonds are forged by her characters for themselves; some are imposed from without, through various ironies of circumstances beyond their control. Alienation and exile are seen as forms of bondage or psychic slavery. In story after story, Laurence depicts an often agonizing struggle to break these bonds, to overcome alienation, to achieve an integration both personal and social which is imaged as a freedom to love and to accept love, to share, to meet, to touch. Such a state, Laurence implies, is our spiritual home, the human goal, the grail. In stories where the mode is primarily ironic and tragic, the focus is upon the forces which block movement towards this goal. In stories where the structure is comic, the characters are successfully engaged, difficulties notwithstanding, in the long trek home.

"The Rain Child" (1962) is an early version of the theme. In many ways, this African story prefigures Hagar's experience in *The Stone Angel,* even to the phrase "Pride has so often been my demon...."[1] Every character in the story save Kwaale, the beautiful young African girl, is and remains an exile. And even Kwaale is excluded, by her youth and limited experience, from the full sharing which her own culture expects and demands. The implacable Kwaale has no pity for Ruth, the African girl who is

* First published in *Journal of Canadian Studies,* Vol. 11, No. 4 (Fall 1976).

culturally white but imprisoned in a black skin; Kwaale has not yet experienced alienation and suffering. She has never been a stranger in the land of Egypt, Violet Nedden thinks, using the archetypal story from the Old Testament which underlies Hagar's name and experience. Both teacher and headmistress are exiles, and Violet's love for the country only deepens her sense of exclusion from it. Other exiles include Ayesha, the child prostitute, and Yindo, the Dagomba boy from the northern desert who expects no mercy from strangers in a foreign land. "'No got bruddah dis place,'" Yindo stammers fearfully, when he is discovered with Ruth. The teachers, Ruth, her equally displaced parents, Ayesha, and Yindo are all strangers in a hard land, outcasts, rain children. One type of rain is tears. In Laurence's poignant image for the human condition, the English climate and the tropical (the cause of Violet's deformity), the contrasting and excluding cultures, and the resulting human suffering, are brilliantly coalesced.

The title image of "The Half-Husky," like the rain child and the stone angel, suggests the paradoxes of human nature and experience. The creature who is half dog half wolf, half domesticated half wild, half loving half vicious, is also Everyman, set in a world which typically evokes both responses. In "The Rain Child," Ruth begins to learn hatred by being hated: "I noticed then how much thinner she had grown and how her expression had altered. She no longer looked like a child. Her eyes were as implacable as Kwaale's" (p. 117). Similarly, Nanuk learns to hate through Harvey's sadistic tormenting. After the pepper incident, Vanessa notices how wolfish Nanuk looks, with his lips drawn back in a devil's grin. Harvey's stone transforms the dog into a demented fury, and its young owner Vanessa into someone who wants to injure Harvey "in any way available."[2]

The stolen telescope forces Vanessa to face the conditions which have spawned Harvey. The ugliness of the human relationships involved are reflected in the physical squalor, the rust, the weeds, the disorder. His aunt's hatred and contempt for her nephew is absolute, and evokes the same feelings in Harvey. Vanessa is like Ruth, reacting to the story of Ayesha's slavery with naive horror, "the look of someone who recognizes for the first time the existence of cruelty" ("The Rain Child," p. 117). Cruelty results in bondage. Nanuk and Harvey are not "safe to go free." Harvey's aunt, along with the rest of mankind, appears to be on the loose thanks to some cosmic laxity or neglect. The sins of the fathers are indeed visited upon the children unto the third and fourth generation. It is a bitter story, reflecting the dark side of Laurence's vision.

"Godman's Master" is my favourite from the African collection, possibly because the dwarf's experience is an analogue for the housewife's, as well as for mankind's.[3] Whether read as a statement on Women's Liberation or simply as a universal parable, the story is both witty and profound. Perhaps Laurence intuits that the seriousness of the theme demands humour. The introductory description of the storm, for example, whimsically compares the egrets, wrapped in their cloak wings, to flocks of sorcerers. The little man squeaks, or scuttles, now a cockroach, now a mouse. And the names! Moses Adu is the dwarf's first deliverer, the one who leads the little man out of slavery yet who cannot bestow freedom. *Moses:* the lawgiver, the Pharaoh-confronter, who led his people towards but not into the Promised Land; *Adu: adieu,* or *à Dieu; Godman,* called "halfman," the little barely human creature or "man-forsaken little god" who aspires to be a free man and who grows into that stature. God-in-man? God's man? In the full context of the story, the name seems to carry these suggestions. Moses' wife is called Mercy. Freedom, in Laurence's fiction, is seen to be a gift which is both a mercy bestowed and also a birthright to be won through infinite desire and struggle, like Jacob wrestling with the Angel, an archetypal narrative which Laurence takes from Genesis and uses repeatedly in her fiction. The witty title suggests both the African who refuses to continue in the role of master, and God, or perhaps human destiny, which includes freedom.

Once free of the village priest, Godman would prefer simply to exchange an unkind master for a kind one. Freedom can be frightening. To work for money, to support himself and be responsible for himself, appears an impossible task. He is quite willing to keep house. If he learned man's work half as well as woman's, Moses tells him, he would be a great success. As Moses begins to understand Godman's dependence, even worship, he is horrified: "'There is more to freedom,' he said, 'than not living in a box.'... He and Godman were bound together with a cord more delicate, more difficult to see, than any spun by the children of Ananse. Yet it was a cord which could strangle" (p. 155).

So the unwilling Godman has the opportunity for freedom forced upon him. And he survives. In Moses' next view of him, a year later, Godman's smallness is his glory: "There sat Godman, flamboyant as a canna lily in scarlet turban and green robe." Man the truant, *pace* Pratt. Godman's story is as flamboyant as his costume. "'I have known the worst and the worst and the worst,'" he concludes, "'and yet I live. I fear and fear, and yet I live'" (p. 159). As must we all, Moses adds. The story closes with the tiny descendant of court jesters taking his place with the other performers "on the broad and grimy stage": the human comedy, African-style.

The stories which make up *A Bird in the House* are linked by character, setting, theme. The primary link is formed by the narrative voice, that of the child-cum-woman Vanessa McLeod. These links are so effective that the collection might be called a novel, and more than one critic has made this claim. Laurence grants that the net effect is similar to that of a novel, but describes the flow-lines as being vertical rather than horizontal, as they are in a typical long fiction. The threads of Vanessa's life are presented separately, not simultaneously. But the narrative voice, with its control over fictive time, is handled in the same way in these stories as it is in Laurence's novels.[4]

Vanessa is a budding writer, curious and observant, who describes herself as "a professional listener" (p. 11). This is obviously a good device for a first-person narrator. Comically, Vanessa sometimes conceals herself by sitting quietly in plain view, and sometimes puts her ear to one of her listening posts, round holes in the bedroom floors which had once been used for stovepipes.

The motif of entrapment is more frequent here than that of achieved freedom. But Vanessa moves through these stories of pain and disappointment, of laughter and love and hatred, on her own path of slow growth, towards the partial freedom of her early adulthood. She will go to university, a freedom denied to her mother. Yet in some indefinable way, Vanessa does not feel nearly as free as she had expected to feel (p. 203). The book ends with Grandfather Connor's death and, in a short epilogue, Vanessa's revisiting (twenty years later) the Brick House that had been both her grandfather's home and his monument.

The Brick House, a central metaphor in the collection, is identified with her grandfather, with his inherited Scots-Puritan culture, and, ultimately, with Vanessa herself. She has feared and fought the old man, yet he proclaims himself in her veins (p. 207). Similarly, Laurence came in maturity to recognize the strengths, the desirable qualities, of a culture she had once despised for its harshness.[5] Fortress or prison?[6] The Brick House is introduced in the first story with military metaphors: it is "sparsely windowed as some crusader's embattled fortress in a heathen wilderness"; its trees are "sternly protective," its guillotine lawn mower beheads the wildflowers and "helmeted snapdragons stood in precision" (pp. 3-4).

The last two views of the Brick House, however, evoke different moods and attitudes. We see, first, its stable-garage, home of the MacLaughlin-Buick: "I remembered myself remembering driving in it with him, in the ancient days when he seemed as large and admirable as God" (p. 206); and second, its neglected state of disrepair. *How are the mighty fallen in the midst of battle.* The trumpets are sounded and Jericho's Brick battlements are fallen down. Once again, the story's title provides the central image and the theme. But Vanessa has come to terms with the Brick House, with her ancestors and her culture, and passed beyond.

A Bird in the House, taken as a whole, is the story of Vanessa's growth. It is her spiritual odyssey, as *The Stone Angel* is Hagar's. Like the novel, its themes are bondage, flight, and freedom. Vanessa is ten in the first story, eleven in the second and third. In the fourth, where her father dies, she is between the ages of twelve and seventeen; in the fifth, between eleven and eighteen; in the sixth, between six and thirteen. She is fifteen in the seventh, and between twelve and twenty in the last. There is a development in the type of suffering, the quality of pain endured, which parallels Vanessa's chronological growth. The first three stories deal with love and loss through death, on a relatively simple level. The fourth connects the death of her father with Vanessa's loss of religious faith. The next three introduce the older adolescent in social evils too complex to be cured by any individual; to psychic depression and breakdown; and to sadism. Finally, the last story treats of two flights to freedom (Vanessa's, and Aunt Edna's) using apocalyptic images of a heavenly chariot and victorious warfare. Near the beginning of the last story, a depressed Vanessa fears that her fictional heroine Marie is trapped for life. Then the twelve-year-old girl clambers into Grandfather's old car and recalls driving with him in early childhood: "*A-hoo-gah! A-hoo-gah!* I was gazing with love and glory at my giant grandfather as he drove his valiant chariot through all the streets of this world" (p. 179). Aunt Edna escapes by marrying a local man. Her suitor works for the C.N.R.: again, the travel archetype. Grandfather's basement rocking chair is a comic chariot which airs his rage. And Vanessa's last action is to drive away from Manawaka. Free?

"The Sound of the Singing" contrasts freedom with bondage through the medium of three personalities. Grandfather Connor's "upright" nature is matched by his brother's "downright" one. Dan is considered by the townsfolk to be downright lazy, downright worthless, a downright fool. Bound by his moral concepts, Grandfather feels like a caged man at the enforced idleness of Sunday, and holds his family in a kind of bondage. Yet he supports his family, and his brother too. Neither man is truly free. Grandfather lacks Dan's *joie de vivre,* a quality to which Vanessa is drawn and which she symbolically pursues at the story's end. Road, journey, quest. Balanced between unpleasant rectitude and irresponsible, child-like gaiety stands Grandmother Connor: "Acceptance was at the heart of her. I don't think in her own eyes she ever lived in a state of bondage. To the rest of the family, thrashing furiously and uselessly in various snarled dilemmas, she must often have appeared to live in a state of perpetual grace, but I am certain she didn't think of it that way, either" (p. 72). The quotation is from "The Mask of Bear." But in the first story, it is Grandmother Connor who rebukes a self-righteous lack of charity in her husband and welcomes Dan back into their house.

The second story contrasts two kinds of spiritual order, one obvious and rigid (which Vanessa rejects), and one subtle, immaterial, free. The latter is large enough to accommodate such radically different personalities as Grandmother MacLeod, her husband, and her son. The description of Vanessa's paternal grandmother, "unaware that her hair was bound grotesquely like white-feathered wings in the snare of her coarse night-time helmet" (p. 40), evokes multiple suggestions of entrapment and freedom. Grandmother's blue Chinese carpet features birds in eternal motionless flight, and water-lily buds "caught forever just before the point of opening" (p. 44).

God loves Order, she tells Vanessa. By *order,* Grandmother means balanced accounts, a well-stocked cellar, and all emotions under lock and key. Fear and expressed weakness are disorders which do not belong in Grandmother's universe. She yearns for social prestige, whereas her husband yearned towards classical Greek drama, and his son, Vanessa's father, for travel to exotic lands. These unfulfilled yearnings are caught up in Vanessa's musings at the story's end, as she thinks of the leather-bound volumes of Greek, the elaborate tea-table, and the pictures of leopards and green seas (p. 59). She knows that her father has lied to his mother about the way in which his brother died, although, in Grandmother's phrase, "the MacLeods do not tell lies" (p. 45). Even the older Vanessa (for the narrative voice speaks from two points in time, simultaneously) understands only that the world before her is not subject to order of the type advocated by Grandmother MacLeod.[7]

Laurence's reader, however, has been given an anagogic image of a spiritual order large enough to embrace this pain and confusion. In the anagogic perspective, everything in the universe is potentially identifiable with everything else; an anagogic metaphor is an image which suggests that it may be identified with the entire cosmos. Laurence's anagoge is the circular rose-window of the MacLeod house. It contains "glass of many colours which permitted an outlooking eye to see the world as a place of absolute sapphire or emerald, or if one wished to look with a jaundiced eye, a hateful yellow" (p. 43). The image picks up such traditional symbols as the circle, and the rose. Even a common phrase such as "seeing the world through rose-coloured glasses" contributes to its ecumenical suggestions. The glasses through which Grandmother views the world are "a hateful yellow," but this colour is transformed later in the story by connecting it with poplar leaves and the sun. Vanessa intuits that the individuals in her family are too different for any simplified system to contain. But sun imagery dominates the closing paragraphs. And the window's rainbow colours are the individual components of light. Even a ladybird, seemingly "unaware that she possessed wings and could have flown up" (p. 59), contributes to the unobtrusive but intricate pattern of images that supports Laurence's theme.

The central four stories focus on pain, fear, entrapment, despite numerous touches of humour. The Haida mask conceals a lurking bewilderment, like Grandfather Connor's pain, untouchable in the cellar retreat. The mask is described as ugly, powerful, with an expression of sullen rage. It is only after her grandmother's death that Vanessa recognizes the mask of anger as a covering for her grandfather's repressed yearnings. The bear has claws, too, sufficient for frightening away Edna's suitor and teaching Vanessa that love and loss belong to Manawaka and not simply to ancient Egypt. The juxtaposition of the two key incidents, the routing of Edna's Jimmy and the death of Grandmother Connor, enrich the symbols of mask and bear and ground them solidly in human experience.

When Vanessa's father dies, the bird trapped between the two layers of her window is not simply an omen of death but an image of trapped humanity, apparently capable only of meaningless movements. The empurpled religious visions of Noreen are as unacceptable to Vanessa as the rigid Puritan code of Grandmother MacLeod. Vanessa, reacting to her father's death by striking Noreen, is also the bird, blindly battling to get out (p. 109).

The loss of her father precipitates a loss of faith which is a kind of psychic death. Where is he now? "*Rest beyond the river.* I knew now what that meant. It meant Nothing. It meant only silence, forever" (p. 110). In a later story, Vanessa thinks of the view of God she has held since her father's death: "Distant, indestructible, totally indifferent" (p. 148). "A Bird in the House" ends with Vanessa's discovery, years later, of an old photo of a girl. There is a French inscription. She remembers what her father has said about the war, and his old unfulfilled desire to travel. Perhaps the French girl had meant some brief and unexpected freedom. But her father is now dead, and the understanding which Vanessa would like to share with him is imprisoned within her. Once again, Laurence returns us to her title image, the bird. The bird, remember, did go free before the father's death. But nothing relieves the severity of the story's ending.[8]

"The Loons" identifies a halfbreed Indian girl and, by extension, her entire people, with the lonely phantom lake birds: "Plaintive, and yet with a quality of chilling mockery, those voices belonged to a world separated by aeons from our neat world of summer cottages and the lighted lamps of home" (p. 121). Two cultures, light years apart. Vanessa's neighbours live in brick houses. The Tonnerres occupy a huddle of lean-tos, ramshackle huts built of materials salvaged from the town dump. At thirteen, Piquette has no interest in the woods around the MacLeod cottage, thereby dashing Vanessa's romantic image of the Indian. Piquette attempts to protect herself from the pain of living by withdrawal. At seventeen, Piquette is engaged to an English boy and her eyes betray "a terrifying hope." Neither before nor after the shack fire which ends Piquette's life can Vanessa forget that look: wild, mocking, yearning, untameable. Incompatible with brick houses. This is Vanessa's first recognition of adult social guilt. Speaking of the story, Laurence traces the alienation of the Métis back to the nineteenth century and identifies the loons with that ancestral past.[9]

Withdrawal is also the protective mechanism used by Vanessa's older cousin Chris in "Horses of the Night." This portrait of an intelligent and imaginative youth crushed by a combination of outer and inner factors strikes me as the bleakest story Laurence has written. Chris craves order and beauty, and is given a family where dirt and disorder prevail. He craves work – the opportunity to create, to contribute to social needs – and is denied a job until the Depression is broken by World War Two. He craves gentleness, and finds violence. After his breakdown, Vanessa remembers "the brave and useless strokes of fantasy against a depression that was both the world's and his own" (p. 153). The title image is beautifully suggestive: of the dread, destruction-laden Horses of the Apocalypse: of the dark and terrifying depths of the mind, fears which are also imaged by the prehistoric monsters who once inhabited the lake near Chris's home and, finally, of his fantasy horses, Duchess and Firefly, "swifting through all the meadows of summer" (p. 135).

The psychic breakdown of Brother Lemon, in the African collection, might be compared with the story of Chris. But the symbols of hope in "The Merchant of Heaven" are more prominent, and the prevailing tone ironic rather than tragic. The American evangelist comes to Africa to acquire souls. Just souls. Bodies –

whether racked with tropical disease, crippled, hungry, or blind – are not Brother Lemon's concern. The metaphors here are blackly comic. Brother Lemon is "replete with faith as a fresh-gorged mosquito is with blood" (p. 51). Like his own water-purifier, the evangelist is a soul-purifier, "sucking in the septic souls and spewing them back one hundred per cent pure" (p. 53). The Jacob archetype, one of Laurence's recurring metaphors, takes a demonic form: "Jacob-like, he came to wrestle for the Angel's blessing, and instead was bent double with cramps in bowels from eating unwashed salad greens." How could his struggle be successful, in this form, as Laurence's ironies make clear?

Brother Lemon's name contains multiple puns, a kind of wordplay which engages the author's wit even when she is most serious. *Leman* is archaic for *lover*: the abstractions of the evangelist's love are even more Manichean than the concept of *cortezia* in Provençal poetry; Danso calls the evangelist his "dear citric sibling"; and, in contemporary slang, a *lemon* is a *failure*.

The final metaphor, and the story's focus, is Danso's picture of the Nazarene, depicted as an African: strong, capable of laughter, and surrounded by diseased beggars. Earlier, we have been given a glimpse of Brother Lemon's deprived childhood in an unpainted American farmhouse. His mental and emotional deprivations match the Africans' physical ones. The epiphany provided by the painting moves beyond its technical limitations[10]: "Sometimes, when I am able to see through black and white, until they merge and cease to be separate or apart, I look at those damaged creatures clustering so despairingly hopeful around the Son of Man, and it seems to me that Brother Lemon, after all, is one of them" (p. 77). And with this, the title expands from the simple level of irony into an apocalyptic reference, with God as the heavenly seeker of souls.

"The Drummer of All the World" deals with freedom and captivity on many levels, personal, national, cultural. Both squalor and beauty are caught in the anagogic metaphor of "the Drummer of all the world, drumming on himself, the Drum of drums" (p. 7). The English narrator loses this vision and is excluded from the country he loves, while the Africans remain excluded from opportunity and a decent standard of living. Freedom here is demonic, the freedom to discard illusion.

The mood in "The Perfume Sea" is quite different. Exile is treated comically, although the pain caused by isolation is not minimized.[11] The story breathes a spirit of reconciliation, expressed in a pattern of baroque and amusing metaphors. The tall gaunt Doree and the plump little hairdresser, Archipelago, are grotesques who nevertheless express the universal pathos and loneliness of human existence. Pigeon and crane, they walk on the African beach "with hands entwined like children who walk through the dark" (p. 49). Each is the other's sanctuary. Their economic and personal freedom has been achieved, as Archipelago puns, "By an act of Mercy," combined with their own courage and love.

In "The Tomorrow-Tamer," Laurence contrasts the types of freedom afforded by two different cultures. Faith, humility, acceptance, and service lie at the heart of the freedom which is to be found within the religious culture of the village of Owurasu. This is curiously close to Grandmother Connor's type of freedom. The service of God, or of the gods, is perfect freedom. The ironically-named Emmanuel, the African bridge-builder, typifies the rootless freedom of a secular, technological culture. Emmanuel's life is "to make money, and spend it" (p. 95). His non-community is the society of those like himself who move from job to job. The lack of understanding between the two cultures is portrayed with humour and pathos. The village elders send Kofi to work on the bridge as a test.

The young man is eventually seduced by a vision of money and power. Laurence sets the gods of the two cultures in ironic juxtaposition. Kofi's silver shillings resemble moons, and the bridge is painted silver, "moon-bright in the kingly sun" (p. 100). Kofi's fall from grace in a moment of exulting self-deification suggests the Icarus myth, and the concept of *hubris* from classical Greek tragedy. Kofi's act is also a betrayal of the values of his own people. His proud ambition is ironically fulfilled when his people weave both his death and the new bridge into their myth.

At the end of the African collection, the mammy trader calls freedom a sun thing, a sweet thing, a piece of free gold. The glory-filled gourd is the common life of these people. Busfare must still be paid, after Independence, yet Mammii Ama confronts the Englishwoman as an equal. A child-like exuberance is common to both characters and symbols here. The story is not one of

Laurence's best, but by placing it at the end of the collection she draws attention to its theme.[12]

Alice Munro has taken issue with an interpretation of literary images which she sees as disembodying her fiction. Munro speaks of "treachery to innocent objects – to houses, chairs, dresses, dishes," while granting that things are symbolic in an infinitely complex way.[13] No quarrel. Nothing that I have said here about the thematic burden carried by Laurence's houses and chairs, windows and what have you, is intended to devalue their solid impact as real objects in a real world. As Northrop Frye states in "Theory of Symbols," the second of the four essays which outline his theory of the shape of literature seen as a single body or form, the metaphoric structure is ironic and paradoxical. A metaphor identifies two things that still retain their own form: "A work of literary art owes its unity to this process of identification *with*, and its variety, clarity, and intensity to identification *as*."[14] Laurence's houses and chairs would signify nothing at all if they did not first of all signify themselves.

The Laurentian theme of exile has received considerable critical attention. George Woodcock, for example, speaks of the "sense of alienation" as crucial in *A Bird in the House*.[15] Clara Thomas sees in Laurence's fiction both "the inevitability of estrangement and the possibility of understanding between generations and among all men and women."[16] But the comic spirit of reconciliation in this body of fiction, and the recurring archetype of the spiritual quest, have not, I think, been sufficiently emphasized.

In an interview with Clara Thomas and Irving Layton published in 1972, Laurence notes a similarity between many of her themes and those of Layton. She describes her work as follows: "When I first began writing, the theme to me then seemed to be human freedom and in a profound sense it still is human freedom. But this is linked with survival, which, as you say, has to be linked with some kind of growth and I would express this in terms of an inner freedom."[17] An author is not always his or her own best critic. But Laurence's self-verdict is, I believe, peculiarly apt. Her fiction is designed to be lived with. It wears well. And with successive rereadings, the underlying concerns become clear. These are survival, growth, inner freedom. The long trek home.

NOTES

1. Margaret Laurence, *The Tomorrow-Tamer,* NCL 70 (Toronto: McClelland and Stewart, 1970), p. 125. All page references to the African stories refer to this edition. Cf. this reflection by the teacher in "The Rain Child" with *The Stone Angel,* NCL 59 (Toronto: McClelland and Stewart, 1968, p. 292), where Hagar thinks: "Pride was my wilderness, and the demon that led me there was fear."
2. Margaret Laurence, *A Bird in the House* (New York: Alfred A. Knopf, 1970), p. 165. Page references in the text to the Canadian-based stories refer to this edition.
3. Cf. Henry Kreisel, "A Familiar Landscape," *Tamarack Review,* 55 (Third Quarter, 1970), p. 91, describes "Godman's Master" as "a microcosm of the human condition in general and of the African experience in particular.... It is still my favorite among the African stories...."
4. See Margaret Laurence, "Time and the Narrative Voice," *The Narrative Voice,* ed. John Metcalf (Toronto: McGraw-Hill Ryerson, 1972), pp. 127-28. Cf. C.E.C., "The Effect of a Novel," *Montreal Gazette,* 25 April 1970, p. 55; William French, "Coming of Age in Manawaka," *Globe Magazine,* 14 March 1970, p. 16: "the cumulative impact is greater than the sum of the parts"; and George Woodcock, "Jungle and Prairie," *Canadian Literature,* 45 (Summer, 1970). p. 84: "...It is hard to know whether to define *A Bird in the House* as a collection of tales or a loosely knit and unconventional novel."
5. See "A Conversation About Literature: An Interview with Margaret Laurence and Irving Layton," taped by Clara Thomas, *Journal of Canadian Fiction,* I, 1 (Winter, 1972), pp. 65-68.
6. Cf. *A Bird in the House:* "'I've had those years with Ewen. I have Vanessa and Roddie. Maybe I can't get out. But they will'" (p. 186); and "'I guess I've got used to being back here in the old dungeon.... But, he's – well, I guess it's just that I have the feeling that the *absolute* worst wouldn't happen here, ever. Things wouldn't actually fall apart'" (pp. 186-87).
7. See Laurence, "Time and the Narrative Voice," pp. 128-29: "It is actually a story about the generations, about the pain and bewilderment of one's knowledge of other people, about the reality of other people which is one way of realizing one's own reality, about the fluctuating and accidental quality of life (God really doesn't love Order), and perhaps more than anything, about the strangeness and mystery of the very concepts of *past, present, and future.*"
8. As a title for the book, however, the image is typically paradoxical. Grandmother Connor's character and her pet bird reinforce the traditional connotations of bird as free spirit.
9. *Ibid.,* pp. 129-30.
10. See "The Merchant of Heaven," p. 76: "'The fact that you've shown him as an African doesn't seem so very important one way or another.'...'Perhaps not,' he admitted reluctantly. 'But could anyone be shown as everything? How to get past the paint, Will?...We will invent new colours, man,' he cried. 'But for this we may need a little time.'"

    Cf. Kent Thompson, review of *A Bird in the House, The Fiddlehead,* 84 (March-April, 1970), p. 109: "With one or two exceptions, they do not employ the revelation of epiphany which we have come to expect since James Joyce. That is, Margaret Laurence is not particularly interested in revealing a point or idea – she *is* interested in revealing a revaluation of a character."
11. George Robertson, "An Artist's Progress," *Canadian Literature,* 21 (Summer, 1964), p. 55: "Everywhere in these marvellously well-written stories the representatives of the old world and the new are thrown into strange and unaccustomed relationships, and Mrs. Laurence has perceived that the most poignant are those who have tried to step from one world into the other, and belong to neither."
12. George Woodcock, "Jungle and Prairie," p. 83, describes "A Gourdful of Glory" as having "much of the blunt pointmaking that has marred officially approved Russian fiction over the past two decades. Yet the awkwardness with which the theme is handled in that particular instance is exceptional."

13. Alice Munro, "The Colonel's Hash Resettled," *The Narrative Voice,* p. 182.
14. Northrop Frye, *The Anatomy of Criticism. Four Essays* (New York: Atheneum, 1967), p. 123.
15. George Woodcock, "Jungle and Prairie," p. 84.
16. Clara Thomas, *The Manawaka World of Margaret Laurence* (Toronto: McClelland and Stewart, 1975), p. 107.
17. Laurence, "A Conversation About Literature," p. 67. Elsewhere, Laurence has described fiction as a vehicle for freedom, the increased freedom which accompanies understanding of oneself and other people; "...writers are creating their private worlds with the ultimate hope of *throwing open the doors* to other humans" ("Time and the Narrative Voice," p. 127, italics mine).

Text and Subtext: Laurence's "The Merchant of Heaven"

W.H. NEW

Margaret Laurence's concern for the Old Testament appears throughout her writing: in her repeated image of Jacob wrestling with the angel, in her stories of Rachel weeping for her children and Hagar raging through her desert, in her critical and cultural observation about Jack Ludwig's novel *Above Ground* that "for most of us in Canada ... the Old Testament legends have more relevance than the classical ones." It is a fascination with the power and the poetry of the Old Testament, moreover, rather than a declaration of belief in any literal truth, which underlies these repeated images and observations. And the function of the Biblical analogues in Laurence's fiction is often to assert this very distinction. Her characters have to learn, when walking through symbolic landscapes, how to recognize the symbols; they have to refuse to be defined by narrow interpretations of life's possibilities; they have to free themselves from an attitude of mind that equates the symbol itself, rather than the understanding evoked by the symbol, with reality. The implications are broadly cultural as well as narrowly theological, affecting political stances and sex roles and other areas of human endeavour where stereotyped patterns can interfere viciously with common freedom.

Laurence's technical means of articulating such distinctions is frequently to build a story around a central allusion or a central "text" (the stories of Hagar and Rachel in *The Stone Angel* and *A Jest of God* offer ready examples) and then to counter this story with what amounts to a "subtext" – a tangential set of allusions that alters its implications and its potential rigidity. A clear instance of this process is provided by the third story in *The Tomorrow-Tamer and other stories,* "The Merchant of Heaven." The allusions here are New Testament rather than Old Testament ones, but they carry the same distinction between the possibilities of "poetry" and the absolutes of literalism. The resulting technical tensions underscore the dilemmas in which the characters find –

* First published in *Journal of Canadian Studies,* Vol. 13, No. 3 (Fall 1978).

or perhaps lose – themselves, and reiterate the cultural perspective which Laurence elsewhere argues openly.

The central narrative is simple. Brother Lemon, proselytizing evangelist for the Angel of Philadelphia Mission, comes to Africa full of a vision that he has learned in America, accepted as gospel, and taken as his duty to teach to pagans. Meeting him in Africa are an extraordinary range of actual African people (bureaucrats, townsmen, the poor, the diseased – none of whom quite fit Lemon's stereotyped expectations) and two individuals who go far to overturning them: Danso, the African artist who despises Lemon even before meeting him, and Will, the narrator, an English architect who hopes to use Brother Lemon's ambitions to further his own career and who ends up moved instead by the individual he comes in some small way to know. Lemon – so American he is almost a stereotype himself: by turns crass and well-meaning, oddly humourless and capable of pity, egocentrically rigid and profoundly naive and vulnerable – cannot, of course, adapt to Africa. Having come with what he accepts as the truth, he cannot accept the multiplicity of truths that Africa unfolds before him, nor can he adequately comprehend the persistence of other points of view. Hence, in one way at least, he is defeated, and he leaves.

Laurence makes the story somewhat subtler by showing how Danso's and Will's perspectives are also imperfect – Will's because of his (never adequately explained) mixed motives, and Danso's because of the anger engendered by feelings of deracination and impotence. The deracination derives from the way, during Danso's own childhood, that colonial European churchmen usurped the African church and took a people's culture away in the name of civilization; the impotence comes from his inability to protect his own family from other religious charlatans or to provide them with the answers and solutions they continue to need. Danso's rigid identification of Lemon as a "pedlar of magic" is equally as inadequate, therefore, as Lemon's own identification of himself as the apostle of the only truth. And both undergo change.

On the surface changes are embodied in the fabric of visual images, sometimes exactly communicated, as when we are told of the "marigold halo" of blonde hair that shines about Lemon's head and the "dove-grey suit of a miraculously immaculate material" that he wears, and sometimes rather desperately strained, as when

Lemon alights from the plane "replete with faith as a fresh-gorged mosquito is with blood." But the contrast which the images insist upon is more important than each image alone. Lemon, living for a European heaven of his own dreams – a blonde, blue-eyed Christ in his own image, and a heaven of crysolyte and jacinth and pearl – is as trapped by dream as the Africans are (Danso says that they live on dreams so much that nothing else matters, hence they cannot face and resolve the realities of poverty and disease), and he finds himself instead in a kind of purgatory. Seeking dragons to kill, he only encounters dragon lizards. Certain he lives in a black-and-white world, he is deluded by his senses and cannot interpret sufficiently what his eyes see. His tourist's eyes are at first charmed by African trinkets, then repelled by African disease; his photographer's eyes value representative colour slides over art, which he neither values nor comprehends; and his evangelist's eyes are so transfixed by his own heaven that he cannot see the limitations he therefore imposes on all experience, all imagination. Danso, too, by rejecting Lemon out of hand, limits another man. But in the process of trying to use Lemon – by painting a picture to sell to his church – Danso commits himself to his art, gets caught up in the visual poetry he is trying to communicate about heaven, and the painting that results (his "best") is a portrait of a powerful black Nazarene with eyes "capable of laughter," surrounded by beggars in pain. Lemon only sees the black skin. Danso, quietly reflective at this point rather than bitterly sardonic, admits the limitations paint imposes on a painter, and observes – Laurence expressing in this early story a conventional white liberal dream herself – "we will invent new colours.... But for this we may need a little time." Lemon cannot accept the notion, of course. When Will had asked him if he ever doubted, Lemon had replied, "'without my religion, I'd be nothing.'" It is all too accurate a statement. To suspect the order he has accepted would be to deny everything he has identified as himself. But for a moment he recognizes that his dream is not all-encompassing, which is, all by itself, more than he can bear.

Various verbal motifs parallel the visual images in the story, and it is here that we return to the idea of the story's text and subtext. Danso's observation that the paint limits the painter echoes the repeated demonstration of how words limit the speaker.

Lemon's text, throughout his mission, is from *Revelations,* and he takes its symbols to Africa – its palaces, beasts, and fountains – as such powerful literal realities that his listeners accept the literalism, too, on faith. In particular, when a group of blind old men demand the feast and the sight Lemon has promised – to Lemon's confusion – what transpires is that they have listened to a Ga translation of a text from chapter seven: "They shall hunger no more, neither thirst any more; neither shall the sun light on them, nor any heat. For the Lamb which is in the midst of the throne shall feed them, and shall lead them unto living fountains of waters, and God shall wipe away all tears from their eyes." When Will investigates, he discovers that

> The interpreter seemed all right, although perhaps not in quite the way Brother Lemon meant. This was his first job, and he was performing it with all possible enthusiasm. But his English vocabulary and his knowledge of fundamentalist doctrine were both strictly limited. He had not put words into Brother Lemon's mouth. He had only translated them in his own way, and the listening beggars had completed the transformation of text by hearing what they wanted to hear.

It is Lemon's problem, too, just as Danso, the "chameleon who felt it was self-betrayal to show his own hues," had seen – until his own symbols had to a degree freed him – only what he wanted to see.

Running through the story is another set of Biblical allusions, however. Lemon is likened when he first arrives to the "apostle landing at Cyprus," and later we are told that he possibly "expected to find an African Barnabas." Throughout, Laurence makes the distinction between apostle and sorcerer, and in the closing paragraphs she identifies these directly as Paul and Elymas. The allusions are to the thirteenth chapter of *Acts,* verses 1 to 12:

> NOW there were in the church that was at Antioch certain prophets and teachers; as Barnabas, and Simeon that was called Niger, and Lucius of Cyrene, and Manaen, which had been brought up with Herod the tetrarch, and Saul.
>
> 2 As they ministered to the Lord, and fasted, the Holy Ghost said, Separate me Barnabas and Saul for the work whereunto I have called them.

3 And when they had fasted and prayed, and laid their hands on them, they sent them away.

4 So they, being sent forth by the Holy Ghost, departed unto Seleucia; and from thence they sailed to Cyprus.

5 And when they were at Salamis, they preached the word of God in the synagogues of the Jews; and they had also John to their minister.

6 And when they had gone through the isle unto Paphos, they found a certain sorcerer, a false prophet, a Jew, whose name was Barjesus:

7 Which was with the deputy of the country, Sergius Paulus, a prudent man; who called for Barnabas and Saul, and desired to hear the word of God.

8 But Elymas the sorcerer (for so is his name by interpretation) withstood them, seeking to turn away the deputy from the faith.

9 Then Saul, (who is called Paul), filled with the Holy Ghost, set his eyes on him.

10 And said, O full of all subtilty and all mischief, thou child of the devil, thou enemy of all righteousness, wilt thou not cease to pervert the right ways of the Lord?

11 And now, behold, the hand of the Lord is upon thee, and thou shalt be blind, not seeing the sun for a season. And immediately there fell on him a mist and a darkness; and he went about seeking some to lead him by the hand.

12 Then the deputy, when he saw what was done, believed, being astonished at the doctrine of the Lord.

If the *Revelations* text articulates the message of the central narrative (Lemon's text, as it were), the "subtext" from *Acts* provides a cross-perspective towards it: both for the other characters (Danso, who sees Lemon as sorcerer, and Will, who makes the Pauline ascriptions) and for the author, who rejects not just Lemon's rigidity but also the *either-or* structure which *Acts* and (initially, at any rate) the various characters alike impose upon morality. The *Acts* chapter echoes the blindness theme upon which the *Revelations* passage hinges. But for Laurence it is not easy to distinguish between those who blind and those who are blinded, a dilemma of recognition that is apparent in the story from the very beginning. The story opens in "the painted light of mid-day" with "No shade anywhere"; bound in tension are the contrary notions that the story later raises: the character of Lemon's heaven ("Neither shall the sun light on them, nor any heat"), with which the airport tarmac clearly does not coincide, and the character of the absolute judgment asserted here ("No shade anywhere") which is Lemon's method for identifying the heaven he offers for sale.

This tension between reference and rhetorical stance, and the incidental ironies in the narrative, supply a means for the author to surmount the limitations that words impose upon her and to reach towards the "poetry" of art. They argue against an acceptance of black-and-white, either-or positions, and they support structurally Will's final refusal to identify Lemon as *either* Paul *or* Elymas. At the end Will tries instead "to see through black and white, until they merge and cease to be separate or apart," and until even Lemon emerges from the confines of absolute definition and seems to him to be more like one of the "despairingly hopeful" "damaged creatures" in Danso's painting, clustered around the Son of *Man.* If this process reduces Lemon in some ways, it also raises him: asserting his ordinary humanness, which for all its imperfection must still be valued.

Pilgrims' Progress: Margaret Laurence and Hagar Shipley

CLARA THOMAS

Who would true valor see,
Let him come hither.
All here will constant be
Come wind, come weather.
There's no discouragement
Shall make him once repent
His first avowed intent,
  To be a pilgrim.
....
No foes shall stay his might,
Though he with giants fight;
He will make good his right
  To be a pilgrim.

Hymn, from Joyce Cary's
To Be a Pilgrim

Hagar Shipley is sustained by her pride and she is made monstrous by her pride. She is ninety years old when we first hear her voice, and she bitterly describes herself as grossly fat, ugly and clumsy, a "perambulating pup-tent." Her body has grown as grotesque as her unforgiving spirit; she is by turns agonizingly constipated and suddenly incontinent, snarling and sarcastic or weak and weeping. Her son and daughter-in-law, Marvin and Doris, themselves in their sixties, have to bear with her hour by hour and day by day, with her stubborn, intractable temper and her massive, unmanageable body. She is humiliated hourly and daily by being so vulnerable, and yet she is implacably unyielding to them in their unhappy, honest efforts on her behalf and to herself in her age and weakness and in her life's failures. Yet in the unbending pride of her spirit there is also enormous strength: she journeys through memory to recall her life, face its failures and admit her

* This article was first published in *Etudes Canadiennes: Revue Interdisciplinaire des Etudes Canadiennes en France,* December 1981. It subsequently appeared in the *Journal of Canadian Studies,* Vol. 17, No. 3 (Fall 1982) and in *A Place to Stand On,* ed. George Woodcock, NeWest Press, 1983.

betrayals; and she makes one last, brief and desperate bid for escape from the chains of age and illness. She comes to her final hospital bed, but she also comes to her moment of truth and liberation, the recognition of the force that warped her own life and her love for others: "Pride was my wilderness, and the demon that led me there was fear. I was alone, never anything else, and never free, for I carried my chains within me, and they spread out and shackled all I touched" (*The Stone Angel,* p. 292).

Hagar's pride is a factor of her background, both ancestral and historical: Jason Currie, her father, was a relentlessly proud and "God-fearing" man, and the battle-cry of the Currie clan, which Hagar took as her own, was "Gainsay Who Dare"; the social fabric of Manawaka, the little western Canadian town built by Jason Currie and other Scottish immigrants like him, was made secure by the pride of its builders, but it was also potentially a prison for its people who were ruthlessly restricted by its "brake of proper appearances." Hagar is herself a "stone angel"; she is also a "holy terror" in the full, literal meaning of those words, and hearing Marvin call her that is her gift of grace at the end of her long life of conflict: "Listening I feel like it is more than I could now reasonably have expected out of life, for he has spoken with such anger and such tenderness" (*The Stone Angel,* p. 305).

In the history of American fiction the publication in 1850 of *The Scarlet Letter* has a landmark place: *The Stone Angel,* published in 1964, holds a comparable place in the lineage of Canadian fiction. Both are not only impeccably crafted works of literary art, but they are also studies of the enclosed "garrison culture" of North American settlements and of the religion that supported and often distorted the spirit of their people. In both, the religion in question is a form of Calvinism – the Puritanism of Arthur Dimmesdale and Salem, the Presbyterianism of Jason Currie and Manawaka. And the overwhelming question at the heart of both these works is one of many-prismed conflict, between the individual's needs and demands and society's, between God's law and man's understanding and interpretation of that law, between the rule of the community and the rule of the heart, between pride and love.

Margaret Laurence is a Canadian novelist and she often calls herself a prairie novelist, but the stress must be placed on the noun in those phrases, and not on the adjective. She is a *novelist,* writing out of her Canadian background and experience – but her first novel, *This Side Jordan,* and her *Tomorrow-Tamer* stories, as well as the autobiographical-travel work, *The Prophet's Camel Bell,* were written out of seven years' African experience. I do not believe that there are direct influences from Canadian authors to her work at all, though, back in Vancouver after her African years and already perceiving that the themes she had abstracted from those experiences were the major themes of her own people as well, she read Sinclair Ross's *As For Me and My House* and realized with joy that first-class fiction could be written out of their common prairie background; she also read and admired the work of Ethel Wilson and was deeply grateful for Mrs. Wilson's friendship and encouragement; but the passion for a sustaining faith and wholeness that infuses and unifies all her works is Margaret Laurence's alone among our novelists. On the deepest, dynamic level she is a religious novelist and all of her works are facets of one whole, a pilgrim's progress towards the complementary and intertwining knowledge of self and knowledge of God.

As she describes it, she wrote *This Side Jordan* in episodes as they came to her and then struggled with the problem of assembling the parts into a coherent whole. To date, it is the only one of her novels written in the third person and, in retrospect, the parallel structure containing the stories of Miranda and Johnny Kestoe and Aya and Nathaniel Amegbe has always seemed too rigid to her. Certainly the ease and seeming inevitability of *The Stone Angel's* telling is a remarkable advance over the earlier work. As Margaret Laurence recollects it, Hagar's voice simply came to her without experimental effort, as a gift. Hagar herself had been developing in her mind and imagination for a period of years; she was always connected for Laurence with the troublesome bondswoman of Abraham and not with the Hagar of Galatians whom William New mentioned in his introduction to the New Canadian Library edition. It is certainly possible that her genesis is connected with the Laurences' experience of the desert people of Somaliland and their nomadic lives, unchanged since Biblical times. The only possible parallel to Hagar's harsh, unyielding spirit in her author's experience, however, was her grandfather Simpson, who was later to be both celebrated and exorcised as Grandfather Connor in *A Bird in the House.* But to Margaret Laurence's conscious knowledge and in her memory there was and is no one model.

When the appointed time came Hagar spoke, in her own voice. At that point Laurence, the creator, became Laurence, the recorder. I once asked her, for instance, if the introductory pages which establish so immediately and unforgettably Hagar's tone, her bitterness, her far-ranging imagination and her energy, required much revision and re-writing. I was especially curious about the line, "Now I am rampant with memory," which establishes such a magnificent bridge between the voice of the old Hagar and the beginning of her journey through her past. The answer was, "None. It all came just like that, as it is now on the page."

There was one novelist at this time, however, whose themes were totally congenial to Margaret Laurence and whose techniques certainly demonstrated to her the possibilities inherent in first person narrative. Back in Vancouver from Africa she had discovered the novels of Joyce Cary. When in 1969 I first asked her about other novelists' influence on her work, his was the only name she gave me; she has recently confirmed this once again. Cary had spent years of his life as a British Colonial administrator in Nigeria, and his *The African Witch,* the first of his novels she read, had an obvious appeal in shared experience. But it was his first trilogy, *Herself Surprised, To Be a Pilgrim,* and *The Horse's Mouth,* whose themes confirmed her own deepest concerns and whose dazzling variations on the first person narrative voice must have expanded her sense of her own options in narrative techniques.

Cary too was a religious novelist and the over-arching themes of all his works are freedom, faith and the revelations of life's meaning and purpose that come as gifts of grace. Writing an introduction to a new edition of his first trilogy in 1957, shortly before his death, he described his purpose thus:

> What I set out to do was to show these people, living each in his own world by his own ideas, and relating his life and struggles, his triumphs and miseries in that world.... Their situation, in short, was to be that of everyone who is doomed or blessed to be a free soul in the free world and solve his problems as he goes through it....
>
> Each of us is obliged to construct his own idea, his own map of things by which he is going to find his way, as far

> as he can, through life. He must decide what he wants and how he shall achieve himself.[1]

Faith, to Cary, is an absolutely necessary concomitant to living: "A man without faith in some value beyond his own advantage sooner or later finds life meaningless and impossible.... It is just because faith is vital to the happiness of every single human being that religious conflict is so bitter and perplexed. Men dare not lose their faith, however fantastic."[2]

Margaret Laurence has written and spoken of freedom as a major theme in her work, notably in the article "Ten Years' Sentences,"[3] but she has publicly explored the foundations of her writing much less than Cary did and she has shown the workings of faith and grace in her characters' lives rather than writing theoretically about these things. She certainly concurs with Cary, however, in the centrality she places on them and his discourse on the meaning of conversion, written in his introduction to *The African Witch* and adopted from William James's *Varieties of Religious Experience,* would find her in complete agreement. Barbara Fisher, Cary's recent critic, has explored the links between James and Cary:

> Of Tolstoy's conversion James says: "Tolstoy does well to talk of it as *That which men live*; for that is exactly what it is, a stimulus, an excitement, a faith that re-infuses the positive willingness to live.... To be converted, to be regenerated, to receive grace, to experience religion, to gain an assurance, are so many phrases which denote the process, gradual or sudden, by which a self hitherto divided, and consciously wrong inferior and unhappy, becomes unified and consciously right superior and happy, in consequence of its firmer hold upon religious realities."[4]

This also describes, of course, the experience that Hagar undergoes and its effect upon her.

In Cary's first trilogy Sara Monday, Mr. Wilcher and Gulley Jimson tell their own stories of lives that touch, intercept, mingle and then flow alone again in voices that are unique to their tellers. Like Hagar, all three are imprisoned by their circumstances and by their own faulty understanding of themselves. As she writes her story, Sara, the cook, is literally in prison for theft from Mr. Wilcher; Wilcher begins his at Tolbrook, his old home, where, old and ill, he has been brought to die; and Gulley, the irrepressible rogue-artist, is just out of prison when he begins his story, but age and illness are overtaking him too, the world he lives in is no nearer to accepting him as the artist he knows himself to be than it ever was, and he is, as always, both stubbornly and self-destructively at odds with that world and enjoying every moment of the struggle. Though there are scenes and situations in all of the three novels that suggest themselves as parallels to Hagar's experience, particularly Gulley's final days in a hospital bed and Wilcher's moving recollection of his sister Lucy's singing of the hymn, "To Be a Pilgrim," it is to Sara Monday's voice and story that one first turns for links to Hagar Shipley.

Sara is writing out her life story after being tried, convicted and imprisoned as a thief. Far from being rampant with memory, impelled as Hagar is into her autobiographical, confessional and finally liberating journey through time, she has been nudged by the prison chaplain to "Know Thyself," and, as she reveals only on the final page, she has also been offered £100 by a newspaper for an account of her experiences. Her purpose is partly therapeutic, partly confessional and partly shrewdly practical and expedient. Neither is the form of Sara's reminiscences similar to the highly dramatic, tension- and suspense-filled juxtaposition of past and present that Hagar's voice records. In contrast, Sara engages in a low-keyed retrospective narrative; once having set her scene and situation, she moves into the past and remains there until her story is finished.

Her tone has nothing of the truculent bitterness nor lacerating scorn of Hagar's; rather Sara's is relatively uncomplaining and only gently self-justifying. She is somewhat bemused by what has happened to her. She has always been used to shifting the responsibility for her actions to circumstances or to other people; she has always taken the easy way out, except in the astonishing tenacity of her relationship with the physically abusive Gulley Jimson. She is rather amazed than bitter to find that a person of such good will and good heart as she believes herself to be could have come to such a pass. But in the process of writing her story she is "herself surprised," impelled to admit responsibility for her choices and, more important, to record and recognize the abiding strands of love that have made her life of such value to her as she lived it and of the grace that makes it still dynamic, precious and to be savoured with hope, though all her fortunes seem to lie in ruins around her.

Like Hagar, Sara is a survivor. Resilience is common to both of them, but whereas adaptation is Sara's natural mode of being, combat is Hagar's. Both women have strongly sensual natures; Sara has drifted in and out of her various vicissitudes motivated by love of living in all its manifestations – sexual love, love of colour, of clothes, food, sensations. She has never differentiated between grades of pleasure, her experience of a new hat or a new lover, of bathing in the river, eating a good meal or caring for a sick child. Hagar has retained her love of possessions and sensations into her nineties, of the look and the feel of them, the texture and colour of a silk dress, the taste of roast beef gravy or the smell of lilacs, but her feelings she has repressed since childhood. She could not, or would not, comfort her brother Matt as he lay dying; she defied her father rather than humbling herself, in spirit when he punished her as a child and in action when she married Bram Shipley. She would never admit or show her sexual pleasure to Bram, much less voice her love and concern for him. The culmination of her tragedy of perversity was the curdling of her love for her son, John, into a meanly possessive pride that connived to deny him Arlene, the girl he loved, and so played its destructive part in their senseless deaths.

Sara's story, like Wilcher's and Jimson's, moves in light compared to the blackness that encircles Hagar – indeed, Cary considered calling his trilogy *The Comedy of Freedom.*[5] The difference is one of both nature and nurture, the difference between their temperaments and characters, exacerbated by the gulf between the social worlds they inhabit and the moral universes that these worlds show forth. A powerful, though largely secularized, Calvinism dominates and has poisoned Hagar's perceptions of the world around her; though in the stories of Cary's characters a strong social criticism is implied, in Hagar's voice that criticism becomes a powerful indictment. Hugh MacLennan, who, like Laurence, carries the Calvinistic heritage into all his work, and who at one time designated John Calvin as "one of the most evil men, if not the most evil man in history," expressed the difference between theologies this way:

> My mortal quarrel with Calvinism was not that it denied realities, but that it inculcated into children the idea that God was each man's personal enemy, and that a man committed a sin merely by existing. Theoretically, the Anglicans also believe this, and so do the Catholics, but the Catholics presume to be able to forgive this sin, and the Anglicans (once they had rid themselves of the puritans) treated God much as they treated parliament. While parliament possesses the right to boil an Englishman in oil at its pleasure, the individual Englishman seems able to live with confidence that it won't do so.[6]

Calvinism, as understood by many of its practitioners, shifted the balance of the Christian gospel from a message of hope, love and redemption, to one of guilt, death and damnation, backwards from the Christ of the New Testament to the Old Testament God of wrath and retribution. It was also particularly compatible with the entrepreneurial spirit of capitalism.[7]

When Hagar Shipley was a child in the 1880s, Manawaka was still close to its beginnings, with board sidewalks, oil lamps, a few successful businesses such as Jason Currie's store, institutions such as the well-tended cemetery, the everpresent undertaker and the churches, especially the Presbyterian church:

> I'd be about eight when the new Presbyterian church went up. Its opening service was the first time Father let me go to church with him instead of to Sunday School. It was plain and bare and smelled of paint and new wood, and they hadn't got the stained glass windows yet, but there were silver candlesticks at the front, each bearing a tiny plaque with Father's name, and he and several others had purchased family pews and furnished them with long cushions of brown and beige velour, so our few and favoured bottoms would not be bothered by hard oak and a lengthy service.
>
> "On this great day," the Reverend Dougall MacCulloch said feelingly, "we have to give special thanks to those of our congregation whose generosity and Christian contributions have made our new church possible."
>
> He called them off, the names, like an honour role. Luke McVitie, lawyer, Jason Currie, businessman, Freeman McKendrick, bank manager, Burns MacIntosh, farmer, Rab Fraser, farmer.

> Father sat with modestly bowed head, but turned to me and whispered very low: "I and Luke McVitie must've given the most, as he called our names the first." (*The Stone Angel*, p. 15)

Pride in financial success, in "getting ahead" was inextricably linked to religion in Hagar Currie's Manawaka. The isolation of small groups of people in a vast land was one of the factors in the growth of a town's personality; in English Canada the other factor was the drive to build a progressive, successful and Protestant community. Ideals of godliness and business enterprise were closely meshed, especially so for those whose religion incorporated the old, passionately-argued Calvinistic doctrines of predestination and of the elect. Though those grim articles of faith were considerably less than ramrod strong in Canadian Presbyterians of the nineteenth and early twentieth centuries, there still existed a residual, crude but powerful belief that the elect of God, the saved, were shown forth by their works and, therefore, that the man who succeeded in the world's terms by his own labours had also succeeded in God's terms, his outward success the sign of his favoured status among the elect. Hence Jason Currie's unremitting drive for success, his pride in it and its link to his religion:

> He was a self-made man. He had started off without a bean, he was fond of telling Matt and Dan, and had pulled himself up by his bootstraps.... *The devil finds work for idle hands.* He put his faith in homilies. They were his Pater Noster, his Apostles' Creed. He counted them off like beads on a rosary, or coins in the till. *God helps those who help themselves. Many hands make light work.* (*The Stone Angel*, pp. 7-8)

Not only Presbyterians came to towns like Manawaka. Methodists, Baptists, Congregationalists and all the other sects who established their churches in the small towns of Canada carried with them religions that balanced far more towards fear than love. Furthermore, everything men and women found in pioneer experience would also confirm their belief that their God required hard service, not rejoicing, as the land demanded battle and did not repay love. The God who presided over their bleak lives must have seemed to the pioneers remarkably analogous to the Old Testament Jehovah, God of war and wrath and judgement. Certainly Hagar in her first words goes one step further still in her indictment, linking the founders of Manawaka with the pharaohs themselves, worshippers of power, wealth and death, and the enslavers of God's chosen people.

Before *The Stone Angel* there had been other novels in Canadian literature that charted the human cost of settling the Canadian west, most notably Grove's *Fruits of the Earth* and *Settlers of the Marsh.* No novel has had a comparable impact to *The Stone Angel,* however; as Margaret Laurence often said, in the United States readers identified Hagar as the archetypal North American old woman: in Canada they identified her as their grandmother. As she also often said, she realized while writing the book that she was reclaiming, as if by a gift, the idiom of her grandparents. Hagar's voice and her language have stamped themselves on her readers with a total authenticity to their time and place.

The settlement of the American west had a pattern of violence, the hard-riding, gun-toting cowboy its symbol to this day; in Canada the law, in the persons of the Northwest Mounted Police, preceded the settlers – our one bloody landmark, the suppression of the Métis and Indians under Louis Riel at Batoche, was seen as the supression of a rebellion against established law and order, not recognized as a desperate last stand by the west's native peoples to hold their land and their way of life. Among contemporary spokesmen for the process of settlement, what we now see as nineteenth-century imperialism was linked to God's will and the missionary enterprise of Protestant Christianity. George Monro Grant (1835-1902), Principal of Queen's University and Head of the Presbyterian Church in Canada, published *Ocean to Ocean* (1873), a classic narrative of western travel:

> The land difficulty has been settled by faith being kept with the half-breeds; a treaty has been made with the Indians that extinguishes their claim to the land.... There is no Jewish law preserving to its family its inheritance forever. The French half-breeds do not like farming, and they therefore make but poor farmers; and as enterprising settlers with a little capital come in, much of the land is sure to change hands.[8]

The Canadian Pacific Railway issued torrents of immigration literature in North America and Europe, painting the west as a new Eden, a "Land of Beginning Again." Writers wrote romances of settlement, especially the Reverend Charles Gordon

(1860-1937), a Presbyterian minister. As "Ralph Connor," our first popular novelist, whose first three novels alone sold three million copies, he tirelessly pictured the settling of the west as an enormous adventure into a new Promised Land, its goal and outcome the foundation of a triumphantly Christian society – according to the ideals of white anglo-saxon Protestantism. These motives and goals, their successes and their failure, are a part of Margaret Laurence's and her Canadian readers' inheritance, a frame of reference that gives depth and density to Hagar's words. Jason Currie and his like were proud, strong men, who performed feats of endurance taming the land in the service of their goals of personal success and social progress. Their pride sustained them, but it was a two-edged sword, its cost reckoned in terms of losses they did not recognize, failures in humanity whose effects were built into the generations after them.

Hagar has inherited their pride and lived by it. It has destroyed her relationships with others, but it also gives her the will to endure and to fight onward. One last time she flings down her challenge in life, "Gainsay Who Dare"; beleaguered by time and mortality, she makes her pilgrimage and she wins through to self-acceptance and peace – and she is finally blessed by the knowledge of love. In the structure Margaret Laurence has built of all her novels, according to her own intuition of life as a gift and pilgrimage, Hagar is the central, tragic figure, finally, at the last moment, redeemed. Coming first in time among Laurence's heroines, she is the keystone among them.

> But all great artists have a theme, an idea of life profoundly felt and founded in some personal and compelling experience. This theme then finds confirmation and development in new intuition. The development of the great writer is the development of his theme – the theme is part of him and has become the cast of his mind and character.[9]

NOTES

1. Joyce Cary, *To Be A Pilgrim,* in *First Trilogy* (New York: Harper Brothers, 1958), Introduction by Joyce Cary, p. ix.
2. *Ibid.*, p. xv.
3. Margaret Laurence, "Ten Years' Sentences," *Canadian Literature,* 41 (1969), pp. 10-16.
4. Barbara Fisher, *Joyce Cary: The Writer and His Theme* (London: Colin Smythe, 1980), pp. 7-8.

5. *Ibid.*, Joyce Cary's letter to Mark Schorer, pp. 2-4.
6. Elspeth Cameron, *Hugh MacLennan: A Writer's Life* (Toronto: University of Toronto Press, 1981), pp. 228-9.
7. Clara Thomas, "Crusoe and The Precious Kingdom," *Journal of Canadian Fiction*, Vol. 1, no. 2 (Spring 1972), pp. 58-64.
8. George Munro Grant, *Ocean to Ocean* (Edmonton: Hurtig, 1967), p. 78.
9. Joyce Cary, *Art and Reality* (Cambridge, 1958), p. 105. Given as the Clark Lectures at Cambridge, 1956.

"All That Happens, One Must Try to Understand": The Kindredness of Tillie Olsen's "Tell Me a Riddle" and Margaret Laurence's ***The Stone Angel***

MICHAEL A. PETERMAN

Speaking at Trent University on the subject of "Books That Mattered to Me," Margaret Laurence gave special praise to a novella and a writer few in that Canadian audience of 1980 recognized. "Tillie Olsen," she reported,

> is an American writer with whom I feel a deep sense of empathy, tribal kinship, sisterhood. Her book, *Tell Me a Riddle,* consists of a novella and three short stories. She has written relatively little because of her personal circumstances. She married young, had four children and for many years had to work at a job outside her home. Her book, *Silences,* explores the circumstances that have prevented some writers, both female and male, from fulfilling their life's work. The Novella, *Tell Me a Riddle,* seems to me to be as close to perfection as any contemporary prose I have read. In just fifty printed pages – fifty! – Olsen communicates the story of a long marriage, an entire family, ancestral roots reaching back into a long ago past in other countries, the ways in which humans suffer and hurt one another and yet support and love one another. In my view, it is a small masterpiece.[1]

The account Laurence gives in that paper is chronological and, not surprisingly, Tillie Olsen's place occurs late on her list. According to Laurence's own recollection, she did not read "Tell Me a Riddle" until years after she herself completed *The Stone Angel,* the work "Tell Me a Riddle" most closely resembles.[2] Thus, although "Tell Me a Riddle" appeared both as a published story and in book form prior to *The Stone Angel* (1964),[3] any attempt to compare the two works must rest upon not the business of influence but what Laurence herself calls "a deep sense of empathy, tribal kinship, sisterhood."

To be useful, comparisons of writers from different countries, cultures, and traditions need to address the particularities that distinguish the work of each writer under discussion. They should help us to consider, to place, and to value each writer more clearly and fully. They should help us to see how (if at all) each approaches the questions of national identity as well as the larger concerns of human understanding. They should alert us to the distinctive ways in which each chooses to tap the potential of a particular subject – what each writer sees and allows us to see in that subject.

Certainly "Tell Me a Riddle" and *The Stone Angel* provide much to compare. Both are stories of elderly women nearing the moment of death. Married 47 years and mother of 7 children, Olsen's Eva is 69 years old and suffering from cancer. Told in the third person, the narrative covers the last few months of Eva's life during which she endures painful surgery and is taken by her husband, against her wishes, to visit her various offspring and their families. Laurence's Hagar Shipley, a proud, independent-spirited woman of more than 90 years, has long outlived both her husband and the more favoured of her two sons. Employing first-person narration, *The Stone Angel* covers the last few weeks of Hagar's life as she struggles against loss of control of her own actions and the growing pain she feels under her ribs. The exact nature of her problem she defines "only [as] a name" that repels and stuns her.[4] Both women are characterized as formidable spirits, both resist the idea of being put into homes for the aged ("the Haven" in Olsen's case, "Silverthreads" in Laurence's), and both are impelled toward unconventional or anti-institutional expressions of meaning and faith as they (voluntarily or involuntarily) review their lives.

Beyond such textual similarities lie the likenesses which led Laurence to remark upon her "deep sense of empathy, tribal kinship, [and] sisterhood" with Olsen. Both are, nominally at least, prairie writers. Born in Omaha, Nebraska, in 1912 or 1913, Olsen seems to have been far less touched by the plains landscape than either fellow Nebraskan, Willa Cather, or Manitoba-born Margaret Laurence. "Tell Me a Riddle" (and the three stories accompanying it) owes virtually nothing to prairie experience. Though set in Vancouver and, like "Tell Me a Riddle" making use of the ocean as suggestive symbol, *The Stone Angel* is Margaret Laurence's richest prairie novel. Not only is Hagar characterized in terms of the prairie but she lives as a struggling farmer's wife for some 24 years, a rugged kind of experience known by none of Laurence's other Manitoba-born but town-raised protagonists.

More compelling grounds for similarity lie in other areas – the problems shared by Olsen and Laurence as women seeking simultaneously to raise families and to pursue writing careers; their attraction to reform-minded, left-wing politics (the Depression looms large in the recollected experiences of both Eva and Hagar); and their shared desire to explore "ancestral roots reaching back into a long ago past in other countries." Both "Tell Me a Riddle" and *The Stone Angel* are explorations into the nature and cost of motherhood. Neither heroine has any sense of being a writer or artist manqué. Rather it has been their fate – in Eva's case a fate imposed by circumstances, in Hagar's case the result as much (or more) or personal pride and temperament as of circumstances – to have devoted most of their mature lives to marriage and/or motherhood. Having endured the deep-rooted "quarrel" of her marriage,[5] and having struggled to raise her children often under difficult and impoverished conditions, Eva has achieved at the story's outset a "reconciled solitude" and a "reconciled peace" (T95, 77). In such a state of mind there is something almost absolute about her personal need and desire to resist at this time the tentacles and pressures of family. "Enough," she thinks. "Now they had no children. Let *him* wrack his head for how they would live. She would not exchange her solitude for anything. *Never again to be forced to move to the rhythms of others*" (T,76). Feeling the larger need to draw her energies inward, she sidesteps the traps that would have her fulfil the image of a good grandmother in the conventional, middle-class, Jewish mode; rather, her mind focusses upon the reclamation of the essence of certain of her girlhood experiences in Russia that made her what she became. She needs to clarify the values she has, in her taciturn way, lived by throughout her life. Like Hagar, she is "rampant with memory" (S,5). Like Hagar, who is described by her son, Marvin, as "a holy terror" (S,304), Eva is "as thorny a flower as ever" (T,91), as thorny in her withdrawal from family as she apparently was within the family in earlier days.

Hagar Shipley also feels much put upon and threatened by others through *The Stone Angel.* "I've never had a moment to myself, that's been my trouble" (S,93), she thinks, but her real trouble, which she struggles to understand and to put into words, is that she's "strangely cast" (S,304). Hers is a temperament torn between impulses of order and disorder, refinement and toughness, propriety and desire, impulses justified in her own mind by her pride in her family and the urgency of her own passions. The struggle of her last days is not only a struggle to maintain independence and control; it is also an almost inadvertent plumbing of "the junkyard of [her] memory" (S,213). In so doing she finds herself at last able to measure the extent of her misjudgments of those closest to her and to break out, to some small extent, of the prison of her nature. Thus, in contrast to Eva who, in the process of recovery, seeks to close herself off from others, Hagar is inwardly impelled to break through her self-imposed toughness so as to express her human and maternal responses more openly, more compassionately.

The politics that underlie "Tell Me a Riddle" are socialistic or communistic. A product of the 1905 revolution in Russia, as were Olsen's own parents, Eva has kept alive vivid memories of her own imprisonment by Russian authorities at Olshana and of the execution of the friend who taught her to read, Lisa, a high-born Tolstoyan who, while in prison with Eva, murdered a traitor to the revolution. Though the details of Olshana appear only as evocative fragments in the text, those Russian experiences years earlier underlie the struggle and the values of Eva's later life. Set in contrast to the opportunities and comforts of contemporary America ("yes, Jeannie, it is more than oceans between Olshana and you" (T,113), she tells her granddaughter), Eva's Russian life stands as a significant human victory over pain, injustice, tyranny, and death. *Her* "fossil memory," *her* "heart of stone" (T,99), is not a function of familial or personal pride; it is the legacy of determined human struggle against almost impossible social odds and conditions. In Olsen's hands, the resilient Eva gives the myth of Sisyphus a particularly Marxist turn: "There was an ancient man who fought to heights a great rock that crashed down eternally – eternal labor, freedom, labor…" (T,99). What Eva learned at Olshana and endured through the Depression years can not be softened by any of the seductions America so readily promises in the present.

Eva's faith lies in the struggle of the proletariat, their ability to sing despite deprivation and tyranny. She will not be deluded by the advertisers' promises in America any more than by the sentimentalized claims of Jewish heritage or the assuaging capacities of religion. Her passion becomes sharply focussed when, in response to her husband's uncritical defense of religion's consolatory benefits, she uncharacteristically breaks her silence:

> "Swindler! does she [her daughter Hannah] look back on the dark centuries? Candles bought instead of bread and stuck into a potato for a candlestick? Religion that stifled and said: in Paradise, woman, you will be the footstool of your husband, and in life – poor chosen Jew – ground under, despised, trembling in cellars. And cremated. And cremated. (T,90)

Refusing religious solace in the hospital, she insists that the staff take her off "the Jewish list ... Tell them to write: Race, human; Religion, none" (T,89).

Cutting herself off from the consolations of religion, from "the passion of tending" (T,92), and holding herself back from her husband, her children, and "their intimate life together" (T,118), Eva may seem pig-headed and cruel. What would impel a "little gnome grandmother," dying of cancer, enduring great pain, to turn away from conjugal and familial comforts so plentifully offered to her. On the one hand she stands, pathetically, as an embodiment of an important Tillie Olsen theme, that of waste, the kind of human waste that comes not from individual squandering of opportunity or talent but from the cruelty of circumstances that prevent opportunity or expression. So thinks her son Lennie, "suffering not alone for her who was dying, but for that in her which never lived (for that which in him might never live)" (T,117). On the other hand, the tiny core of Eva's spirit resists waste and defeat; it seeks reclamation in a way Lennie cannot see. Drawn backward to her youth, she seeks to articulate the spirit or belief that kept her always from despising or despairing of life, however it might have wearied and frustrated her (T,113). Having struggled so much, she will not become "a memorialized wraith" simply to comfort those who will outlive her:

> Surely that was not all, surely there was more. Still the springs, the springs were in her seeking. Somewhere an older power that beat for life. Somewhere coherence, transport, meaning.

> If they [her family] would but leave her in the air now stilled of clamor, in the reconciled solitude, to journey on (T,93).

Heroically, then, Eva pursues an "older power" or pole star. "Coherence" for her lies not in personal relief but in a larger honesty and knowledge that puts suffering in perspective. What was denied her in the books she respected but always had so little time for or access to, she has garnered from hard experience. Aware of "the monstrous shapes of what had actually happened in the century" (T,120), she strives toward knowledge of "what humanizes" (T,90). Her personal credo is perhaps best suggested in her phrase, "All that happens, one must try to understand" (T,113). Pursuing this larger, less personal vision, Eva resolves to "Let the living comfort themselves" (T,113). Like a sensitive organ, an ear exposed and unprotected, her urgency to know and to feel is so great that, in Tillie Olsen's hands, Eva stands as a challenge to conventional and sentimental images of solicitous motherhood, particularly in the Jewish tradition.[6]

Tillie Olsen's experiences as a child within a family committed to socialistic goals and as a writer and activist for the Communist cause in America in the 1930s and 1940s contrast sharply to the privileged, middle-class upbringing of Margaret Laurence.[7] While her "feelings of anti-imperialism, anti-colonialism, anti-authoritarianism, had begun, probably, in embryo form" in her childhood,[8] it was her experience first with the old Left of North Winnipeg in the 1940s and then her life in Africa from 1950 to 1957 that nurtured her sympathies for the victims of prevailing power-structures. Despite the gathering force of Laurence's left-wing sympathies, despite her growing desire to address issues of dispossession and social injustice, *The Stone Angel* is very much a novel of middle-class aspiration, action, and folly. Proud descendent of a family that could claim clan connections, a lapsed Scottish baronetcy, and self-made success in pioneering Canada, Hagar (Currie) Shipley has little time for the larger questions of social order and justice. Though she oscillates like a pendulum between her personal impulses (S,202), so strong is her ethic of self-reliance that she fails to see clearly the plight of farmers she knows during the Depression of the 1930s or the dispossessedness, sense of loss, and desperation of the local Métis of Manawaka. Indeed, the novel very carefully suggests that Hagar's blindness to larger issues of social justice was typical of and deep-rooted in many people of her generation. As close as she was to the actual effects of the Depression on farmers and to the Métis friends favoured by her husband Bram and her son John, she steeled herself against any potential awareness of or empathy in such experience. Her "respectability" threatened by them, she needs to hold herself aloof from, superior to the "bunch of breeds and ne'er-do-wells and Galicians" (S,114) she is obliged to feed during harvest-time. Pride both blinds and sustains her when her social identity is in question.

A study of a feisty individual forced to endure circumstances grotesquely at odds with her self-image, *The Stone Angel* enacts a more capacious view of fate than Olsen's novella. *Tell Me a Riddle* implies that fate is largely a matter of the "punitive difference in circumstance,"[9] of being born to the wrong circumstances or being a victim of tyranny or oppression. *The Stone Angel* presents fate as an amalgam of character and circumstance, the two forces interacting complexly. The individual is certainly the victim, in Laurence's phrase, of the jokes or jests of God (S,60). Those "jests", however, often have their root in individual character. In Hagar's case, it is the pendulum-like oscillation between impulses of order and disorder, respectability and passion, dynastic pride and individual need that dictate the unfolding of her life and characterize her "blindness." God's great joke is that "one discovers so many things too late" (S,60), most notably the wilderness that pride can make of a life and the self-enclosure that is the outward aspect of self-reliance. It never occurs to Hagar to ask the serious question "why" when it comes to the tyranny of social circumstances.

What struggles to find expression in the dying Hagar is the mothering side of her being that she was never, by circumstance, allowed to know and never, by temperament, willing to acknowledge. Though she remains – or at least a side of her insists upon remaining – "unchangeable, unregenerate" (S,293), she moves closer to the greater openness, warmth, and rejoicing that Laurence seems to locate in her belated tapping of her capacity and need to speak what is called "the mother-word": "There, there" (S,66).[10] It is this buried or frozen dimension of herself that Hagar struggles to bring to life. In pursuit of this personal and humanizing self-knowledge – so different from Eva's more generalized and larger-scale recoveries – she, like Eva, seeks no consolation from institutional religion. "I've never had much use for prayer," she tells her daughter-in-law's clergyman (S,119). Far more conscious of "the terrible laughter of God" (S,234) than the promise of "God's infinite mercy" (S,120), she takes an attitude similar to Eva, who can offer no riddles to her grandchildren. "If God's a crossword puzzle, or a secret code," says Hagar to her daughter-in-law's minister, Mr. Troy, "it's hardly worth the bother, it seems to me" (S,119).

Though both protagonists ostensibly reject riddles, each seeks "*to live within*" (T,77), pursuing "the thing inside" (S,118) toward some coherent sense or understanding of life's meaning. Music, young women (in particular granddaughters), and the ocean help, among other sources, to release in them a flood of memories that are the clues to that "transport." Working within the economies of the novella, Olsen summons up Eva's recollections as fragments – vivid, often poetic fragments – that the reader must follow, interpret, and link together. As befits Olsen's emphasis upon the need to recognize and humanize man's cruel and tyrannous tendencies – at work particularly against the Jews, the poor, and women – Eva's memories are decidedly impersonal. What matters is a social interpretation of truth. Operating on the larger scale of the novel, Laurence is both much more personalized and detailed in her selection of memories and more deliberate – almost over-organized – in her presentation of Hagar's past. While the richness of *The Stone Angel* lies in Hagar's extraordinary spirit and feisty personality – at once destructive and trivial, she refuses to be less than her proud, life-embracing self – the novel suffers structurally. Hagar's memories unfold in chronological order, packaged in linear prosaic sections that, in their careful organization, belie the quick jumps from association to memory that effectively characterize *Tell Me a Riddle* and the operations of memory in general.

Of final concern is the emphasis upon ancestral consciousness shared by Tillie Olsen and Margaret Laurence. *Tell Me a Riddle* is clearly a celebration of Olsen's Russian and Jewish roots. Eva's "coherence," her proletarian vision, is built upon her Russian girlhood and substantiated both by twentieth-century experience in general and her own difficult struggles as a mother in America. In terms of characterization and humour in the novella, the Jewish roots have predominance. Eva and her husband may have come to America from Russia but they are Jews in either place. Their cadences and marital sarcasms vividly distinguish them and help to embody their deep-rooted quarrel. The husband's comic euphemisms for Eva (Mrs. Word Miser, [T,73] Mrs. Unpleasant [T,79], Mrs. Live Alone [T,83]) are a measure of his frustration with her and his inability to see her as she sees herself, while her sardonic remark – "Vinegar he poured on me all his life; I am well marinated; how can I be honey now?" (T,84) – is both characteristically American-Jewish in its phrasing and indicative of her refusal to accept his self-serving solutions to the problems of *their* old age.

The idea of dynasty does not, however, affect Eva's vision, despite the size of her family. By contrast, Hagar Shipley is preoccupied by the significance of her Scottish roots. Quick to criticize the dynastic impulse in others, be it her father or her slovenly, unpretentious husband, she is herself deeply influenced by the Currie legacy of clan, (temporary) nobility, and self-made success, of familial significance in both the old world and the new. To the Currie grandeur she grafts, out of her own energy and need for self-justification, the lesser Shipley legacy just as she defies personal history by linking the family names on a single pedestal in the Manawaka cemetery. At the same time, Hagar's sharp tongue and categorical judgments owe much to her father's unyielding masculine toughness and Scots pride. "Gainsay who dare" is a kind of life motto Hagar delights in enacting upon the people she encounters just as she carries her father's attention to orderly appearances and to careful control of money throughout her own life.

In attending so tenaciously to the tight-fisted, unyielding, and proud Scottish spirit, Laurence tapped a major nerve in the Canadian sensibility. *The Stone Angel* is unabashedly middle-class, Scottish, and small-town in its emphases. As such, it captures something essential about the energy, enterprise, mood, and pattern of the settlement and development that have characterized not only the growth of Manitoba but of Canada as a whole. Though but one of Manitoba's and Canada's many cultural threads, the Scots middle-class outlook incarnated in Jason Currie and passed on to his rebellious daughter is the firm base upon which, in her later Manawaka novels, Laurence was able, without inconsistency, to integrate her developing left-wing concerns, particularly her empathy with the victims and the dispossessed who have been cast aside in the province's and the country's growth.

Little wonder then that Margaret Laurence's work is so prominent in Canada by contrast to Tillie Olsen's reputation in the United States. *The Stone Angel* was voted the most important novel in Canada at the University of Calgary's infamous "Taking Stock" conference in 1978, a fact not to be overlooked especially in the light of Laurence's own relative lack of prominence south of the border. Such particularized recognition suggests the success with which Laurence shaped her novel to present a compelling version of formative stages of Canadian identity. In linking her vision to that of her friend, historian W.L. Morton, she "assimilated Morton's work with her own experience and the past of her people," in Clara Thomas's phrase.[11] Not surprisingly, in the same essay in which she praises Tillie Olsen's achievement, Laurence cites Morton's *Manitoba: A History* (1957) as the book about my land "that has meant the most to me." "When I first read [it]", she adds, "it was with a tremendous sense of excitement, combined with an angry sense of having been deprived, when young, of my own heritage. I have since done a great deal of reading of prairie history, but it was Morton who first gave me the sense of my place's long and dramatic past."[12] In *The Stone Angel* the dream of dynasty, in itself both compelling and destructive, becomes a map of Manitoban and Canadian heritage.

Tillie Olsen's *Tell Me a Riddle* provides no such culturally significant mapping. Despite the recent interest generated in her work by the women's movement (Margaret Atwood remarks upon the "reverence" with which *Silences* has come to be treated)[13] and despite the very high quality of her small output of fiction, Olsen remains a neglected American writer. Various criticisms have been registered about her work but no single argument, indeed no cumulative account, adequately explains the relatively minimal recognition granted so talented an author. At risk of oversimplification, I am inclined to think that Olsen's low estate owes much to both her politics and her placelessness. Writing out of a proletarian vision and not particularly concerned with the relation of setting to personal experience and outlook, she has not spoken as powerfully to the American public as Margaret Laurence has to Canadian readers. Still, however much they differ in their attitudes to class, to fate, to politics, and to place, Olsen and Laurence share much in common. When Laurence speaks of their "tribal kinship" she stresses their shared struggles as writers, and in particular as women writers. When she speaks of empathy, she emphasizes that shared vision of the ways in which individuals "suffer and hurt one another and yet support and love one another." The phrasing deftly embraces the long quarrels which characterize the relationships of the protagonists in both *Tell Me a Riddle* and *The Stone Angel.* What Laurence doesn't add is that both books share above all an unflagging quest to know more, to understand better, to recover and recognize what is best and most worthwhile in human experience.[14] "All that happens, one must try to understand" (T,113): so thinks Eva as her world shrinks "into one room like a coffin" (T,107). Struggling to "understand why" she resists and tries to close off the sentimental force of her familial relationships. She must make her journey alone. Hagar also remains a fighter to the end even as her world shrinks to "a needle" (S,307). Caught in her characteristic tension, and almost against her conscious will, she struggles to open the channels of mothering she has for so long kept blocked. One side of her insists upon control, grasping "the shiny steel grail" (S,301) in her hospital bathroom, proving to herself she can still do things self-reliantly. "There I'm there, I knew I could," she thinks (S,301). The other side, maternal, giving, meek, increasingly breaks through, the "there, there" of control merging with the compassionate "there, there" of the motherword. In both protagonists, however different, the process of and the emphasis upon recovery, the struggle to understand what has eluded knowing, is made heroic, heartening, and significant.

NOTES

1. "Books That Mattered to Me," *Friends of the Bata Library,* ed. F.A. Hagar (Trent University, Peterborough, Ontario, 1981), n.p. Laurence also discusses the impact upon her of Arthur Conan Doyle, Rudyard Kipling, Robert Louis Stevenson, Nellie McClung, L.M. Montgomery, Sinclair Ross, W.O. Mitchell, Adele Wiseman, the French psychologist O. Mannoni, Canadian historian W.L. Morton, Frank Scott, Joyce Cary, Kurt Vonnegut, Gabrielle Roy, Rudy Wiebe, Robertson Davies, and Timothy Findley.
2. Margaret Laurence in conversation with Michael Peterman in May 1986.

3. "Tell Me a Riddle" first appeared in *New World Writing 16,* ed. Stewart Richardson and Corlies M. Smith (Philadelphia: Lippincott, 1960), pp. 11-57. It won the O. Henry Award as Best Story of the Year and was included in the collection of four pieces under the title, *Tell Me a Riddle,* published by J.B. Lippincott in New York in 1961. Laurence later met Tillie Olsen in Toronto and is mentioned along with several other Canadian writers in a footnote in Olsen's *Silences* (New York: Laurel, 1978).
4. Margaret Laurence, *The Stone Angel* (Toronto: McClelland and Stewart, 1968), p. 254. Further quotations from *The Stone Angel* will be designated S in the essay.
5. Tillie Olsen, *Tell Me a Riddle* (New York: Dell, 1976), p. 72. Further quotations from the novella will be designated T in the essay.
6. Jacqueline A. Mintz, "The Myth of the Jewish Mother in Three Jewish, American, Female Writers, *Centennial Review,* 22 (1978), pp. 346-50.
7. Olsen's father was State Secretary of the Nebraska Socialist Party. She became a member of the Young Communist League and participated in various labour disputes during the 1930s and 1940s. Her earliest writing appeared in the *New Republic* and the *Partisan Review* in 1934. See Abigail Martin, *Tillie Olsen* (Boise, Idaho: Boise State University Western Writers Series – Number 65, 1984).
8. Margaret Laurence, "Ivory Tower or Grass Roots?: The Novelist as Socio-political Being," in *A Political Art: Essays and Images in Honour of George Woodcock,* ed. William H. New (Vancouver, B.C.: University of British Columbia Press, 1978), p. 24.
9. Olsen uses the phrase in describing the fate of women in history. I take the liberty of applying it more widely still. *Silences,* p. 46.
10. Laurence uses the words "There, There" on numerous occasions in the text, sometimes with carefully modulated application to Hagar's two-sided nature. See pp. 76, 85, 258, and 308 for example.
11. Clara Thomas, "Myth and Manitoba in *The Diviners,*" *Journal of Canadian Studies,* 13 (Autumn 1978), p. 63.
12. "Books That Mattered to Me," n.p.
13. Margaret Atwood, "Obstacle Course," *New York Times Book Review,* 30 July 1978, p. 1.
14. Blanche Gelfant, *Women Writing in America* (Hanover and London: University Press of New England, 1984), p. 60. In the preface to her Olsen essay, Gelfant remarks upon the belated feeling of kinship Olsen felt for Willa Cather's work. "I began to sense then, dimly perhaps, what has now become clear: that women writers have common roots, not necessarily geographic, as in this instance; that they inspire and give strength to each other; that when one finds or recovers her voice, she enables many others to speak." This essay echoes that perception.

The Religious Roots of the Feminine Identity Issue: Margaret Laurence's ***The Stone Angel*** *and Margaret Atwood's* ***Surfacing***

EVELYN J. HINZ

Spearheaded by the 1973 publication of Mary Daly's *Beyond God the Father,*[1] a key contention of many Liberationists is that a major factor in preventing women from achieving a genuine sense of identity has been the "dominant male" philosophy embedded in Judaeo-Christian theology. Accordingly, women are urged to expose the sexual politics inherent in the Bible and to construct a new "thealogy" based upon matriarchal cults and upon the real experiences articulated by contemporary liberated women.

Two modern Canadian novels which would seem to serve as key texts on both accounts are Margaret Laurence's *The Stone Angel* and Margaret Atwood's *Surfacing*; indeed, the latter, in particular, has been read in this light.[2] Actually, however, as much as these two works *do* explore the connection between religious issues and female identity, they also have the effect of calling into question many of the premises and conclusions of feminists.

* * *

Published in 1964 – almost a decade before Daly's critique[3] – *The Stone Angel* is the story of a ninety-year-old woman's last days, with flashbacks designed to provide the causes of her present loneliness, her self or gender alienation, and above all her fear of death. Though played out on sociological, psychological, and historio/cultural levels, all of the protagonist's problems are shown to stem from the religious climate in which she has been raised. Thus Laurence, in seemingly feminist fashion, dramatizes the extent to which religious ideology permeates even secular aspects of human existence.

Although Hagar could be described as the damaged product of

* First published in the *Journal of Canadian Studies,* Vol. 22, No. 1 (Spring 1987).

an education that emphasizes mental/male talents, for example, that such a "logos" orientation is relatable to the "Logos" of the Judaeo-Christian tradition is made clear through the name – specifically the initials – of her prime mentor, her father: *J*ason *C*urrie. Similarly, though Hagar's relationship with her father could be studied as a modern version of the Electra Complex, her sense that her husband has committed a sacrilege when he urinates on the front steps of her father's store suggests the religious implications of the episode and so prevents any simple Freudian interpretation of her response.

Or again, if what has prevented Hagar's acceptance of her own femininity has to do with the biological fact that her mother died in giving her birth and with the culturally upheld ideal of the slim, virginal female, these too are shown to have their roots in the Judaeo-Christian tradition. Her religious role models are her mother's monument, an "angel of pure white marble," and the sisterly Madonna of Michelangelo's "Pieta" – the latter being iconographically evoked when Hagar refuses to hold her dying brother and to drape him and herself in their mother's shawl.[4]

Finally, if Hagar's sexual prudery and inability to articulate her delight in carnal love are symptomatic of the Victorian ethos of her time, Laurence also traces the problem to the spiritual orientation of Christianity. Thus it is in the context of her recollection of the line "His banner over me was love" that Hagar in retrospect acknowledges the way in which she – like the commentators who allegorized the erotic *Song of Solomon* – refused to let her husband sense her sexual response.[5]

Yet to see *The Stone Angel* purely as a Dalyesque critique would be to miss Laurence's equal concern with the implications of the decline of the Judaeo-Christian tradition. If Jason Currie's initials suggest the Saviour, for example, his first name also allies him with the questor for the golden fleece. His donations to the church proceed from no religious piety but rather from a desire to broadcast his financial superiority. For him, the importance of the angel tombstone is that it had been bought "at terrible expense" and that of all the angels in the cemetery it was "the first, the largest, and certainly the costliest" (3). Therefore, if like his classical namesake he sacrifices the female for his own interests, he also represents the materialization of spiritual values.

Similarly, far from it being her father's use of religious authority to sanction his notions of dominance, it is his lack of a sense of hierarchy that bothers Hagar. Recalling how in church the congregation sang the psalm "Unto the hills around do I lift up/ My longing eyes" to "GOD the LORD, who heaven and earth hath made," Hagar then continues:

> Auntie Doll was always telling us that Father was a God-fearing man. I never for a moment believed it, of course. I couldn't imagine Father fearing anyone, God included, especially when he didn't even owe his existence to the Almighty. God might have created heaven and earth and the majority of people, but Father was a self-made man, as he himself had told us often enough. (16-17)

Conversely, Hagar's real tragedy lies in her "feminist" confusion of spiritual and secular authority figures. Equating God and her father, she stops going to church because of the way she feels her husband has *disgraced* her in her father's eyes: "I preferred possible damnation in some comfortably distant future, to any ordeal then of peeking or pitying eyes. But now when time has folded in like a paper fan, I wonder if I shouldn't have kept on going. What if it matters to Him after all, what happens to us" (90).

Also serving to call into question the feminist position is the fact that what bothers Hagar about Christianity is not its "masculinity" as much as its "effeminacy." Here Laurence seems to be suggesting that the New Testament constitutes a decline from the Old. Hagar's husband is also a Christ figure – like Jesus, he was "born in a barn" (125) – and although his "feminine" association with the earth strikes a sympathetic cord in Hagar, it is also his lack of masculine assertiveness that is responsible for the failure in their relationship. This recognition comes to him in his last delirious moments when he muses: "That Hagar – I should of licked the living daylights out of her, maybe, and she'd have seen I could. What d'you think? Think I should of?" Hagar's response in turn is "I could not speak for the salt that filled my throat and for anger" (173) – not anger at her husband for such a male chauvinist statement, but anger over the realization of how different things might have been if Bram had been a stronger mate.

Furthering her critique of the effeminacy of the New Testament and its degeneracy, moreover, is Laurence's characterization of the surrogate God figure, the minister, whom Hagar's very "religious" daughter-in-law feels will bring the old woman "comfort" in her last days. Far from evidencing any "Trojan" qualities, the Reverend Mr. Troy is "plump and pink, and if he met John the Baptist in tatters in the desert, stuffing dead locusts into that parched mouth for food, and blazing the New Kingdom out of those terrible eyesockets, he would faint" (38). Or again, "He speaks of prayer and comfort, all in a breath, as though God were a kind of feather bed or spring-filled mattress. . . . He prays a little prayer, and I bow my head, a feather in his cap or in the eiderdown of God" (53). Not only is modern Christianity too soft, finally, it is also essentially too materialistic:

> Even if heaven were real, and measured as Revelation says, so many cubits this way and that, how gimcrack a place it would be, crammed with its pavements of gold, its gates of pearl and topaz, like a gigantic chunk of costume jewelry. Saint John of Patmos can keep his sequined heaven, or share it with Mr. Troy, for all I care, and spend eternity in fingering the gems and telling each other gleefully they're worth a fortune. (120)

Yet what is ultimately most problematic about the Judaeo-Christian tradition, as Laurence sees it, is the egocentricity and concept of individual uniqueness which it inculcates by reason of its monotheistic and anti-archetypal ideology – and here, of course, the Old Testament comes under attack equally with the New. To emphasize this point, at the moment of Hagar's greatest sense of loneliness, Laurence has her protagonist ponder the twin issues of identity and the fear of death: "Hard to imagine a world and me not in it. Will everything stop when I do? Stupid old baggage, who do you think you are? *Hagar.* There's no one like me in this world" (250). Not Logos in the sense of its patriarchal orientation, but Logos as the masculine principle of separateness and distinctness is the ultimate feature of the Judaeo-Christian tradition, which makes it such a self-destructive religion for women whose orientation is toward Eros or the principle of connectedness and toward a sense of the communal and cyclic nature of experience.[6]

Accordingly, one of Laurence's major strategies in *The Stone Angel* is to evoke biblical prototypes for Hagar, whereby she disproves her protagonist's claims to uniqueness at the same time that she demonstrates that the Bible is merely the Judaeo-Christian rendition – or "signature" – of mythic or eternally recurring experiences.[7] Just as the biblical Hagar was the Egyptian concubine of Abraham, taken by him because his first wife, Sarah, was childless, so Laurence's Hagar, who likens herself to "Pharaoh's daughter" (43), is the second wife of "Bram," whose first wife, Clara, had provided him with no male heirs. Just as a key episode in the Abraham story is Jehovah's command that he sacrifice his son, so Hagar is subjected to a test of faith when she watches Bram one day "cut a slab of waxen honey and hold it out" to their son, who "opened his mouth, afraid to do otherwise, and stand stock-still and white, while the honeyed butcher knife rammed in . . . offering sweetness on a steel that in another season slit pigs' carcasses" (125).

In turn, with a view to denying chronology – which is the historical equivalent of separateness – Laurence also finds a precedent for Hagar in the succeeding biblical generation: just as Isaac's wife, Rebecca, helped her son, Jacob, to cheat his brother out of his birthright, so Hagar wants her second son, John, to be the true heir of her father's line. Similarly, to demonstrate the universal and therefore non-sex-differentiated nature of archetypal experience, Laurence does not limit Hagar's prototypes to women. Bereft of everything, faced with the seemingly unjust ways of God, constipated Hagar is like "Job in reverse" (40).

Most important of all, however, are the variations Laurence plays on the story of Jacob and the angel, by which Hagar becomes identified not only with another masculine type but also with the spirit of Jehovah Himself. On the one hand, like Jacob who came to realize that his chief pursuer and opponent was not his brother but Jehovah, so Hagar must realize that her identity crisis stems not from secular issues but from religious ones – from "the lack of a proper foundation garment" in a metaphorical sense. On the other hand, she must come to realize that she is the antagonistic force in her relationship with her son John. As he tries to upright the toppled angel in the graveyard, she compares him to Jacob "wrestling with the angel and besting it, wringing a blessing from it with his might. But no" (179). Rather it is her other son, Marvin, who plays this role, gripping her hand as she lies in her hospital bed: "Now it seems to me he is truly Jacob, gripping with all his strength, and bargaining. *I will not let thee go, except thou bless me.* And I see that I am thus strangely cast, and perhaps have been so from the beginning, and can only release myself by releasing him" (304).

In contrast to feminists who argue that the Bible has absolutely nothing to say to women, therefore, *The Stone Angel* argues that it is only the Judaeo-Christian "signature" that is problematic.[8] Nor would Laurence appear to agree with those who argue categorically that what women need is a religion which reverses the Judaeo-Christian alignment of pride and self-assertion with sin and conversely of self-sacrifice with virtue.[9] To the exact contrary, when Hagar explicitly connects her situation with that of her biblical prototype, it is precisely in terms of hubris and of the extent to which she has internalized the egocentric value system of a monotheistic deity: "Pride was my wilderness, and the demon that led me there was fear. I was alone, never anything else, and never free, for I carried my chains within me, and they spread out from me and shackled all I touched" (292).

"Nothing can take away those years," Hagar concludes, anguishing over the guilt she feels for the love she has withheld, but with Laurence pointing to what Hagar has missed most of all in her essentially Protestant upbringing: namely, rituals of atonement and exorcism. To provide these is Laurence's purpose in having Hagar escape to an old fish cannery where she encounters a seedy "life assurance" salesman, just as Laurence herein recovers the pagan or Dionysian figure of the redeemer and his cults which lie beyond or have degenerated into the more Apollonian Christian signature. Significantly, the episode takes the form of a descent to "Shadow Point," which would seem to imply both that it is not consciousness-*raising* but *lowering* that modern women need, and that such lowering needs to have a religious dimension.

Evocative of a shift from logos to eros, Christian to pagan, the episode begins when Hagar removes her hat and adorns herself with June bugs and rowanberries. And it is in this maenadic attire that she is found by Murray Ferney Lees, himself fleeing in scapegoat fashion from two dogs who would "have torn [him] to pieces" (222). In keeping with his surname, Lees produces a jug of wine and, with Hagar making her offering of soda biscuits, the two enjoy their "Eucharistic Banquet." Lees then tells her of the "nothing meek" lusty-singing form of "early Christian" evangelicalism he had practiced and of how in this spirit he had met his wife and come to understand the divine ecstacy of sex: "in those days she could have prayed the angels themselves right out of heaven, if she'd been so inclined, and when she lay down on the moss and spread those great white thighs of hers, there wasn't a sweeter place in this entire world" (227). Unfortunately, like Hagar who responds, "Well, that's a mighty odd combination . . . prayer and *that*," Lees's wife too felt that "God is love, but please don't mention the two in the same breath" – as a long-range result of which their son dies in a housefire while he and his wife are at a church service on the theme of the end of the world. Clearly, then, to Laurence, men like Lees and Bram have suffered as much from the other-worldly orientation of Christianity as have women.

Laurence's immediate point, however, is that Hagar is "not alone" in her grief, as the Reverend Troy had earlier tried to convince her, and unsuccessfully because he was speaking purely theoretically. Lees' confession leads to Hagar's own therapeutic recollection of the night her son died. In this recollection, Laurence further emphasizes the way in which lack of rituals and of such a religious role model as the "Sorrowful Mother" result in Hagar's turning into "stone," while at the same time she ironically evokes a classical prototype for her protagonist, namely, Niobe, another "hubristic" woman who suffered the wrath of Apollo's mother for boasting about her procreative abilities, and who wept for her lost children until her eyes and body became "dry."

Provided with the advantage of confession and, significantly, not conscious of the fact that she has done so, Hagar is able to weep, the purgative aspect of which is also accompanied by her very real fit of vomiting.

The final phase of this revitalized ritual occurs when Hagar, again unconscious but this time in an actual physical manner, acts out her atonement with her son and, with Lees acting as his surrogate, receives her son's forgiveness. As a result, Hagar "could even beg God's pardon this moment, for thinking ill of Him some time or other" (248). Designed to express her gratitude to God, Hagar's comment also suggests an understanding of what the Divine Parent may have felt in sacrificing His Son.

Yet ultimately it is indeed "God the Mother" who comes to Hagar's aid in her last days, not in any individualized or other-worldly form but rather in the collective experience of love and maternity shared by the dying women who make up "the mewling nursery of old ladies," as Hagar at first sarcastically describes them – but with Laurence thereby emphasizing the coincidence of birth and death (264; see also 307). Significantly a trio – evocative of the Trinity and the triple aspect of the goddess in pagan mythology – each of these women has something in common with Hagar, which, however, they manifest in positive and archetypal forms. Most articulate of the three is Elva Jardine, a skinny old crone of a woman who like Hagar stems from "Freehold," whose name is etymologically evocative of the first "garden" mother, and who finds her sustenance in her love for her husband. Second is Mrs. Dobereiner, whose foreign tongue – like Hagar's logos education – isolates her from her kind but who finds consolation in singing hymns about the true "home country" she expects to find after death; to these hymns the other women respond even without understanding the words. Finally there is Mrs. Reilly, like Hagar a tun of a woman but whose obesity makes her a type of "Great Mother" and whose prayers are addressed to the Roman Catholic equivalent of that primordial figure.

Reluctant at first to join the group, Hagar finally subconsciously acknowledges her sisterhood and her affiliation with these women's mysteries when she joins the nightly litany:

Tom, don't you worry none–
Mother of God, pray for us now and at the hour of–
Mein Gott, erlöse mich–
You mind that time, Tom? I mind it so well–
I am sorry for having offended Thee, because I love–
Erlöse mich von meinen Schmerzen–
Bram! (275)

And having found this kind of religious support system, Hagar can also acknowledge the Judaeo-Christian deity without lapsing into the role of a suppliant daughter: "Ought I to appeal? It's the done thing. *Our Father*–no. I want no part of that. All I can think is–*Bless me or not, Lord, just as You please, for I'll not beg*" (307).

* * *

If Margaret Laurence could therefore in retrospect be termed a "revisionist" or "reformist" – a feminist who finds many faults with the Judaeo-Christian tradition but still feels it possible to discover or recover a viable female ideology within that religious framework – Margaret Atwood might at first glance appear to be a "radical" or "revolutionary" – one who espouses a total break with biblical tradition and encourages women to create their own "thealogy" out of their experience.[10] For unlike Hagar, the protagonist of *Surfacing* has been raised an atheist: Jesus is to her "a wooden Christ" and "the alien god"; she has been raised to believe that "Jesus was a historical figure and God was a superstition, and a superstition was a thing that didn't exist."[11] Yet far from being conducive to a well-adjusted feminine psyche, the narrator's lack of religious upbringing and its consequent secular reverberations have left her totally nameless, totally passive, and unable to form any meaningful relationships.

Of course to be raised without "God the father" is not necessarily to be raised without the Logos-value system He represents. Up to a point this certainly is the narrator's problem; like Hagar's, her education appears to have been a cerebral one, and though she does not suffer from the Electra Complex and is not a motherless child, her love affair is with an older married man and it is in obedience to his suggestion that she aborts her fetus.

At the same time, however, the narrator's father is an ecologist – a man with great respect for "Mother" nature – just as he is also a pronounced critic of Judaeo-Christianity. If such attitudes are quite in keeping with feminism, they are also the twin characteristics of eighteenth-century philosophy, a point which Atwood emphasizes when the narrator examines her father's books, observing that they consist on the one hand of technical do-it-yourself guides and on the other of

> . . . the King James Bible which he said he enjoyed for its literary qualities, a complete Robert Burns, Boswell's *Life*, Thomson's *Seasons*, selections from Goldsmith and Cowper. He admired what he called the eighteenth century rationalists; he thought of them as men who had avoided the corruptions of the Industrial Revolution and learned the secret of the golden mean, the balanced life, he was sure they all practised organic farming. (42)

A believer in "reason and benevolent order," he has returned to nature on the Rousseauistic premise that animals are more consistent and predictable than so-called civilized people and that there he would be free of all external ideologies (204, 63). Similarly associated with the Augustan Age is the narrator's lover, whom she recalls as "writing his own initials on a fence, graceful scrolls to show me how, lettering was one of the things he taught. . . . I lean beside him, admiring the fall of winter sunlight over his cheekbone and the engraved nose, noble and sloped like a Roman coin profile. . ." (51). Taking her home after the abortion, "His flexible hands on the wheel. It turned, perfect circle, and the gears interlocked and spun, the engine ticked like a clock, the voice of reason" (95). Even more specifically linking the narrator's problem to the age of "Enlightenment" are the recurrent references to the city of the abortion as a "tiny company town, neatly planned with public flower beds and an eighteenth century fountain in the middle, stone dolphins and a cherub with part of the face missing" (12; see also 94, 154).

Atwood's point, in short, is that the roots of the narrator's identity crisis go back not to the Bible but rather to the eighteenth-century Rationalist attack on traditional religion and related concepts of man, nature, and society. What the attitudes of the narrator's father and lover reflect are the view that man is a rational animal and that when he acts irrationally he is acting unnaturally; that God is merely a name for the principle of order in the universe, that He works through the fixed laws of nature, and that the Bible is therefore not the word of God since it contains too many miraculous events; that man in a state of nature is good; and that what corrupts man is a faulty form of society, one based on the traditional hierarchical Christian concept that man is a fallen creature who needs controls.

To Atwood, therefore, if the feminine is allied with the irrational, so also is pre-Enlightenment religion. Thus the chief instrument of women's oppression is not the Judaeo-Christian tradition *per se* but rather the eighteenth-century demystification of religion. In turn, to the extent that feminists are against traditional religion, to the extent that they have reduced the spiritual truths of the Bible to sexist politics and ascribe to a Rousseauistic notion of societal evil, they have themselves, ironically, contributed to those forces which to Atwood are responsible for woman's identity crisis.

Similarly, if Atwood's narrator must discover her own religious value system, it is not that traditional religion has become nonviable because it empowers the male but because it has lost its truly "religious" power altogether.[12] Thus the background sections of *Surfacing* focus not merely on the atheistic nature of the narrator's upbringing but also on the decadence of religious rituals and symbols, with both factors, significantly, being related to anti-Catholic attitudes and involving the emergence of unattractive female figures.

As a child, for example, the rationalistically-raised narrator is especially intrigued by the "mysteries" of Catholicism, which are ridiculed by her brother as a birthday party where all they eat is "soda crackers" and by other boys as a worship of the "B.V.M." (59, 60). When her father finally allows her to go to Sunday School – on the grounds that "reason would defend [her]" from the distortions of Christianity – she is taught by a woman who tells her students "a lot about her admirers and their cars" and who hands out "pictures of Jesus, who didn't have thorns and ribs but was alive and draped in a bed-sheet, tired looking, surely incapable of miracles" (59). Subsequently she has lunch with one of these Christian families and observes the way in which the saying of "Grace" is followed by the "Pork and Beans" scatological refrain, after which the "mother, who had a bun of greying hair and prickles around her mouth like a schmoo, would frown and ask me what I'd learned about Jesus that morning, and the father would grin feebly, ignored by all" (60).

Decadent at the time she was growing up, Christianity has become totally defunct by the time the narrator returns to the place of her childhood. On the road to the village, political and commercial advertisements mingle indiscriminately with graffiti saying "Fuck you" and "Jesus saves" (15). When she arrives, "waiting for the nostalgia to hit, for the cluster of nondescript buildings to be irradiated with inner light like a plug-in creche," all she finds is that the "white dollhouse-sized church . . . is neglected, peeling paint and a broken window, the old priest must be gone. What I mean is dead" (19).

Further dramatizing religious decadence are the blasphemous

expletives which punctuate the speech of the narrator's companions. Thus Atwood explores a variant of the association of God and Logos: that is, the frequency with which his name is taken "in vain," of the way the "holy triple name" has "shrunken to swear-words" (155) is symptomatic of the extent to which god is dead. That these swearwords come from the mouths of characters whose own names derive from the Judaeo-Christian tradition – David, Anna and Joseph – makes the usage doubly effective.

But of course Atwood's major way of illustrating the death of Christianity – and of its connection to the narrator's problem – is the conflation of imagery in her climactic encounter with the dead heron. The bird, which must have been caught "before it had time to rise" (125), and which is "hanging upside down by a thin blue nylon rope tied round its feet" recalls her aborted fetus; its suspension from a tree with its wings fallen open evokes the configuration of an inverted crucifix. Reinforcing this connection between the aborted fetus and a decadent Christ, moreover, is the narrator's vision of the former as "suspended in the air above me like a chalice, an evil grail" (153), and her confession that "instead of granting it sanctuary" she allowed the fetus to be killed. In short, although feminists have argued that it is the spiritualizing tendency in Christianity – the denigration of the body and things earthly – which has occasioned the current ecology crisis, Atwood seems to relate crimes against nature to the loss of vibrant Christian symbols. What precipitates the narrator's quest for a new spiritual vision is the fact that "no power remained in [the] bland oleotinted Jesus prints or in the statues of the other ones, rigid and stylized" (155).

Though a new religion is therefore necessary, Atwood does not make this her major concern until she has first explored the innate need of the individual to believe in something "eternal" beyond the self; the failure of secular substitutes to answer to this need; and the way in which a loss of religious authority has a domino effect, undermining all forms of authority and leading ultimately to total anarchy and utter loneliness.[13]

"If you tell your children God doesn't exist they will be forced to believe you are the god," observes the narrator; "but what happens when they find out you are human after all, you have to grow old and die" (112). One answer suggested by the narrator's companions is that you "disown your parents": "Joe never mentions his mother and father, Anna says hers were nothing people and David calls his 'The Pigs.'" Another answer, provided by the narrator and her brother, is the turning to superheroes. In her brother's childhood scrapbooks, the narrator finds "flying men with comic-book capes and explorers on another planet" rescuing a man with "flamethrowers, trumpet-shaped pistols, ray-guns. In the background was their spaceship, bristling with gadgets" (97). For the narrator herself, the substitute deities were movie stars; "I believed in glamour, it was a kind of religion and these were my icons" (46). At a later age, her response was to project godlike qualities on her lover: "I worshipped him, non-child-bride, idolator, I kept the scraps of his handwriting like saints' relics" (158).

Anna's would-be solution is the reading of palms, and of "mystery" novels which, according to the narrator, provided "cold comfort but comfort, death is logical, there's always a motive. Perhaps that's why she read them, for the theology" (182). Additionally, Anna has become committed to self-discovery and liberationist philosophy: "she told me once you shouldn't define yourself by your job but by who you are. When they ask her what she does she talks about fluidity and Being rather than Doing" (62); "'I say there are these basic emotions,'" Anna tells the narrator; "'if you feel something you should let it out, right?' It was an article of faith, she glared at me, challenging me to affirm or deny. . ." (106).

The misplaced religious instinct is even more evident in the case of Anna's husband, David, whose nationalism has all the earmarks of a crusade. With delight he envisions a war between Canada and the United States over water, evoking in the process the kind of carnage which characterized the French revolution, the putting into practice of the "revolutionary" ideals of the eighteenth century. The narrator herself has little faith in the "Movement," however, for she has seen in David the extent to which national symbols are incapable of commanding loyalty when their religious sanction has become degenerate. Thus punctuated by Anna's "Oh Christ . . . don't get going on that," David had described "the latest national flag" – "Nine beavers pissing on a frog" – and then asked whether they realized "that this country is founded on the bodies of dead animals? Dead fish, dead seals, and historically dead beavers. . ." (43).

To make the connection between religious decadence and cultural disrespect even closer, Atwood has her narrator reveal that David had wanted "to be a minister" and had sold "Bibles door to door to put himself through theological seminary" (30). Moreover, it is this same frustrated religious instinct which explains his chauvinistic attitude toward his wife. When the narrator suggests that he and Anna should discuss their marital insecurities, David answers:

> "What would we talk about? She's too dumb, she can't figure out what I'm saying to her, Jesus, she moves her lips when she watches T.V. even. She doesn't know anything, every time she opens her mouth she makes an ass of herself. I know what you're thinking," he said, almost pleading, "but I'm all for the equality of women; she just doesn't happen to be equal and that's not my fault, is it? What I married was a pair of boobs, she manipulated me into it, it was when I was studying for the ministry, nobody knew any better then. But that's life." (148)

Yet that Anna herself may have married him as a godly substitute is suggested when the narrator overhears the couple in their bedroom:

> . . . Anna breathing, a fast panic sound as though she was running; then her voice began, not like her real voice but twisted as her face must have been, a desperate beggar's whine, *please please.* I put the pillow over my head, I didn't want to listen, I wanted it to be through but it kept on, *Shut up* I whispered but she wouldn't. She was praying to herself, it was as if David wasn't there at all. *Jesus jesus oh yes please jesus.* (88)

Similarly, that sex is no substitute for a relationship with the divine and, moreover, that love is impossible without belief in a principle of transcendence is the import of Joe's statement – "'Do you love me, that's all. . . . That's the only thing that matters'" – and of the narrator's response – "'I want to. . . . I do in a way.' I hunted through my brain for any emotion that would coincide with what I'd said. I did want to, but it was like thinking God should exist and not being able to believe." Joe's final expletive therefore summarizes the situation very well: "Fucking jesus" (115).

If religion to Atwood is thus essential to survival, the "new" religion she advances also takes the form of a survival – in keeping with the definition of religion as that which answers to man's need to believe in something immortal and eternal. A key episode in this respect is the one extended "fishing" episode in the novel, which begins when David, ignorant of the linguistic degeneration of the word "rood," tells Anna to lie down so that he can use his own "rod," to which she replies "Oh Christ" (37). When the narrator baits the hook, Anna further expostulates, "God, you're cold-blooded," thereby bringing into sharp focus the significance of the narrator's fish theology: "I believe in them the way other people believe in God: I can't see them but I know they are there." The point, in short, is that in discovering this "new" symbol of God, the narrator is really recovering the ancient vision of Christ as *ichthyos*. In turn, one understands why in the description of the dead Christ symbol, the heron, emphasis was placed on the fact that it smelled like "decaying fish." And in this context of recovery one might also note that in its upside-down position the heron-crucifix emphatically suggests the death of the Christian symbol, just as the inversion also makes the heron positively evocative of the Hanged Man of the Tarot – the ancient cards thought to contain all religious wisdom and used to divine the "rising" or surfacing of the waters of the Nile.

To return to the fishing episode, the narrator recalls how as a child she "fished by prayer" – "Our father who art in heaven / Please let the fish be caught" – but how later she changed her prayer to a simple "Please be caught." If this change signals a shift in the locus of the divine, it is also in accordance with the primitivistic belief that reverence for what one sacrifices not only entails forgiveness in advance but also turns killing into a ritual of participation in the life of the creature/god being killed. In the present instance what also makes for a successful catch is the narrator's use of her "magic" frog, the amphibious nature of such a creature functioning as a natural symbol for the dual nature of Christ.[14] Finally, when they eat the fish the next morning, in David's parodic prayer – "Good food, good meat, Good God let's eat" (74) – Atwood simultaneously evokes both the degeneration of the Eucharistic Banquet and the totemic ritual which lies behind the Judaeo-Christian signature.

Accordingly, what Atwood finds most problematic about the

Judaeo-Christian tradition is not so much its spiritualizing tendency as its monotheistic character and claim to uniqueness. Moreover, she demonstrates that herein lies the seeds of its own demise as well as the roots of the egocentricity which characterizes the modern alienated individual. In negative fashion, this is dramatized in the godlessness of the narrator's companions: raised, as it were, to identify all religion with the Judaeo-Christian variety, when this God dies they assume all religion has become defunct. This being the case, there is an advantage to the narrator's having been raised an atheist; unlike her companions, she can distinguish between archetype and signature, a situation which enables her not only to countenance the death of Christian symbolism but also to revitalize it. Thus, just prior to and precipitating her redemptive dive into the lake, she encounters one further symbol of decadent Christianity: "Overhead a plane, so far up I could hardly hear it, threading cities together with its trail of smoke; an X in the sky, unsacred crucifix." But this dead symbol has its living correlative in the heron, which cannot die because it does not have a single identity: "The shape of the heron flying above us the first evening we fished, legs and neck outstretched, wings outspread, a bluegrey cross, and the other heron or was it the same one, hanging wrecked from the tree." Accordingly, instead of concluding that Christ is dead she concludes that "anything that suffers and dies instead of us is Christ . . . . hunters in the fall killing deer, that is Christ also . . . . dead Christ-flesh resurrecting inside us, granting us life . . . . even the plants must be Christ" (150). At the same time that Atwood uses ecology to call into question the concept of a unique redeemer, so does she also demonstrate how such religious ecology differs from the rationalistic variety of the narrator's father; similarly, at the same time that she roots her new theology in primitivism, she also, unlike many feminists, does not utterly divorce this primitivism from Christianity.

Nor indeed does Atwood align this primitivism solely with a feminist world view; if what the narrator encounters at the depth of her dive is the death of her father and if, as a consequence, she is able to confess to her abortion or crime against motherhood, it is to the "gods" of the shore and water that she gives thanks. Furthermore the "primitives" whose religious practices the narrator emulates are Indians, scarcely a matriarchal culture. And finally, if it is important to recognize that Christ is the Judaeo-Christian signature for the archetypal redeeming principle, so it is important to realize that the "Indians did not own salvation" (155).

Where Atwood would seem to sound most feminist is in her subsequent depiction of the narrator's descent into madness and in her related process of recovery. For the point of departure here is her observation that her father gave her "only knowledge and there were more gods than his, his were the gods of the head, antlers rooted in the brain." Yet when she adds that what she requires is "Not only how to see but how to act" (163), Atwood is also making the point that what the narrator needs are rituals – and rituals are enactments of divine models.

Nor is this recovery of religious models from *within* the Judaeo-Christian tradition belied by the seemingly heretical childhood drawing which serves as the narrator's guide:

> On the left was a woman with a round moon stomach: the baby was sitting up inside her gazing out. Opposite her was a man with horns on his head like cow horns and a barbed tail.
>
> The picture was mine, I had made it. The baby was myself before I was born, the man was God, I'd drawn him when my brother learned in the winter about the Devil and God: if the Devil was allowed a tail and horns, God needed them also, they were advantages. (169)

If it is important to note that this drawing was made before the narrator reached the "Age of Reason," as it were, it is equally important to realize that a similar configuration characterizes paintings of the "Holy Family" in Medieval religious art.[15]

In turn, if what the narrator subsequently enacts with Joe is the primordial hierogamous union, and if she envisions herself later as parthenogenetically giving birth to a furry Pan-like god, that the putative father is a man named after the "cuckolded" father of Jesus, and that Christ in Medieval iconography is frequently pictured as a stag, suggest once again that Atwood is able to recognize the archetypes which lie embedded in Christianity.

Or again, if the image of the Great Mother as "Our Lady of the Beasts" and "Lady of the Plants" and as the "Ship of Life" is suggested by the narrator's symbiotic vision of herself – "My body also changes, the creature in me, plant-animal, sends out filaments in me; I ferry it secure between death and life, I multiply" – one also finds such depictions of the Madonna in pre-Reformation religious art, just as this ecological symbiosis also revitalizes by sacramentalizing the original meaning of the concept of Atonement.

Furthermore, if the narrator's slashing with an "X" everything connected with history indicates her awareness of the way the Judaeo-Christian tradition has fostered a linear and hence irreversible concept of time, whereas she in her madness has indeed gone back to the beginning, one should also notice that the time span of the narrator's descent and resurfacing coincides with the six plus one days of the creation. For good reason, therefore, the opening words of *Surfacing* are "I can't believe" and the plot of the novel takes the form of a return to beginnings.

* * *

Although Margaret Laurence and Margaret Atwood are thus extremely concerned with the relationship between woman's identity and religious issues, *The Stone Angel* and *Surfacing* do not seem to support many feminist contentions but rather point to dimensions which have largely been ignored: namely, the way in which the Judaeo-Christian tradition fosters egocentricity and in turn alienation and loneliness by reason of its monotheistic character; the extent to which the decline of religious authority reverberates in the secular spheres, and the extent to which this decline can be traced to the aftermath of Renaissance individualism or to the Rationalism of the eighteenth century; the need to distinguish between forms of Judaeo-Christianity and to recognize that the problematic element for women largely resides in Protestant varieties – with Catholicism, until recently perhaps, evidencing a pro-female emphasis in its sacramental basis and devotion to "Holy Mary, *Mother* of God"; and the importance of going beyond a mere criticism of the "Written *Word*" and the value of exploring religious iconography and pictographs.

NOTES

* This essay is based on a paper delivered at the XVth Congress of The International Association for the History of Religions, Sydney, Australia, August 1985. For financial assistance facilitating the research of the paper and attendance at the Congress, I am indebted to the Social Sciences and Humanities Research Council of Canada.

1. Mary Daly, *Beyond God the Father: Toward a Philosophy of Women's Liberation* (1973; Boston: Beacon Press, 1985).

2. Carol P. Christ, "Margaret Atwood: The Surfacing of Women's Spiritual Quest and Vision," *Signs: Journal of Women in Culture and Society*, 2, 2 (Winter 1976), pp. 316-30.
3. Actually, the real pioneer in exploring the connection between feminism and religion was D.H. Lawrence, as I have demonstrated in "*The Rainbow:* Ursula's 'Liberation,'" *Contemporary Literature*, XVII (Winter 1976), pp. 24-43. See also my "Le Féminisme, les Femmes et la Sexualité," in *L'Arc* (Special Issue on D.H. Lawrence), 96 (Spring 1985), pp. 48-57, for a further discussion of this issue, as well as an explanation of why feminists have not merely refused to recognize Lawrence's contribution but have also attacked him.
4. For a discussion of the negative character of this sculpture, see Evelyn J. Hinz and John J. Teunissen, "The Attack on the Pieta: An Archetypal Analysis," *Journal of Aesthetics and Art Criticism*, XXXIII (Fall 1974), pp. 43-50.
5. Margaret Laurence, *The Stone Angel* (Toronto: McClelland and Stewart, 1964), p. 80. Further references to this work are indicated by page number in the text.
6. In my use of the terms Logos and Eros and their respective alignment with the masculine and feminine, I am following Carl Jung. See especially "Women in Europe," *Contributions to Analytic Psychology* (New York and London: Pantheon Books, 1928), p. 176. For the particular relevance of these concepts for an understanding of female psychology, see M. Esther Harding, *Woman's Mysteries: Ancient and Modern* (New York: G.P. Putnam's Sons, 1973), especially pp. 32-43.
7. In his "Introduction" to the New Canadian Library edition of *The Stone Angel*, William H. New notes some of these prototypes, but he believes that Laurence's purpose is to suggest that Hagar is indeed "unique." More in keeping with my approach are Sandra Djwa, "False Gods and the True Covenant: Thematic Continuity between Margaret Laurence and Sinclair Ross," *Journal of Canadian Fiction*, I/4 (Fall 1972), pp. 43-50, and Leslie-Ann Hales, "Spiritual Longing in Laurence's Manawaka Women," *English Studies in Canada*, XI (March 1985), pp. 82-90.
8. This inability to distinguish between archetype and signature is particularly evident in Naomi R. Goldenberg, *Changing of the gods: Feminism and the End of Traditional Religions* (Boston: Beacon Press, 1979).
9. See Valerie Saiving, "The Human Situation: A Feminine View," in *Womanspirit Rising: A Feminist Reader in Religion*, ed. Carol P. Christ and Judith Plaskow (New York: Harper & Row, 1979), pp. 25-42.
10. For this distinction, see the "Introduction" by Christ and Plaskow to *Womanspirit Rising*, pp. 9-11.
11. Margaret Atwood, *Surfacing* (1972; Markham: Paperjacks, 1980), pp. 14, 112. Further references to this work are indicated by page number in the text.
12. For a discussion of this religious decadence in a slightly different context, see my essay, "The Masculine/Feminine Psychology of American/Canadian Primitivism: *Deliverance* and *Surfacing*," in *Other Voices, Other Views: An International Collection of Essays from the Bicentennial*, ed. Robin Winks (Westport, CT: Greenwood Press, 1978), pp. 75-96.
13. It is this dimension of *Surfacing* that Plaskow misses entirely when she complains that Atwood does not relate the narrator's "spiritual" quest to a "social" one. See "On Carol Christ on Margaret Atwood: Some Theological Reflections," *Signs*, 2, 2 (Winter 1976), pp. 331-39.
14. The frog is also a symbol of her fetus – which is amphibious in the sense that it is a potential land creature which lives in amniotic fluid.
15. The significance of this iconography, as well as a discussion of the narrator's psycho-religious development which includes issues not addressed in this essay, may be found in Evelyn J. Hinz and John J. Teunissen, "*Surfacing*: Margaret Atwood's 'Nymph Complaining,'" *Contemporary Literature*, XX, 2 (Spring 1979), pp. 221-36.

Politics and A Jest of God

KENNETH JAMES HUGHES

> To be sure, the aesthetic transformation is *imaginary* – it must be imaginary, for what faculty other than the imagination could invoke the sensuous presence of that which is *not* (yet)?
>
> – Herbert Marcuse

> Margaret Laurence has written that *A Jest of God,* as some critics have pointed out disapprovingly, is a very inturned novel. I recognize the limitations of a novel told in the first person and the present tense, from one viewpoint only, but it couldn't have been done any other way, for Rachel herself is a very inturned person. She tries to break the handcuffs of her own past, but she is self-perceptive enough to recognize that for her no freedom from the shackledom of the ancestors can be total.[1]

Here "inturned person," "handcuffs of her own past," and "shackledom of the ancestors" are popular, metaphorical and non-technical literary phrases substituting for the standard language of psychology in which "inturned person" means something like "introvert" and "handcuffs of her own past" etc. "repression." Notwithstanding the avoidance of technical terminology, the novel has been reduced to categories of the psychological.

There can be no quarrel initially with Laurence's psychological emphasis. For in *A Jest of God* she clearly has created a series of characters the key to whom, in terms of the individual *qua* individual, really is through psychology. As we shall see, there is a definite Freudian influence in *A Jest of God.* If the characters have been created with Freud in mind they can obviously be interpreted through Freud. The problem still remains, however, that having accepted the validity of the psychological approach, it becomes necessary for us to insist that psychological categories alone cannot account for the full range of the novel since they leave so much unexplained.[2] Because the dominant assumption about the "nature" of character in the psychological approach is that of

* First published in the *Journal of Canadian Studies,* Vol. 13, No. 3 (Fall 1978).

the isolated individual in the bourgeois tradition, psychology quite naturally seems the most applicable key to understanding. But such an assumption isolates the individual, in life and in literature, from society by making society a background against which the individual acts out a personal role. In Laurence's account of her novel, society tends to be reduced to "the ancestors," ghosts of the past who haunt Rachel's mind in the present. In the case of Rachel's mother, a very real ghost of the past in the present does the haunting. A careful reading of the novel, however, does not reveal society to be retreating into the background. Rather, society keeps up on centre stage with and through the main characters, and it is this feature, what I shall call the political side of *A Jest of God,* that causes the work to transcend the psychological while yet taking it into account.

Speaking specifically of politics and her novel, Laurence has said:

> I don't feel that you shouldn't make political statements but I personally feel disinclined to do it through my work. But what I'm dealing with in my work in fiction is that whole cultural background and characters which start in my case with a small prairie town. This may be political in a different sense.[3]

The argument here will be that the political in *A Jest of God* is not only "political in a different sense," but political in the profoundest sense of all because the politics seem to cover all traces of their tracks. No politician could wish a better situation for himself.

What does Laurence mean by the phrase "political in a different sense"? Raymond Williams has noted Gramsci's observation about the necessity of distinguishing between the kinds of power in class society,

> between 'rule' *(dominio)* and 'hegemony'. 'Rule' is expressed in directly political forms and in times of crisis by direct or effective coercion. But the more normal situation is a complex interlocking of political, social, and cultural forces, and 'hegemony', according to different interpretations, is either this or the active social and cultural forces which are its necessary elements.[4]

Certainly there is no War Measures Act invoked in *A Jest of God* to illustrate "rule" or "dominio," the naked use of political power.

In the "more normal situation" of the novel, however, Rachel experiences the authoritarian, hegemonic push and pull of her mother, of Willard Siddley, the principal, and of others who wish to dominate her. By such means Manawaka society reproduces itself as it moulds individuals to accept the *status quo* and their place within it.

Of domination, subordination and hegemony, Raymond Williams observes that hegemony

> sees the relations of domination and subordination, in their forms as practical consciousness, as in effect a saturation of the whole process of living – not only of political and economic activity, nor only of manifest social activity, but of the whole substance of lived identities and relationships, to such a depth that the pressures and limits of what can ultimately be seen as a specific economic, political, and cultural system seem to most of us the pressures and limits of simple experience and common sense. Hegemony is then not only the articulate upper level of 'ideology', nor are its forms of control only those ordinarily seen as 'manipulation' or 'indoctrination'. It is a whole body of practices and expectations, over the whole of living: our senses and assignments of energy, our shaping perceptions of ourselves and our world. It is a lived system of meanings and values – constitutive and constituting – which as they are experienced as practices appear as reciprocally confirming. It thus constitutes a sense of reality for most people in the society, a sense of absolute because experienced reality beyond which it is very difficult for most members of the society to move, in most areas of their lives. It is, that is to say, in the strongest sense a 'culture', but a culture which has also to be seen as the lived dominance and subordination of particular classes.[5]

The sort of situation described here seems to explain what Laurence probably means by "political in a different sense." In any event, as I hope to show below, the politics are so structured into the characters that the interaction and conflict of these characters in everyday life become aspects of the political. As Georg Lukacs observes, in the successful novel "general, typical phenomena must at the same time be particular actions, the personal passions of definite individuals."[6] So we can well see how what Laurence treats primarily on the psychological level may well have other, deeper and more significantly "*political*" cultural dimensions. In order to understand this phenomenon more fully it will be necessary to examine Laurence's concept of character in *A Jest of God.* For the purposes of analysis, we shall have to distinguish between four different dimensions of character in the novel: the individual character in relation to the prototype, the individual as individual, the individual as Lukacsian type, and the individual as type of social class.

II

For much of its history, Canada has been in different ways a colony of Great Britain, this latter an imperial society well known for its severe class divisions and remembered, amongst other things, for the way in which its representatives throughout its far-flung empire often "lorded it" over the natives, black or white. It is perhaps hardly surprising that in Canada – one of the inferiors in the imperial relationship – a popular cultural tradition developed whereby certain phenomena were interpreted to produce an understanding quite the opposite of that which obtained among the imperial "Lords of human kind."[7] Thus, an early nineteenth-century diary about experiences in Canada draws on Shakespeare's *The Tempest,* and the writer, a British officer, quite literally sees himself as an imperial Prospero with a divine right to superiority over the despised French-Canadian Calibans. By contrast, Laurence's *The Diviners* (1974) rejects the values of an anglophile Prospero and exalts those of an outcast Métis Caliban.[8] One main line of the Canadian literary tradition between these two tendencies strongly supports and develops the disjunction between the "noble" British imperial concept of the heroic, which is rejected, and the Canadian low-key, ordinary and Calibanish heroic, which is taken to be an admirable Canadian norm. This popular Canadian tradition permeates *A Jest of God.* The rejection of the grand heroic and the exaltation of the ordinary and everyday as heroic not only defines Canadian character but is political in its anti-imperialist opposition to hierarchy and authoritarianism and in its upholding of the values of egalitarian democracy.[9] To begin to see this clearly, we must examine the individual characters of *A Jest of God* in relation to their prototypes.

The *Oxford English Dictionary* defines prototype as "The first or primary type of anything; the original (thing or person) of which another is a copy, imitation, representation, or derivative, or to which it conforms or is required to conform; a pattern, model, standard, exemplar, archetype."[10] Individual characters as prototypes (e.g., Abraham, Odysseus) and the stories in which they are enshrined (the Bible, classical literature) have long permeated western European culture and served as models for imitation by writers. Indeed, so powerful has been the presence of these characters and stories, they have often been imitated whether or not writers were fully conscious of doing so.

We find that the Canadian experience represented in *A Jest of God* either does not fit the patterns set by traditional prototypes and stories, or the experience fits only in part. Laurence's purpose in drawing attention to the prototypes, therefore, seems to have been to imply by means of contrast the definition of the post-colonial Canadian reality. Conscious purpose or not, that is what happens as we can readily see in the novel.

There is in the novel a minor character named Miklos. Miklos and his Parthenon Cafe offer a sense of the remote past living on into the present. The name of the Cafe, The Parthenon, instantly recalls the auguste tranquillity of the ancient Greek temple on the Acropolis. The Parthenon's architectural structure stands in sharp contrast with the bustling greasy-spoon in the prairie town of Manawaka. Yet Laurence makes the connection between past and present without any sign of satiric irony. She accepts the greasy-spoon in all its concreteness for what it is, rather than looking back wistfully to supposedly better days and aristocratic traditions.

No obvious irony emerges either when we read that "Outside the Parthenon Cafe, Miklos is sponging his windows dawdlingly, spinning the job out to last the morning while his wife waits stoically on the customers inside."[11] The scene offers a sense of the "real," for we have seen it, or something like it, before in "real" life. Yet even as these few words draw on common Canadian experiences to create a convincing feeling of reality, even so do they refer to the remote past and enrich the scene by defining character and situation through subtle ironic contrast. For a Greek, a wife who "waits stoically," and the word "spinning" may cause us to recall *The Odyssey* and in particular Odysseus and Penelope, even if it is the male here who does the "spinning." Miklos, Greek-Canadian heir to the whole Greek tradition, serves to suggest a Canada rooted in the Greek and European tradition.

But Miklos is not Odysseus. The association of the little bourgeois businessman with this traditional epic and heroic figure can only remind us of the differences between the two. For through the association with Odysseus comes a simultaneous dissociation which tells us that the grand heroic belongs in the past. Like the aspect of Canada he represents, Miklos becomes the transformed past in the present. He is the ordinary and everyday in contrast with the grand heroic Odysseus of epic fame so often celebrated by Victorian imperialists, and this emphasis on the ordinary and everyday is characteristic of that Canadian literary tradition with roots in the pioneering nineteenth century which rejects the old notions of the grand heroic.

Much like Miklos, the ageless Chinaman, Toy – proprietor of the Regal Cafe[12] and inscrutable as the proverbial Chinese philosopher whose prototypal shadow stands behind him – symbolically represents in his person the inheritance in Canadian culture of at least parts of the Chinese tradition. But here again the tradition is transformed into the ordinary and everyday. Miklos and Toy bring with them a suggestion of a grand past transformed and living on in present-day Canada in ordinary and everyday characters. Laurence, however, does not lament the former glories of these pasts. Rather she emphasizes the very ordinary Canadian present in this novel, a present containing transformed elements of a dialectically opposite past that help to define it.

We have not left Greek prototypes behind when Miklos disappears after his brief showing. For we meet with the polar opposite prototypes, Apollo and Dionysus, in *A Jest of God,* and we do so within the framework of what passes for the Christian religion in Manawaka. The calm tranquillity of Reverend MacElfrish and his establishment congregation is Apollonian. Rachel tells us that "if the Reverend MacElfrish should suddenly lose his mind [i.e., turn Dionysian] and speak of God with anguish or joy, or out of some need should pray with fierce humility as though God had to be there, Mother would be shocked to the core. Luckily, it will never happen" (p. 41). Here a glimpse of the Apollonian past of ancient Greece, with its tight control over emotion, has been embodied in the Canadian present of the novel.

Whereas in the past, Apollo had been the god of the Greek landed and ruling aristocracy, in Manawaka he represents the less than grand bourgeois ruling class of merchants and salesmen. This we see through the art objects by which Laurence makes the Manawaka bourgeoisie define and reveal themselves. Their church's "stained-glass window shows a pretty and clean-cut Jesus expiring gently and with absolutely no inconvenience, no gore, no pain, just this nice and slightly effeminate insurance salesman who, somewhat incongruously, happens to be clad in a toga, holding his arms languidly up to something which might in other circumstances have been a cross" (p. 41). It is not that the Manawaka ruling class are supposed to look silly when compared with their heroic opposite, the Apollo prototype, god of the old Greek landed aristocracy. The novel simultaneously rejects the ancient Apollonian values, the modern Apollonian values of the Manawaka businessmen, *and* the values of *their* Christ. But, through a comparison between a diverse past and the present, an aspect of Canadian middle-class mentality has been defined. (If irony is absent in the comparison between the ancient and modern Apollonian, it surely presents itself when we think of Christ, for the passion of Christ has been neutralized, presumably on the grounds that passion is a threat to the best of all possible worlds for it is the preserve of those wild people over the tracks.)

In contrast with the solidity of the "Apollonian" Church, its salesman Christ, and its respectable Manawaka middle-class congregation stands the shaky Dionysian Tabernacle, home to the less than respectable lower orders and outcasts of Manawaka. If Apollo was the rational god of the Greek landed and ruling aristocracy, Dionysus was his opposite, the irrational god of the dispossessed in ancient Greece. Not surprisingly, the portraits of Christ in the Tabernacle are Dionysian. Rachel tells us that "Two large pictures are hanging, both Jesus, bearded and bleeding, his heart exposed and bristling with thorns like a scarlet pincushion" (p. 30). The simile, "like a scarlet pincushion," neatly reduces emotive pathos to ludicrous bathos. Here again, however, Laurence does not create an ironic and satirical contrast between any idealized Dionysian past that stands behind the peculiar Tabernacle variant of Dionysianism. She rather defines through the dramatic action a specific Canadian and modern reality in which the one-sided

Dionysian (and irrational Christianity) has no accepted place. As with the Apollonian Church congregation, so with the Dionysian Temple group: we move from an imaginative depiction of Canadian reality to a dramatically structured criticism of it by the author.

In an emotionally and sexually repressed state, Rachel, of course, feels the pull of the Dionysian, her polar opposite. This we gather when she fearfully asks herself, "Will there be ecstatic utterances and will Calla suddenly rise and keen like the Grecian women wild on the hills..." (p. 31), and when she says, "Let the Dionysian women rend themselves on the night hills and consume the god" (p. 36). These things she says as she momentarily begins to lose her inhibitions. Finally, however, she – as individual and as the embodiment of a new Canadian ideal – rejects both the Tabernacle and Dionysianism in general because it is one-sided. The Dionysian implies a split existence as much as the Apollonian. Wholeness – individual or national – cannot be achieved by that route.

In the Tabernacle sequence of the novel we find mention of the seer, Tiresias, as a man who has the gift of voices, of prophecy. Rachel says: "I see him. He is standing now. He is not old. His face is severe, delicate, and his eyes are closed, like a blind seer, a younger Tiresias come to tell the king the words that no one could listen to and live. The words. Chillingly, I realize. *Galamani halafaka tabinota caragoya lal lal ufranti.* Oh my God. They can sit, rapt, wrapped around and smothered willingly by these syllables, the chanting of some mad enchanter, himself enchanted" (p. 35). Without exalting the prototypal Tiresias by doing so, Laurence puts her modern Tiresias into the world only to undercut him and reduce him to a misguided and unwitting fraud. The modern Canadian world has no room for the prophetic, for here, in the face of the unknown, Canada and Canadians must work out their own destiny in history. That kind of "heroic" prophetic past cannot come into the ordinary secularized present.

Earlier we met with references to Odysseus in the little scene with Miklos and the Parthenon Cafe, while in the Tabernacle scene we meet with, amongst others, references to Tiresias and Dionysus. Connecting these two scenes is the mind and person of Rachel who, we observe, is also on a quest, in search of herself so to speak, just as Odysseus was on the quest which led him to define himself through his adventures. Like Odysseus, Rachel goes on a special journey and meets a Tiresias of sorts. It would not be going too far, with this basic pattern in mind, to suggest that Rachel is an Odysseus figure on an Odyssian quest. However, since the large gap between the grand heroic Odysseus and the little neurotic petty-bourgeois spinster is only too obvious, we must be careful not to assume any irony, for Laurence conceives of the low-key heroic in positive terms when she places it at the centre of her vision. This matter of a *female* Odysseus will be dealt with when we examine the implications of the concept of woman as hero.

Nick Kazlik combines three biblical prototypes: the Cain of Cain and Abel, the Prodigal Son, and Jacob. Nick stands as Cain in relation to his dead twin brother, Steve, or Abel (perhaps Plato's twins of the *Timaeus* are here, too), and like Cain he is in exile and alienated from his parents. Yet what a difference we discover between the original Cain and Nick. For Nick can in no way be held responsible for his brother's death from polio, having indeed suffered from it himself. So while grounds exist within the prototypal story for the exile of Cain, these original grounds do not explain Nick's guilt or exile in the novel.

Nor does the situation change when we consider Nick as the Prodigal Son. Clearly he is the Prodigal Son, yet no one kills a fatted calf for him when he returns, neither does he repent (although the fatted calf would be killed for him if he were repentant). Moreover, he absolutely refuses to accept the inheritance his father has available for him, the farm. Here again the compelling necessity of prairie and Canadian society cannot be contained by the original prototype and story. Representing as Nick does the shift from a rural ethnic mosaic to urban assimilation, he cannot go back. The dynamics of Canadian history, of which he serves as a representative figure, prevent him from doing so. (We meet this figure also in the form of Jackson Stake, Jr., in Robert J.C. Stead's *Grain.*[13]) With Nick we witness a radical discontinuity between prototypes of the past and a present filled with new experiences which the past can neither contain nor explain. Nick, who is the Jacob to Rachel's role as the biblical Rachel, presents differences also. Whereas the original Jacob had two wives, Nick has none, although Rachel initially believes she may become his wife, and Nick with deception suggests that he already has one.

As we become fully aware of Rachel's unhappiness and note carefully her name, we cannot help but recall the Rachel of the Bible. Both in the original and the novel we find women concerned with love and the bearing of children, so we may safely assume the validity of an initial identification. Yet here again differences soon emerge. For indeed, Nick coldly uses the Rachel of the novel for his own selfish gratification, and in the process he misleads her about his marital status. And where the biblical Rachel died giving birth to her first son, the novel's Rachel undergoes the false pregnancy occasioned by the tumour and moves from a spiritual death-in-life in Manawaka to life itself elsewhere. In giving death, so to speak, to the tumour, she achieves life.

If we discern a discontinuity between the prototypal Rachel and the Rachel of the novel, and if this marks a disjunction between the past and the present, the night scene in which Rachel descends into Hector Jonas' land-of-the-dead suggests a continuity with the Persephone myth. From death Rachel will work her way back up to life, having achieved knowledge. Yet even here there are discontinuities as Canadian experience refuses to match that of the prototype. One critic labours to demonstrate a one-to-one relationship between the Demeter and Persephone pattern and *A Jest of God.* Failing to note that the myth is modified to suit Canadian needs, he is led to say, "In view of May Cameron's heart condition and tyrannically demanding attitude to Rachel, it might seem odd to refer to her as a fertility figure...."[14] It seems in fact more than odd, for May Cameron is a spiritually dead woman who lives in a dead past and "fertility" is the last word we would ever associate with her.

In the descent scene we see Hector Jonas "perch" and note his "owlish" eyes, the owl being the symbol of Minerva or knowledge. As well, the name "Hector" recalls one of the heroes of *The Iliad.* These are heavy prototypal loads for the bourgeois undertaker to carry, but Laurence sets him up only to undercut all notions of the heroic by describing his ridiculous funeral parlour and by making his wife laugh at his fumbling efforts in bed. Hector emerges as a considerably less than heroic figure, yet he is a figure that we recognize and sympathize with.

The prototype of Cinderella also looms large in *A Jest of God.* When Rachel returns home at midnight, having been out with Nick, we encounter the following conversation:

'Hello, dear. Have a nice evening? What time is it?'

...

'Very nice, thanks. It's just twelve.'

'Oh, you are a Cinderella, aren't you?'

Mother cries with a carolling laugh. (p. 113)

Of course, at this point Cinderella really believes that she has just been out with Prince Charming. She has yet to learn that Nick is less than a prince (although the novel devalues princes) and finally much short of being charming. Moreover, the novel hardly ends Cinderella-fashion. It concludes with an ordinary-and-everyday Rachel who looks forward to controlling her own destiny rather than resting under the protection of a Prince Charming. This will not be an age or country of grand heroic princes.

The Cinderella prototype connects with two, perhaps three, other prince prototypes. The first of these is the shadow prince of Rachel's first sexual fantasy, the second the sexual fantasy where Rachel identifies herself with a lascivious Queen Cleopatra who throws herself on Antony, and the third where she plays Ophelia to Nick's vacillating Hamlet. As with Cinderella, so here does Laurence reject the grand heroic. For Rachel neither allows herself to be swallowed up in blackest night with the shadow prince (though she is tempted), any more than she poisons herself like Cleopatra (though she tries and unheroically fails) or drowns herself like Ophelia (indeed she jokes about it). This democratic Canadian Cinderella does not desire palaces.

Through these various, selected persons and scenes we see that Laurence begins with contemporary Canadian society and its problems. In this society there are continuities as well as discontinuities with the past. The connection between characters and prototypes in the novel serves the dual function of enriching the individual characters as individuals while defining, through contrast with distinctive prototypes, the peculiarly Canadian essence of these characters. When the universal prototype and the essentially Canadian come into conflict, however, it is the prototype that is abandoned. During the process of defining characters by contrast with prototypes, Laurence time and again sets off the old imperial grand heroic against the democratic, low-key, ordinary and everyday heroic which is her norm for a post-colonial Canadian society.

This process of definition is itself one of the dimensions of the political in the novel, for one set of political values is set off against another, with Laurence on the side of the progressive, democratic set.

III

The concept of character as individual in the broadest current of literature in the modern era requires the creation of highly particularized, psychologically rounded and well-motivated characters who exude a credibility such that a reader can accept the illusion of reality in which the individual character is presented as reality itself. The word must truly be made flesh. Notwithstanding some criticism, there seems to be a fairly broad consensus that *A Jest of God* succeeds because it meets these requirements. This success is a triumph over the limitations of the novel form, for the form itself limits the extent of particularization of character, no matter how long a specific novel may be. Since the protagonist must somehow stand out from the rest, it follows that in one way or another he or she must be more highly particularized than the rest. For this reason, precisely because of the necessities of the novel form, the artist must create a hierarchy of credible characters,[15] some major, some minor, but all of some importance to the plot and themes. It is surely a sign of the craftsmanship of *A Jest of God* that, while we find an hierarchy of characters there, even the minor ones are credibly alive and somehow individually "real."

The hierarchy of characters in *A Jest of God* implies that there are major, intermediate, and minor characters of different degrees of particularization. And it is precisely with the intermediate and minor characters – who must be accounted for either directly or implicitly in any interpretation – that the psychological approach gets beyond its depth. What connects all the individual characters in the novel and makes them all relevant is the fact that they are social beings involved in struggle, and it is this perception that leads us to the concept of character as Lukacsian type. Lukacs tells us that

> The created character can be significant and typical only if the artist succeeds in disclosing the manifold connections between the individual traits of his heroes and the objective

> general problems of his time, if the character himself experiences the most abstract problems of his time as his own individual problems that are a matter of life and death for him.[16]

If we substitute feminine for masculine pronouns in this statement, we see that it fits perfectly Laurence's *A Jest of God.* At this point we might note one other matter of extreme importance: while the novel has a heroine rather than a hero, the most significant level of meaning of the novel subsumes women's liberation beneath it because Rachel represents all of us in the twentieth century. Laurence is a liberationist, not simply a *women's* liberationist.[17] It is the very centrality of Rachel as human type rather than simply as woman that explains her relationship to the Odyssian quest discussed earlier.

The "individual traits" and the "general problems" that Rachel experiences are concretely Canadian and are of such a kind as to make her the *type* of a post-colonial search for identity in a changed world. Basically, Rachel must be seen from three different angles, as individual, as woman, and as the symbolic representation, the "type" of Canada in a process of transformation. Readers in other countries will readily see how Rachel embodies different aspects of their own post-colonial experience. On all three sides of Rachel's character, the picture emerges of an attempt to come to terms with the past, to transform the present, and to earn the right to create a future, a future in which she will actively seek to make her own destiny.[18] When Rachel says, "There are three worlds and I'm in the middle one, and this seems now to be a weak area between millstones" (p. 94) she certainly speaks as an individual who begins to see a way out of the inner and outer repressive psychological situation in which she as an individual finds herself. But she speaks at the same time as the type or voice of a country that can begin to see its own way clear from a colonial past into an independent national future. In an historical context, Canada has been a world caught between two other powerful worlds.

As individual, as woman, and as the symbolic representative of a new Canada, Rachel will reject the old authoritarian family and society, and its ideas of religion and God.[19] For good measure Laurence, as we shall see, includes a rejection of modern consumer society also. Rachel will, in short, reject alienation in all of its social and political manifestations and escape from the psychologically troubled subjective world which underlies a stable society in the novel. She will earn the right as individual, and as "type" of the country, to struggle in order to recreate herself and the world in which she lives.

The Manawaka in which Rachel, the individual, lives is both a prairie small town and a microcosm of Canada. It is a divided society. We are told of the split between the rational and middle-class side of the tracks and the lower-class physical or passionate side. Rachel tells us that "No one in Manawaka ever dies, at least not on this side of the tracks. We are a gathering of immortals. We pass on, through Calla's divine gates of topaz and azure, perhaps, but we do not die. Death is rude, unmannerly, not to be spoken to in the street" (p. 13). We learn that her side of town "is known as a good part of town. Not like the other side of the tracks, where the shacks are and where the weeds are let grow knee-high and not dutifully mown..." (p. 11). Over there they do not know the middle-class conception of order and duty. That side of the tracks is as unknown as passion on her side of the tracks; it is known "only from hearsay, distorted local legend, or the occasional glimpse from a child's words" (p. 11).

Although Laurence tells us about life on the lower-class side of the tracks, she does not pursue the matter directly. Nor does she need to, since she collapses the whole mind versus body and the middle- versus lower-class problem into her characters. Indeed, considered as type, Rachel's mind-body conflict represents in microcosmic form the larger social class and value split in Manawaka society. This is but one aspect of the typicality of the individual character Rachel. The split in society is the external socio-macrocosmic dimension of the internal microcosmic division in Rachel's consciousness.

No one on the middle-class side of the tracks in Manawaka "ever dies." In this figurative sense, of course, it is impossible for the dead to die. Having created a narrowly rational, sternly controlled society,[20] one in which passion or the emotive side of life has been left to the lower classes, the middle classes have repressed the emotive side of life and developed a death-in-life existence which makes death impossible. Death is a meaningless concept if it is not seen in relation to life, and here there is no life. This middle-class society, in fact, has created human commodities, finely machined and honed identical products. All that is needed when physical death actually occurs is to wrap the commodities in neat and respectable packages. And this is precisely Hector Jonas' function as he himself defines it. In fact, we see in the shift of the name of Hector's business from the personalized Cameron Funeral Chapel to the impersonal Japonica Chapel[21] a symbol of the development of the economic system into a commodity-producing system and of persons into commodities. As Hector Jonas says somewhat ironically of his new organ: "I can positively guarantee you it won't be loud enough to wake the living" (p. 127). The point of the irony is, of course, that in this land of the dead (Manawaka) there are no persons living. This emphasis on the reification of human beings, the turning of them into commodities, reminds us that the novel is not only a dramatic critique of the old Victorian world which comes into the twentieth century but of the new consumer society also.

If Manawaka is a microcosm of Canada, the funeral home becomes in turn a microcosm of bourgeois Manawaka. The distinction between the lower floor, where the physically dead lie, and the upper floor, where the dead-in-life live, is strictly marginal. With regard to the lower floor Rachel tells us of "The blue light, and the chapel purged of all spirit, all spirits except the rye..." (p. 127). Life on the upper floor represents in concrete individualized form the life-in-death existence of the whole of middle-class society in Manawaka, Canada, and, by extension, anywhere in this alienated modern industrial and consumer world.

Rachel's family church serves as an extension of the funeral home for it is simply a mausoleum where the dead-in-life stretch themselves out at prescribed intervals, with the firm assurance that nothing will be said to disturb their slumbers of death. Rachel's avoidance of the church as she begins to come to terms with herself suggests the beginning of a refusal to accept death-in-life or alienation. Historically, this act by Rachel reflects the decline of a church apparently unable to change and find a new function, evidenced in real life in reduced church attendance towards the middle of the twentieth century.

Rachel not only rejects the church, however; she also rejects the notion of a transcendent god, the god of her tribe. For this god is nothing less than an idol, a reflection of the authoritarian society that she also refuses to accept. From a remote and transcendent authoritarian god of fear whom she seeks to bribe, even as she does not believe, she moves to the concept of an immanent spirituality as she repatriates the self she has alienated and realizes her own integrity and wholeness.

This authoritarian God and the repressive social value system do not, of course, simply exist "out there." Both are thoroughly internalized at the beginning of the novel, and the outer conflict thus finds its place in the inner, divided psyche of Rachel Cameron. The internal struggle is thus the counterpart of her struggle with external society. But since she is a type, this inner struggle also represents the struggle between others like her and a decadent, life-denying set of social values. As the embodied essence of new values and change, as a type, Rachel must be made to change herself and her values; the process is a literary way of delineating a change in society and its values, since social values cannot finally exist and survive except in the persons of those who collectively constitute society.

The dominant Mrs. Cameron exercises a defensive tyranny over Rachel that is, on the individual and inter-personal level, at once the essential expression of a conservative "don't rock the boat" philosophy on the national level, and symbolic of an increasingly effete mother-daughter power relationship on the imperial-colonial plane. For Mrs. Cameron, the passionate barbarian hordes are just over the tracks and must be kept there in a subordinate position within a system dominated by class power and bourgeois rationality. When she learns that Rachel has met Nick she says unbelievingly, "You mean the milkman's son?" (p. 67). Her question is symptomatic of her general attitudes as individual and type. What she represents as a type appears in her own individual make-up: reason, narrowly conceived, dominates, and emotions are repressed. The middle-class emphasis on mind must protect itself from the lower-class emphasis on body. This is the world vision which, in the process of social reproduction, she seeks to pass on to Rachel, the next generation. Characteristic of her Victorian conservatism is an equally Victorian racism which assumes certain others to be naturally inferior. She believes that Ukrainians and Scots, like oil and water, cannot mix. For this reason she cannot approve of Rachel's relationship with Nick Kazlik.

In the realm of appearances Rachel is similar to her mother at the beginning of the novel. As she remarks of herself, "How can it happen, still, this echo of my mother's voice?" (p. 4). No medieval scholastic conservative was quite so obsessed with "saving the appearances" as she is, even though certain of her feelings and certain facts speak against the narrow system of order of which she is both the embodiment and upholder. The inner dimensions of Rachel are, however, very different; there is an essence inside her which seeks to realize itself in action, and this desire to act stands in contrast with the ideal of passively receiving and suffering the authoritarian values from the past which live on into the present. Indeed, the contradiction between internalized and restraining objective circumstances on the one hand and powerful but repressed desires on the other motivate her into action. In Freudian terms, a powerful superego – the internal component of external authority – limits and deforms the ego. However, the age which had given rise to this kind of external authority and internal superego is now decadent and we are into a new age with new possibilities.[22]

When Rachel descends into the Hades of Hector Jonas' Japonica Chapel, she descends, within generally Freudian categories, into an objective representation of her own subconscious in order to come to terms with her personal past, and thus to escape her alienation. In this instance Laurence does not so much modify Freudian categories as add a new and fulfilling dimension to them. For as Rachel descends in a psychological sense, she also descends as the *type* of a new Canada, in a socio-historical sense, into the national past. In both senses Rachel's father appears as a key figure. In the individual psychological sense there is the incestuous Electra fantasy which we see in Rachel's king dream. Her father's ghost must obviously be put to rest for Rachel to achieve personal wholeness. The father figure dominates her. In the socio-historical and national sense, the father is the type of old Canada who came back dispirited from the First World War and who says of the Second World War as the Camerons march away, that the pipes tell lies. His escape to liquor and isolation serves as a personal solution on the individual level of character and represents, on the level of character as *type,* the attempt of a colonial country to escape from, rather than face, the beginnings of the collapse of the British imperial system. When Rachel learns that her father, as individual and type of the old Canada, chose his own destiny *out of history,* she also learns that she can – as individual and as type of new Canada – choose her own destiny *in history.* For she, as individual and as type, must escape from the unfinished process which is the world her father bequeathed to her.

Frank H. Underhill catches the essence of Rachel's situation in his 1963 Massey lectues, "The Image of Confederation," when he describes the dilemma of Canada in the light of the modern decline of British imperial power. He remarks: "So we are now out in the world on our own.... Somehow or other we have put a distinctive meaning into the declaration that we are Canadian. This is a hard world in which we live. We can no longer creep back into our British mother's womb."[23] This well describes Rachel as both individual and as type, and Underhill's statement serves as a correspondence,[24] in the discipline of history, of the same "spirit" that was to find expression in Laurence's novel.

Rachel's society, a major instrument of which is the institution of the family, causes sexual repression, the measure of which we see in Rachel's sexual fantasies. One aspect of Rachel's attempt to achieve a new kind of wholeness by escaping from her alienation will be to come to terms with sex and the mind-body problem.[25]

Rachel, the individual, meets Nick who, not without some distress, gives her a sexual education. But sex is only one aspect of her problem, and when we consider some other dimensions of her alienation we can understand why Nick is finally less than suitable for her. Nick, as individual, has a major flaw. The prodigal son cannot come to terms with his past, for he rejects as an embarrassment the Ukrainian family and culture into which he was born. Thus, he is left as an isolated and alienated individual pursuing illusions about himself into a future over which he can have no control. At this point he can be seen as a specifically prairie type who represents the divided nature of the Ukrainian community. The split between the Ukrainian nationalist father and the politically leftist uncle symbolizes a split that, in the real world, has taken the life out of the prairie Ukrainian community. In essence, the inability of Nick as type to come to terms with his past is the inability of the Ukrainian community to come to terms with its own history. And by virtue of this inability, the only path open for the ethnic community is a steady assimilation and the loss of its cultural heritage. Nick as type represents this "path" perfectly. At a higher level of abstraction, Nick represents perhaps all the ethnic minorities in Canada in the first half or more of the twentieth century.

When Nick, as individual, misleadingly allows Rachel to believe that the picture he shows her is of his own son, we see one manifestation of his alienation. He uses her; to him she is an object to be consumed, fit only to satisfy his sexual desires. She is not for him a whole person with whom he is capable of having a lasting spiritual and physical relationship. Indeed, he seems incapable of the spiritual. In Martin Buber's terms,[26] Rachel seeks an I-thou relationship between fully-rounded thinking and feeling beings, while Nick, because of his failure to come to terms with himself and his past, must be involved in "ego tripping," instrumental I-it relationships of power in which Rachel serves simply as another "it," another object or commodity for consumption. This instrumental relationship with people Nick reveals when he says of the young students he teaches: "Trample their egos firmly" (p. 63). He pretends to be joking, but his subsequent behaviour leads us to realize that his alienation has made him very much like Willard Siddley. Nick's failure as an individual, therefore, is also his failure as type, for while Rachel can be seen as the type symbolic of a Canada seeking to free itself from an authoritarian colonial past and to make its own future, Nick cannot serve this function because he, along with the ethnic community that he represents, has not been freed from the past by coming to terms with it so as to prepare for a future.

As Rachel is defined by her relationship with Nick, so is she also defined by her relationship with Calla. Calla, in fact, appears to be another Rachel who has not gone far enough in her attempts to escape her situation. She has settled for something less than the range of possibilities available to her. With Calla we see a straight reason (narrowly defined) and emotions split, and this division reflects her social-class status (middle class) and social function (schoolteacher). Calla finds an outlet for her repressed emotions in the Tabernacle, but her regular attendance at the Tabernacle, her surrogate satisfaction in it, reveals that she can never escape her alienation. It is as if she had fractured a leg and chosen to walk on crutches for the rest of her life instead of setting the bones and returning to wholeness. She is a less than satisfactory symbol for the country as a whole as it moves into a new age. Her bird Jacob obviously symbolizes her state. He climbs up and down Jacob's Ladder, between heaven and earth, but being so unhappy, he will not sing. Moving between life as she narrowly conceives it and the substitute emotions of the Tabernacle, Calla cannot be happy either. Her one-sided and unhappy state is suggested by her latent lesbianism.

Rachel as individual and type is also defined in relation to Willard, the principal, as we see in the incident involving her pupil, James Doherty. Doherty is defined by a symbol of the free spirit for he "always seems about to take off like a sparrow" (p. 3). Willard on the other hand is a predator "like a picture of a vulture" (p. 23). "His eyes have the reptilian gift" (p. 45). We find him "peering foxily" (p. 196). He wants Rachel when she leaves the school to say that she has "always been as happy as a veritable meadowlark" (p. 197) but she cannot. Willard is a sadistic authoritarian who does not realize it, and thus, along with Nick and Mrs. Cameron, is involved in power relationships with people of an I-it kind in contrast with Rachel's desire for I-thou relationships. When Rachel herself strikes James Doherty she becomes at that moment the exact replica of all that Willard stands for. More characteristically, she sees the inner sensitivity of her student while Willard only perceives an external object to be moulded in conformity with an *a priori* conception of what for him is desirable, right, and necessary.

Rachel's desire to touch Willard's hairy hand is at once an expression of her sexual frustration as an individual and a sign of her temptation as an individual and type to accept the authoritarian *status quo* and her alienation. However, Willard is finally more than just an old-fashioned authoritarian as we gather when Rachel tells us that "He reads books on Time-Motion Study and draws charts on how to make your head save your heels" (p. 7). Willard is a composite type embodying both the old authoritarianism and the new authoritarianism of time and motion management study in the tradition of Taylorism.[27] This latter aspect stresses the fact that he sees persons as instruments of power to be manipulated.

Rachel's false pregnancy and the surgical removal of her tumour brings all the levels of her character together. In terms of the individual Rachel, the tumour represents symbolically the internalized psychological watchdog of an external repressive society; the surgery marks the removal of a paranoic and paralyzing self-consciousness which frees Rachel for action as a self-moving, whole individual. In terms of Rachel as the type of post-colonial Canada, the tumour is the colonial past and its authoritarian values. The removal of the tumour signifies the end of an acceptance of repressive society itself, and the end of the colonial state of mind.

We are left, therefore, at the end of the novel with a vision of Rachel as a self-moving, cautiously optimistic individual who goes into the future and attempts to create her own destiny. If we read the novel simply as an imaginative representation of the trials and tribulations of an isolated, neurotic individual or of a liberated woman, we are bound to conclude that she has escaped one phase of bourgeois individualism only to fall victim to a new set of bourgeois illusions, i.e., that she is, in primitive Rousseauist fashion, "freed" from the "chains" of civilization and reawakened to some original and "free" human nature. Rachel's development, however, is not away from society, for in one special sense she has never been in society as an active being. Her escape is not *from* society, but from a passive role in a static society out of history into a dynamic role in society and *in* history. Seen as type, we have presented to us in Rachel a vision of a post-colonial Canada moving uncertainly yet with hope onto the stage of the world.

IV

Scrutiny of Rachel as a type of Canada in the post-colonial period does not exhaust all the dimensions of her typicality. We have only to ask about her social class to realize that she is a national type seen from a particular class point of view, and clearly the view is not that of the ruling financial bourgeoisie. One aspect, therefore, of Rachel's typicality is her social class, which takes us back to the *Oxford English Dictionary* definition of type as "A person or thing that exhibits the characteristic qualities of a class; a typical example or instance." Indeed, all the characters are types in this sense, for they embody different qualities and tendencies of the social classes to which they belong.

The Camerons are the type of the Canadian independent petty-bourgeois family in decline, and they represent the fall of the petty bourgeoisie in Canada as a whole in the twentieth century as Leo A. Johnson has described it. Johnson notes that now "Some 83 per cent of Canadians depend upon wages and salaries for their income...." Of the remains of the petty bourgeoisie he remarks: "With their numbers reduced from their numerical and political dominance of the 1850s to a mere 10.9 per cent of income earners in 1968, it is clear that the whole petite bourgeoisie is reaching the last stages of destruction." He goes on to add: "It would be difficult to over-estimate the economic and historical significance of the destruction of the independent petite bourgeoisie and in particular of the independent commodity producers. For the past century, Canada's history has been shaped by their losing struggle against the maturing capitalist economy."[28]

Whatever else they may be about, *A Jest of God* and the other Manawaka novels have at their heart the concept of social class, class in decline, and the petty bourgeoisie. We think of Hagar in *The Stone Angel* who declines in status from Victorian bourgeois respectability to become an egg woman and a housekeeper – without ever admitting any change in her rank and condition. Bram, her husband, is an independent commodity producer who will no longer compete and is therefore the type of all those small Canadian farmers in an advanced stage of decline earlier in the century. Stacey in *The Fire-Dwellers* hovers on the edge of the abyss of her social class, her husband reduced to the most menial type of salesmanship. Young Morag in *The Diviners* drops immediately in class when her parents die and she is forced to go and live with the lumpen-proletarian, Christie Logan. And so it is throughout Laurence's works.

The decline in *A Jest of God* begins with the death of Niall Cameron and the sale of his business. For if Niall was an independent businessman, free from dependence upon any employer for wages, Rachel works for and falls dependent upon others for her income. By comparison with her father, Rachel has a reduced social status, although her mother, with the typical false consciousness of one of her time and kind, refuses to recognize change of any kind.

Nick Kazlik's father is an independent businessman who gets

by financially in the country, even if he is not exactly rich. Nick, however, will have nothing to do with his father's "independent" farm and business life; rather he prefers the city and the salary of one dependent upon others. He lives in the city, and Rachel will go to live in another city, the pair of them representing the Canadian rural-urban shift that accompanied the decline of the petty bourgeoisie.

We seem to run into a problem here. If decline in social class is at the centre of Laurence's novels, and if she draws imaginatively on the reduction in status of her immediate ancestors, we would surely expect her vision to be a tragic one. And indeed it almost becomes that in *The Stone Angel.* Yet all her novels conclude with varying degrees of cautious optimism and affirmation. How is this optimism (or "hope," as Laurence calls it) to be explained?

Certainly cautious optimism is characteristic of the main line of Manitoba novels. We think of Gander Stake going happily to wage-labour in Winnipeg at the end of *Grain,* Judith Gare in *Wild Geese* cheerfully settling down to a small house, children and the scrubbing of floors, and Niels Lindstadt united with Ellen (whose name in Greek means "the light") when he returns from prison. Even Craig in Douglas Durkin's *The Magpie,* defeated by the forces of urban capitalism and corruption, returns in a cautiously optimistic fashion to the land and his first love. There is precedent enough for cautious optimism in the tradition of the Manitoba novel.

The question becomes: If there was room in the past prairie experience and in the experience of Canadian society for an optimistic vision of reality to be embodied in the literature, is such optimism justified in the present when Johnson has assured us the petty bourgeoisie is nearing total decimation? And if it is not justified, why has Laurence again and again created cautiously optimistic conclusions? We should perhaps begin to answer these questions by noting that Canadians, according to one persuasive argument, have never been as enamoured of the rugged individualist ethos of competitive capitalism as the Americans, that all along Canada has been much more of a social country than the U.S.[29] If this indeed has been the case, then the loss of business "independence" would not seem so much of a sacrifice.

The key to Laurence is that she creates major characters who are either active beings to start with or who move, as in *A Jest of God,* from passivity to activity. As impossible as the situation may sometimes be, her characters fight with whatever weapons they have available. Why do we admire Hagar in *The Stone Angel* so much if not because she is a type who will not accept what a narrow world has in store for her? Why do we follow the mental meanderings of Rachel with such interest if not because we know that she seeks a freedom, a concrete freedom, that most people do not have in a dominated and administered, advanced capitalist society? Rachel is, in fact, a genuine modern hero who, in Goldmann's words, is in search of authentic values in a degraded world.[30] If she represents a declining class, she can be optimistic because the future is hers and this time she will be on the winning side. For as Johnson says:

> Over the past seventy years fundamental changes have occurred in all aspects of class relations in Canada. With the decline of the petite bourgeoisie and the consolidation and maturation of capitalism, a new situation – one more closely resembling Marx's delineation of a capitalist economy – has emerged. Today we are entering a new era of Canadian history where the primary conflict of social forces is moving from one between the capitalist and petit bourgeois modes of production, to a conflict of capital and labour within the capitalist production system.[31]

Rachel the type moves out into the world to face this conflict. She is at once the embodiment of petty bourgeois society in the process of transformation and she is a model to inspire the reader to action.

If we look carefully at the world in which we live, we see monopoly capital, through advertising and other hegemonic means, attempting to isolate individuals from group and class interests and to play on them as passive consumers. If we assume Rachel to be simply an individual character, *A Jest of God* leaves us with a person who is, notwithstanding her illusions of freedom, natural prey for these very large and powerful forces. Only if we see Rachel as type does the novel escape this problem. In this light Rachel is a fully realized individual character who is, in Lukacs' terms, "significant and typical"; through her Laurence succeeds "in disclosing the manifold connections between the individual traits of [her heroine] and the objective general problems of [her] time," because this character experiences in most convincing fashion "the most abstract problems of [her] time as [her] own individual problems that are a matter of life and death [for her]." The psychological and apparently unpolitical surface of *A Jest of God* conceals a powerful political essence.

NOTES

1. Margaret Laurence, "Ten Years' Sentences," in *Margaret Laurence,* ed. William New (Toronto: McGraw-Hill Ryerson Limited, 1977), p. 21. Since I am going to object, finally, to Laurence's interpretation here, I had better make clear that only in certain areas and in a special sense is the author a privileged person when it comes to the interpretation of one of his/her own creations. As T.S. Eliot indicated years ago, there is always more to a work of art than its author knows. We must therefore distinguish between a work of art and its creator's interpretation of the work. If the author's interpretation does not account for all the evidence, and if an opposing interpretation accounts for more evidence, then the latter must take precedence, all other things being equal.
2. For example, Miklos, the cafe owner, is a very minor character that most readers would not remember, a bit of local colour, of no significance at all from the point of view of a psychological approach. As I shall argue, however, appraoched from a different angle, Miklos achieves significance and serves a definite function in the novel. To account for Miklos, more is needed than a simple psychological approach.
3. Laurence, *op. cit.,* p. 27.
4. Raymond Williams, *Marxism and Literature* (Oxford: Oxford University Press, 1977), p. 108.
5. Williams, p. 110.
6. Georg Lukacs, "The Intellectual Physiognomy of Literary Characters," in *Radical Perspectives in the Arts,* ed. Lee Baxandall (Harmondsworth: Penguin Books, 1972), pp. 94-5.
7. The phrase is from Goldsmith's *The Traveller* (1765) and is used by V.G. Kiernan as the title of his 1969 study of British imperialism.
8. See my "The Noble Savage and the Imperial Gentleman," *Canadian Dimension,* XI, No. 7, and "Divining the Past, Present and Future," *Canadian Dimension,* X, No. 7. The former deals with the imperialist ideology of George Bond Head's diary of 1814 (published 1829). In an 1865 novel, a Westmount English lawyer plays a less than idealized Prospero to a very brutalized bastard Caliban son of his by a French-Canadian woman. See my "Heavy-sege's *The Advocate:* The Art of Failure," *Journal of Canadian Fiction,* II, No. 3 (Summer 1973), pp. 95-8, and my review article on *The Diviners,* "Divining the Past, Present, Future" in *Canadian Dimension,* Vol. 10, No. 7 (March 1975).
9. The skeleton of this tradition can be found in two long narrative poems and a prairie novel, short passages from which will serve as illustrations:
   (a) No long line of bards and sages
   Looking to us down the ages;
   No old heroes sweeping by
   In their warlike panoply.
   Yet heroic deeds are done
   Where no battle's lost or won;
   In the cottage in the woods,
   In the lonely solitudes....

(b) Inglorious? Yes; they [the fields] make no promises
Of Star or Garter, or the thundering guns
That tell the earth her warriors are dead.
Inglorious? Aye, the battle done and won
Means not – a throne propp'd up with bleaching bones;
A country sav'd with smoking seas of blood;
A flag torn from the foe with wounds and death;
Or Commerce, with her housewife foot upon
Collossal bridge of slaughter'd savages,
The Cross laid on her brawny shoulder, and
In one sly, mighty hand her reeking sword,
And in the other all the woven cheats
From her dishonest looms. Nay, none of these.
It means – four walls, perhaps a lowly roof;
Kine in a peaceful posture, modest fields;
A man and woman standing hand in hand
In hale old age....

(c) The eleventh of April, 1896, is not generally known to be a date of special significance, yet it was on that day, or, to be more exact, that night, that the hero of this narrative made his entry into a not overhospitable world. Perhaps the term hero, with its suggestion of high enterprise, sits inappropriately upon the chief character of a somewhat commonplace tale; there was in Gander Stake little of that quality which is associated with the clash of righteous steel of the impact of noble purposes. Yet that he was without heroic fibre I will not admit....

The first two passages are from McLachlan's "The Emigrant" (1861) and Crawford's "Malcolm's Katie" (1884), in *Nineteenth-Century Narrative Poems*, ed. David Sinclair (Toronto: McClelland and Stewart, 1972), pp. 116 and 160 respectively. The third passage is the opening paragraph from Robert J.C. Stead's *Grain* (1926). The low-key heroic and anti-imperialist theme is immediately evident in each of the quotations.

10. The term "archetype" has been taken over by the Jungians since the *O.E.D.* was written. I wish to avoid that word for reasons that will become obvious below.
11. Margaret Laurence, *A Jest of God* (Toronto: McClelland and Stewart, 1974), p. 60. Hereafter page references will be in parentheses following a quotation.
12. While in Neepawa helping to set up a local arts council in 1975, I discovered that the local Bamboo Cafe was the original of the Regal, and the name Toy in the novel is a variation on the name of the preceding proprietor.
13. This inexorable rural to urban migration is captured also in Osteno's novel *Wild Geese* (1925), in which Judith Gare is a type representative of this shift.
14. Warren Stevenson, "The Myth of Demeter and Persephone in *A Jest of God*," *Studies in Canadian Literature*, I, No. 1 (Winter 1976), p. 122.
15. Lukacs, *op. cit.*
16. *Ibid.*
17. "I'm 90% in agreement with Women's Lib. But I think we have to be careful here ... for instance, I don't think enough attention has been paid to the problems men have and are going to have increasingly because of the changes taking place in women.... The change must liberate them as well." Margaret Atwood quoting Laurence in "Face to Face," in *Margaret Laurence*, ed. William New, p. 36.
18. Laurence speaks frequently of the "survival" of individuals and at other times of the need for a cultural coming to terms with the past, understanding the present and preparing for the future. The cultural process, of course, is embodied in the character type of Rachel. After all, has not the history of Canada been one of "survival" and does this history not in essence parallel the personal, doubt-ridden history of Rachel?
19. See Alexander Mitscherlich, *Society Without the Father* (New York: Schocken Books, 1970). Originally published in German in 1963, this study preceded *A Jest of God* by three years. Had Laurence known about it, Mitscherlich might well have prompted her in part to develop the character of Rachel. As it is, we can see that certain ideas

were in the air owing to changes in western culture. In the precise and correct words of Lewis A. Coser in the blurb on the back cover, "The title" of Mitscherlich's book "refers to his major organizing idea, that paternal and paternalistic authority has broken down under the impact of modern industrial and urban trends. Hence modern man is no longer controlled by a tradition-bolstered superego. The task before us is the building of a more enlightened society in which the ego rather than the superego, rational consciousness rather than unthinking submission to authority, will guide the behaviour of men." This is, in effect, an abstract of the main theme of *A Jest of God,* and we can well understand now why the novel transcends its Canadian base to constitute a universal statement within the framework of a generalized western European civilization. In the haste for universality, however, we ignore at our peril the concrete particularities of Canadian life in the novel.

20. Laurence's focus on and criticism of this alone would make *A Jest of God* essentially a political novel, for, through her characters and her depiction of society, she attacks the narrow technological rationality of capitalist society for its inhumanity. In this way *A Jest of God* comes to belong to the tradition of critical realism, of which Arnold Kettle writes:

    > By *Critical Realism* I assume we mean literature written in the era of class society from a point of view which, while not fully socialist, is nevertheless sufficiently critical of class society to reveal important truths about that society and to contribute to the freeing of the human consciousness from the limitations which class society has imposed on it. (Arnold Kettle, "Dickens and the Popular Tradition," in *Marxists on Literature,* ed. David Craig [Harmondsworth: Penguin Books, 1975], p. 214.)

    Certainly *A Jest of God* reveals "important truths about that society" and in Rachel we see "the freeing of the human consciousness from the limitations which class society has imposed on it."

21. It may be of some significance that the Japonica plant is not native to the harsh climate of Manitoba and is ill adapted to it.
22. Mitscherlich's thesis, *op. cit.*
23. Frank H. Underhill, *The Image of Confederation,* The Massey Lectures (Toronto: CBC, 1964), p. 72.
24. "At one level correspondences are resemblances, in seemingly very different specific practices, which may be shown by analysis to be both direct and directly related expressions of and responses to a general social process." Williams, *op. cit.*, p. 104.
25. See Peter T. Cominos, "Late-Victorian Sexual Respectability and the Social System," *International Review of Social History,* VIII (1963), pp. 18-48 and the following issue, pp. 216-50. Cominos deals with the sources and function of the kinds of values against which Rachel reacts. Evidence for all the basic patterns in the novel can be found here.
26. Martin Buber, *I and Thou,* Trans. Ronald Gregor Smith, 2nd ed. (New York: 1958).
27. For a description and analysis of Taylorism see Harry Braverman, *Labor and Monopoly Capital: The Degradation of Work in the Twentieth Century* (New York: Monthly Review Press, 1974).
28. Leo A. Johnson, "The Development of Class in Canada in the Twentieth Century," in *Capitalism and the National Question,* ed. Gary Teeple (Toronto: University of Toronto Press, 1972). Quotations from pp. 153, 151, and 151 respectively.
29. "We should not believe that ... Canada has made a simple choice for individualism against its opposites – communality and what are called traditional views of society as a fabric made up of organically interdependent groups. Both in English Canada and in Quebec, it may be argued, individualism has been severely questioned and, ultimately, rejected for other views of man and society." Robin Mathews, "Le Roman engage – The Social/Political Novel in English Canada," *Laurentian University Review,* IX, No. 1, p. 15.
30. Lucien Goldmann, *Pour une sociologie du roman* (Paris: Gallimard, 1964), pp. 24-6.
31. Johnson, *op. cit.*, p. 178.

Language, Body and Identity in Margaret Laurence's ***The Fire-Dwellers***

CHRISTL VERDUYN

Relative to the critical attention given other of Margaret Laurence's works, *The Fire-Dwellers* has not received close scrutiny in recent years. Indeed, its paperback cover precis proclaiming "a poignant novel of a [forty-year-old wife and mother of four] searching desperately for new love" suggests a view of *The Fire-Dwellers* as a somewhat dated 'housewife story'. If that were so, concentrated and sustained critical re-appraisal of the text would perhaps not be warranted. In fact, however, *The Fire-Dwellers* reflects a number of the predominant themes which have emerged in contemporary feminist writing and criticism.

Feminist inquiry into representation – literary, linguistic, or generally artistic – has led to a recent explosion of writing by women. In this writing, language is scrutinized from women's perspective, particularly in relation to questions about reality as women experience it. This experience has been dissected in three ways: physically (through the body), psychically, and in terms of human identity. Much of the writing by women in English Canada and Québec today has been informed by the work of sophisticated theoretical analysts such as Luce Irigaray, Julia Kristeva, Hélène Cixous, and Dale Spender. One sees the results in the work of contemporary Canadian and Québec writers such as Nicole Brossard, Daphne Marlatt, Louky Bersianik, Lola Lemire Tostevin, and Madeleine Ouelette-Michalska. They and many others issue bold challenges to received notions of reality, to the language and literature that describe it, and to the concept of identity prescribed within it.

It is fascinating to discover the extent to which writers of the 'previous generation' were moving towards grappling with these ideas, albeit in a more halting and less complete way. Close examination of Laurence's *The Fire-Dwellers,* for example, discloses a subtext wherein language is repeatedly shown to be an inadequate vehicle of expression for the protagonist Stacey MacAindra. At this level of disclosure, *The Fire-Dwellers* reads much more like a contemporary feminist exploration of language and "reality" than as a 'somewhat dated housewife story'. This essay will examine the extent to which *The Fire-Dwellers* contains a subtext illustrating three themes which dominate contemporary feminist critical thinking: language, body and identity.

Foreign Language

The exploration of language is at once an exploration of the reality – and the fiction – of the body and human identity, since language serves to construct reality and/or fiction. This construction is not a neutral process, as modern theorists such as Michel Foucault have shown. The awareness that words are never neutral is an awareness of the extent to which language inscribes the (perhaps unconscious) assumptions about the dominant values within a particular group. In a world shaped and described predominantly by men, the values of their own gender group prevail in and through the dominant discourse. The possibly different values of the "other" gender – of women – are thus minimized, marginalized, or muted. Women's perspectives remain largely unarticulated – unspoken, silenced, outside of language. The struggle then is with language, the frustration arising from language's deficiencies when it comes to women's (self) expression, the goal in many cases being quite simply to "put it into words."

Doubts about language are introduced at the outset of *The Fire-Dwellers*. The novel opens with the Ladybird refrain, acknowledged as one of *The Fire-Dwellers*' key motifs, indicative of the recurrent fire imagery throughout the story. The protagonist Stacey has the "crazy rhyme ... on the brain this morning,"[1] as a result of having tried to teach her two-year-old daughter Jen, "a few human words yesterday"(1). Stacey questions the soundness of this instruction, given that the rhyming words are frequently very frightening. At this early stage of her inquiry, however, Stacey merely speculates that "maybe it's okay, though. Prepares them for what they can expect"(1).

The reader is prompted to wonder just what *can* children expect? That which Stacey has come to expect: daily life in the adult world otherwise known as reality? The latter, Laurence suggests, must be entered deliberately, precisely because it is not done 'naturally', either by Stacey or by children. There is nothing particularly infantile or childish about Stacey. The fact is that she recognizes a considerable distance and resistance between reality as she experiences it and as it is given to her. Newspapers, radio, and television – Laurence's "ever-open eye" – are instrumental in this transmission. Stacey finds the words they transmit as alarming and problematic as those of the children's rhymes:

> – The Ever-Open Eye. Western serial. Sing yippee for the days of the mad frontier. Boys were sure men in those days all right and men were sure giants. How could they miss? Not with them dandy six shooters. *Tak! Tak! Splat!* Instant power. Who needs women?
>
> The program ends, and then the News. This time the bodies that fall stay fallen. *Flicker-flicker-flicker.* From one dimension to another. Stacey does not know whether Ian and Duncan, when they look, know the difference.
>
> – Everything is happening on TV. Everything is equally unreal. Except that it isn't. Do the kids know? How to tell them? I can't. Maybe they know more about it than I do. Or maybe they know nothing. I can't know. (51)

The images of reality that the television and other vehicles of language project into the brain – a recurring and significant physical site in the novel – create a pool of reflections in which Stacey feels increasingly she is drowning. The motif of water that overcomes persists throughout the novel, culminating in young Duncan's near drowning and Stacey's horrified understanding of "words' total lie"(263).

While musing about nursery rhymes, Stacey looks into the full-length mirror on the bedroom door, where she "sees images reflected [there], distanced by the glass like humans on TV, less real than real and yet more sharply focused because isolated and limited by a frame"(1). The principal image in the mirror is Stacey's "own self in the present flesh"(2), her body framed by the mirror and distanced, to be seen "objectively" as aging and overweight by at least ten pounds. Stacey's alienation from her body is manifest in her acute sense of an "outside" and an "inside" which splits her experiences of self and reality into separate and opposing realms of existence. Her struggles with this divided self, and the separated spheres of body and brain, are paralleled and illustrated by her struggles with language. Time and again Stacey engages language in an effort to repair, reunite, rejoin separate(d) entities – husband and wife, mother and child, woman and friend, body and brain, inside and outside. This struggle unfolds against a backdrop of silence – her husband Mac's, her son Ian's, and her daughter Jen's. Even at two years old, Jen appears "determined not to communicate"(3).

In the opening sequences of the novel, Laurence provides a neat parallel between a young daughter's unwillingness to talk and a mother's critical hesitancy and uncertainty about language. She indicates additionally the complexity as well as the breadth and depth of woman's interrogation of language. Finally, she suggests how an interrogation of language can be related to an analysis of reality, to woman's body, and to human identity in general. Stacey's story illustrates these concerns as she participates in, and is frustrated by, a language which is deficient in expressing reality as she experiences it. Overwhelmed by "too many people" and "too many crises" in her life, Stacey protests inwardly against "too few words that tell any of us a damn thing about any of the others"(189). Shaken by her son Duncan's near drowning, "she is suddenly aware of the words' total lie. They are rune words, trinket charms to ward off the evil eye, and that is all. There is nothing she can do"(263).

If Stacey's experiences with language leave her powerless, for others there is leverage in linking language and knowledge, words and reality. As happens to the people in one of Luke's science fiction stories, to lose language is to lose all knowledge of the past (178). One can be reasonably confident that the brain will bridge language and knowledge and that there exists a logic of the mind. One can *know,* as Buckle knows, that "the other guy is going to [give way]" in one of his games of play chicken(136). Incredulous, Stacey asks, "You know them [the other truckers] all well enough to be able to tell?"(136). It appears, however, that Buckle doesn't have to know who the other truckers are: "I'm okay while my luck's in and it's in because of what I know, see?"(137). Stacey does not see, anymore than she can "take in the reality of Mac's words"(208) when her husband announces some weeks later Buckle's death in a head-on collision. She confronts unanswered questions rather than knowledge and certainty. Words remain forbidden lest she "say the one wrong or fuselike word which may make something explode in [Mac's] head or heart"(210).

Mac would appear to share some of Stacey's reservations about the efficacy of language. But his reservations result in an attitude to language diametrically opposed to Stacey's. In Mac's mind, "there is absolutely no use in talking"(99). But neither he nor neighbour Jake Fogler, a radio actor "fond of talking about the breakdown of verbal communications and the problems of semantics in mass media"(72), seems prepared to probe the possible problematics of the system of beliefs and structures of experience underlying language. Neither man wants to deal with the potential madness that is involved in confronting these problematics. As Tess Fogler undergoes a mental breakdown, and as Stacey approaches one, their husbands draw further and further away as a survival strategy. A semblance of sanity is to be maintained at all costs along with some belief in "reality", no matter how flimsy and misleading.

In Mac's case, for instance, one simply keeps the faith, especially as an employee of Thor Thorlakson of the new Richalife vitamin company. Based on a vision of a New Concept and a New Way of Life (28), Richalife promotes "a healthy mind in a healthy body". This is to be accomplished through individualized programmes of consumption of Richalife pills. Mac seems willing to embrace the easy promises of a richer life with Richalife. Stacey, however, is reluctant to commit herself to this pseudo-religion. The religious overtones of the Richalife programme are paralleled in other of society's attempts to improve her body and mind as distinct entities in her existence. At her weekly visit to the hairdresser, she is attended by "priestesses" for whom grateful customers lean their heads back "to receive the benediction of the shampoo"(87). Shopping for groceries, she strolls with the other consumers along "the long aisles of the temple. Side chapels with the silver-flash of chrome where the dead fish lie among the icy strawberries. The mounds of offerings ... music hymning from invisible choirs"(65). In her conversations with God, Stacey expresses her growing uncertainty about "reality" and religion alike:

> At the Day of Judgment, God will say, *Stacey MacAindra, what have you done with your life?* And I'll say, *Well let's see, Sir, I think I loved my kids.* And he'll say, *Are you certain about that?* And I'll say, *God, I'm not certain about anything any more.* So He'll say, *To hell with you, then. We're all positive thinkers up here.* Then again, maybe He wouldn't.

> Maybe He'd say, *Don't worry, Stacey, I'm not all that certain, either. Sometimes I wonder if I even exist.* And I'd say, *I know what you mean, Lord. I have the same trouble with myself.* (8)

> God knows why I chat to you, God – it's not that I believe in you. Or I do and I don't, like echoes in my head. It's somebody to talk to. Is that all? I don't know. (57)

Through all of this, Stacey is filled with a growing sense of estrangement. Everyday experiences take on an unreal quality. The hairdresser, the grocers, religion, business, health – both the banal and the profound have become alienating. Yet others appear to accept these realities without question. Stacey can only conclude that she is "cracking up"(3) – 'out of her mind'.

Stacey's mind would indeed appear to be a site of weakness, judging by her experiences at night school. The courses in which she enrols – Ancient Greek Drama, Mythology and Modern Man, Man and His Gods, Aspects of Contemporary Thought, Varying Views of Urban Life – serve to measure the extent of her confrontation with the reality of the dominant discourse. In describing and inscribing "reality" through and in language, these experiences prescribe Stacey's doubts and questions as those of a "birdbrain"(21), a "dimwit"(26), a "mini-mind"(39). To fail to live by the word and the mind is to be belittled and beleaguered. Stacey's young Ph.D. instructor undermines her reading of *Clytemnestra*:

> Young academic generously giving up his Thursday evenings in the cause of adult education. *Mrs. MacAindra, I don't think you've got quite the right slant on Clytemnestra.* Why not? The king sacrificed their youngest daughter for success in war – what's the queen supposed to do, shout for joy? *That's not quite the point we're discussing, is it? She murdered her husband, Mrs. MacAindra.* (Oh God, don't you think I know that? The poor bitch.) Yeh well I guess you must know, Dr. Thorne. Sorry. *Oh, that's fine – I always try to encourage people to express themselves.* (27)

In a similar fashion, young Duncan is accused of having no brains (191) by his older brother Ian, who uses "his brains to plan attack"(13), and struggles to be like his father, echoing Mac's own words in the process: *"Can't you just leave me alone?"* (193).

Beset by words – her son's, her husband's, her instructor's –

Stacey remains outside of language. This only serves to reinforce the uneasy dichotomy she experiences between the "reality" *outside* her and the personal experiences *inside* her. The tension between "outside" and "inside" comes to threaten her mental stability as it plays itself out in an additional physical site – her body. A central motif in *The Fire-Dwellers,* woman's body is also a key consideration in contemporary feminist writing and criticism.

Body Experience/s

Many feminists have posed woman's body at the centre of their investigation of language and representation in the dominant discourse. They have engaged language in a "writing of the body", wherein woman's body becomes the springboard of female creativity and cultural production. The female body is thereby liberated from its limited role as reproducer to a new and exciting role as producer and source of expression and representation from woman's perspective. Without subscribing to the notion that anatomy determines women's destiny, numerous theoreticians suggest that the body remains a powerful reference for understanding female (and male) experience. In *Boundaries of the Self: Gender, Culture, Fiction*[2], Roberta Rubenstein identifies the body not only as the site of experiences of gender, ethnicity and language, but also as an important measure of the boundaries of those experiences. The categories of "inside" and "outside" arise as configurations in these experiences of body and self. Arguing that interpersonal boundaries mirror and are mirrored in the larger social body, she notes that the latter "constrains the way the physical body is perceived. The physical experience of the body, always modified by the social categories through which it is known, sustains a particular view of society. There is continual exchange of meanings between the two kinds of bodily experience so that each reinforces the categories of the other."[3]

This is an issue Laurence deals with directly in *The Fire-Dwellers.* Stacey experiences in an acute way this continual exchange of meaning between "inside" and "outside". She likens her experience of this to "a disease I've picked up somewhere": "What goes on inside isn't ever the same as what goes on outside" (28). The dichotomy of "inside" and "outside" is fused with the rift between "reality" and "unreality": *"Everything drifts. Everything is slowly swirling, philosophies tangled with the grocery lists, unreal-real anxieties like rose thorns waiting to tear the uncertain flesh, nonentities of thoughts floating like plankton ...*" (28). In this, Stacey's experience of her body is one of uncertainty, alienation, and constraint. The latter, as noted above, arises largely from the attitude of restriction with which the greater social body perceives the physical body. For women in general, and for Stacey in particular, these restrictions are translated into rules of appearance having to do with body weight and shape, colour coordination, age, and so forth. In an effort to meet these standards, Stacey compares herself constantly to the images of the ideal woman ('s body) that she sees reflected all around her in magazines, on the television, in the figure of her neighbour Tess Fogler.

> Tess is still in her housecoat, but being tall and slender looks as though ready to receive the Peruvian ambassador. Tess's hair is honeyblond and even this early in the day is done in a flawless French roll. Stacey, who is shorter than she would like to be, is wearing her pale-blue last year's spring coat and, because her dark unruly hair needs doing, a small white veil-enfolded straw hat which she dislikes.
>
> – My God I look awful how does she always look so
>
> (3)

Her apparent failure to measure up is translated into self-addressed words of admonition: "Come on, fat slob, get up off your ass and get going"(2); "Sometimes I feel like a beat-up old bitch ... I feel about a hundred"(11); "Oh Cleopatra. You old swayback ... filled in with the slow accumulation of flesh. Not flesh. Fat. F.A.T."(15). Language underscores what repeated glances into mirrors reflect: Stacey's body as a separate, unreal self, a reflection from outside, which somehow delineates for the world at large the totality of her self. Of the young woman who sits beside her on the bus, Stacey wonders:

> – What's she seeing? Housewife, mother of four, this slightly too short and too amply rumped woman of yesteryear, hemlines all the wrong length as Katie is always telling me, lipstick wrong color, and crowning comic touch, the hat. *Man, how antediluvian can you get?* Is that what she's thinking? I don't know. But I still have this sense of some monstrous injustice. I want to explain. *Under this chapeau lurks a mer-*

> *maid, a whore, a tigress.* She'd call a cop and I'd be put in a mental ward. (9)

Stacey's struggle is to get beyond the too narrow dominant definition of self and to "make [her]self real", as she puts it, when she makes love with Luke(183).

For Laurence, then, the psychic tension women experience between "outside" and "inside" is made concrete in the physical realm, in the body. This central consideration in contemporary feminist thought is a major theme in *The Fire-Dwellers.*

Identity and 'Self'

The concept of self as a separate, coherent, and centered unit(y) of subjecthood has come under the scrutiny of many feminist scholars. Julia Kristeva has expressed deep suspicion about the notion of identity as it is traditionally understood: "What can "identity," even "sexual identity," mean in a new theoretical and scientific space where the very notion of identity is challenged?"[4] In *Speculum of the Other Woman*[5], Luce Irigaray asserts that theories of the subject have always been appropriated to the "masculine". When woman submits to these theories, she abdicates unawares her specific relationship as woman to the imaginary. Woman is excluded from (male-defined) subjectivity as she is exiled from (ma(i)nstream) representation. Nor can she easily construct subjectivity and representation from a female perspective insofar as these concepts postulate a subject that is capable of reflecting (on) its own being. Irigaray argues against what she sees as the fundamentally narcissistic "specularization" underlying Western discourse, in which that which exceeds the reflective circularity is that which is unthinkable and unrepresentable. Such a male specular logic can only represent woman as the negative of its own reflection, the other in a system that seeks sameness. For Irigaray, woman is not only the Other, as Simone de Beauvoir demonstrated, but she is quite specifically man's Other – his negative or mirror-image. Femininity is then analysed as non-specular (in that it does not work on an either/or model), as inclusive, plural or multiple, and uncentered. Woman's efforts to center herself as a unique, coherent, and separate subject thus become an exercise in frustration.

In *The Fire-Dwellers,* Laurence puts Stacey through such an exercise. She is continuously assaulted by the directive to cultivate her individualized self. For example, in one women's magazine article she reads, women are encouraged to express themselves as individuals by painting their front doors lilac. "What a fool I was," Stacey reflects in hindsight, "'Want To Be a Little Off-Beat?' Here's ten ways, the article said. A lilac door was one. So off I tripped to the nearest hardware store to assert my unique individuality with the same tin of paint as two million other dimwits. Conned into idiocy"(26). Mac communicates a similar message through the "icy calm"(14) that separates him from Stacey and keeps even the children at a distance. Rather than see herself as separate from her children and husband, Stacey thinks of herself in terms of them, as extensions of them, so much so that she is periodically overwhelmed with a sense of having no self at all:

> I can't go anywhere as myself. Only as Mac's wife or the kids' mother. And yet I'm getting now so that I actually prefer to have either Mac or one of the kids along. Even to the hairdresser, I'd rather take Jen. It's easier to face the world with one of them along. Then I know who I'm supposed to be. (83).

Tension arises for Stacey when this way of being is measured against a concept of subjecthood which posits the mature self as an autonomous and distinct unity, and, upon comparison, found wanting. Tension subsides given a redefinition of identity which perceives others less as distanced Other than as self including. Stacey speculates how strange it would be to "stop thinking in terms of *them* and *me*"(183) and wonders if she ever could, given the accepted definition of identity.

An alternative concept of identity tells a different story of the search for self. In the traditional narrative, the young hero finds himself by separating himself from his community in order to undergo on his own tests and challenges which serve to prove his manhood and reveal his selfhood. Stacey's adventure with Luke tests the appropriateness of this story in her search of self. She takes leave of her family and is encouraged by Luke to set out with him on an adventure which would afford her the opportunity of finding out who she is as someone quite separate from children and husband. Stacey turns down the invitation; she "can't leave ... my kids and and "(204).

The heroic approach to self-discovery is thus aborted. But

Stacey's desire for selfhood is retained and pursued, in less spectacular and adventurous ways, although in more woman-defined terms. After the trials and tribulations of Buckle's death and Duncan's near death, Mac's accusations of infidelity and his confrontation with Thor Thorlakson, Stacey finds reconciliation with both family and self. This reconciliation takes place through the rejection of a self which is definite – defined and finite. Instead, Stacey comes to an understanding of self as an ever-evolving experience, one that is constructed as an ongoing process. "The truth is that I haven't been Stacey Cameron for one hell of a long time now. Although in some ways I'll always be her, because that's how I started out"(272). But the unfolding of self goes on and extends to those around her so that Stacey can comfortably say "it's myself I'm thinking about, as well as them... Temporarily, they are all more or less okay"(276-277). The new perspective does not encompass certitude, resolution, or infinity. Rather it admits confusion, irresolution, and temporariness: "I stand in relation to my life both as child and as parent, never quite finished with the old battles, never able to arbitrate properly the new, able to look both ways, but whichever way I look, God, it looks pretty confusing to me"(40).

Stacey's sense of self not only suggests an alternative concept of identity; it also suggests some new possibilities for language. Listening to Mac's and Ian's minimalist exchange after Duncan's near miss with death, Stacey realizes: "That's the most Mac will ever be able to say. They're not like me, either of them. They don't want to say it in full technicolor and intense detail. And that's okay, I guess. Ian gets the message. It's his language, too. I wish it were mine. All I can do is accept it is a language, and that it works, at least sometimes. And maybe it's mine more than I like to admit. Whatever I think that I think of it, it's the one I most use" (265-266). This reconciliation of sorts with language is underscored by Jen's coming to language, a "brass bands and banners"(269) event for Stacey, a celebratory moment for mother and daughter.

Conjunctions

Margaret Laurence's *The Fire-Dwellers* suggests that there is a conjunction of language and identity in woman's understanding and expression of self. This is an idea which reverberates in the work of other contemporary women writers. Hélène Cixous, among others, has envisioned writing "in the feminine mode" as a way of re-establishing a spontaneous relationship to the physical *jouissance* of the female body in a truly non-oppressive and non-sexist society. More than just a vehicle of liberation, writing is posed as the very enactment of it.[6]

> To write. An act which will not only "realize" the decensored relation of woman to her sexuality, to her womanly being, giving her access to her native strength; it will give her back her goods, her pleasures, her organs, her immense bodily territories which have been kept under seal; it will tear her away from the superegoized structure in which she has always occupied the place reserved for the guilty (guilty of everything, guilty at every turn: for having desires, for not having any; for being frigid, for being "too hot"; for not being both at once; for being motherly and not enough; for having children and for not having any; for nursing and for not nursing...) – tear her away by means of this research, this job of analysis and illumination, this emancipation of the marvellous text of her self that she must urgently learn to speak.[7]

Many other writers see work to be done on and with language as the springboard for a new vision of human understanding and human identity. In this work the woman writer, or quite simply women writing, has a particularly vital role to play. Not surprisingly, in an increasing number of contemporary works by women in Canada as elsewhere, the woman writer or woman as artist is presented as the central character. She turns up in Laurence's work immediately following *The Fire-Dwellers,* first in *A Bird in the House,* and then in *The Diviners.* The interrogation of language and its constructs of the female body and human identity, so intensely undertaken by Stacey in *The Fire-Dwellers,* unfolds in full force in Laurence's subsequent works. It also appears as a compelling challenge in the work of women writers both of Laurence's generation and since, whose writing works with and against language in an attempt to reconstruct reality – and fiction – as women experience them.

NOTES

1. Margaret Laurence, *The Fire-Dwellers* (Toronto: McClelland & Stewart-Bantam Ltd., Seal Books, 1981). All references in this essay to *The Fire-Dwellers* are to this edition and appear bracketed in the text.
2. Roberta Rubenstein, *Boundaries of the Self: Gender, Culture, Fiction* (Urbana and Chicago: University of Illinois, 1987). See introduction, pages 3-10.
3. Rubenstein, p. 4, quoting Mary Douglas, *Natural Symbols: Explorations in Cosmology* (New York: Pantheon, 1970), p. 65.
4. Julia Kristeva, "Woman's Time," quoted by Toril Moi in *Sexual/Textual Politics: Feminist Literary Theory* (London and New York: Methuen, 1986), p. 163.
5. Luce Irigaray, *Speculum de l'autre femme* (Paris, Minuit, 1974). For these and other considerations of Irigaray's work, see Moi, chapter 7: "Patriarchal reflections: Luce Irigaray's looking glass," pp. 127-149.
6. Moi, p. 121, p. 125.
7. Hélène Cixous, "The Laugh of the Medusa", in Elaine Marks and Isabelle de Courtivron, eds., *New French Feminisms,* (Amherst: University of Massachusetts Press, 1980), p. 250.

The Chariot of Ossian: Myth and Manitoba in ***The Diviners***

CLARA THOMAS

For the past eight years, since she came back to Canada in 1969 as Writer-in-Residence at the University of Toronto, Margaret Laurence's work has been two-fold. Tens of thousands of people have read her books, and these will remain her timeless achievements in literature. Thousands of people have also heard her speak. Neither her readers nor her audiences could possibly doubt the sincerity of her convictions about Canadian nationality. Since 1969 she has spoken on hundreds of occasions to clubs, classes and seminars, in public lectures and at university convocations. She has a powerful public presence, developed through intense self-discipline, for the solitude of writing, not the spot-light of speaking, is her natural preference. But from a sense of mission, she has made herself available to groups of all ages. Anyone who has watched her with students knows that her presence operates on them with the force of a benign psychic phenomenon. Always her message centres around the importance of our literature as a necessary foundation-link with generations of Canadians in the past, with one another in the present and with all the generations of the future.

Speaking at Simon Fraser's Convocation in the spring of 1977, she reiterated the convictions that are basic to her.

> The calibre and scope of our literature now is such that it can be read and taught simply because it is interesting, worth reading and worth teaching. But for us it has an added dimension as well. It is our own; it speaks to us, through its many and varied voices, of things which are close to our hearts; it links with our ancestors and with one another.... [we do] have a great need to possess our own land, to know our own heritage, to value ourselves in relation to a world community [*S.F.U. Week,* vol. 8, no 5].

The words "ancestors" and "heritage" are keystones in that statement and their importance to individuals and communities is a basic

* First published in the *Journal of Canadian Studies,* Vol. 13, No. 3 (Fall 1978). Also published in *Here and Now,* ed. John Moss, NC Press, 1978.

premise in all of Laurence's work, the early *Tomorrow-Tamer* stories and the Ghana-set novel, *This Side Jordan,* as well as each of the five Canadian works. Her Scotch-Irish tradition and family background, her experiences in Somaliland, in the emergent nation of Ghana, and later with the great group of writers who first celebrated the independence of Nigeria, the strength of her own roots in Manitoba and her deep involvement in Canadian cultural nationalism, all these have combined to convince her that a writer's opportunity and responsibility includes weaving the past of his place and his people into "a feeling of our own people, of our place of belonging.... It is important to know that we all come from different sources, originally, but that in this diversity lies our true strength as a people" (*S.F.U. Week, Ibid.*). In a conversation with Irving Layton in 1970 she first recorded her belief in the close interweaving of history and myth in our literature. "People like my grandfather, or like the character of Harvey Lepage in *Stud-Horse Man...* – These people are our myths. This is our history. And perhaps not consciously, but after awhile consciously, this is what we are trying to set down."[1]

In *The Diviners,* the most complicated and structurally complex of her novels, she writes out in full the process of Morag Gunn's education into her personal and cultural heritage – by implication the need of every child. To the adult Morag, remembering, her awareness widened in well-marked stages, from her early acceptance of outside authority to her revolt against it and finally to her confidence in her own inner integrity and sufficiency. The authority of Christie's voice, of the printed word, of the conventions of Manawaka, of her own age group, and of Brooke Skelton was finally replaced by her own authority and her own truth. Similarly, Morag finally knows where her place is. She has escaped the town of Manawaka, but she carries it with her always. The true land of her ancestors is, finally, "Christie's real country. Where I was born" (p. 391).[2] As Laurence knows that writers must work out of their own roots in place and time, so, for her, both personal identity and nationality begin with place and region – any literature must, first of all, be in this sense regional or local and must reach the universal through first being local.

Christie Logan shows Morag the two large books of Ossian when she is twelve years old. In the narrative sequence of *The Diviners,* this incident occurs between Christie's telling of the first and second tales of Piper Gunn. This is a signal to the reader of one of Laurence's intents in *The Diviners,* the offering of an extended lesson on the transference of folk-lore into literature, history into myth, and these into the development of a child. It happens when Morag is well into the hands of the public school system – the printed word, not Christie's voice, has become her authority. When he finds her copying out Wordsworth's "Daffodils" (a poem which has become a cliché for British educational imperialism, especially as practised on children of the tropics who never saw a daffodil), Christie counters with his copy of James Macpherson's Ossianic Poems, a printed authority that he recognizes:

> "In the days long long ago," Christie says sternly, "he lived, this man, and was the greatest song-maker of them all, and all this was set down years later, pieced together from what old men and old women remembered, see, them living on far crofts hither and yon, and they sang and recited these poems as they had been written down over the generations. And the English claimed as how these were not the real old songs, but only forgeries, do you see, and you can read about it right here in this part which is called Introduction but the English were bloody liars then as now. And I'll read you what he said, then, a bit of it" [p. 63].

There is a mountainous literature on James Macpherson and the probable authorship of the Ossianic Poems. Amongst all the controversy that has raged since their publication in 1760, however, no one has been able to deny their power and influence, not only in Scotland, but in Europe and America as well. Andrew Hook, a recent cultural historian, is well aware of these far-reaching effects, whatever the poems' ratio between folklore and individual imagination may have been:

> Genuine or fraudulent, a product of the Gaelic bardic tradition, or an artificial literary exercise, there is a note in these poems which found a response in contemporary readers everywhere, and which lingers there for the unprejudiced reader of today. Beneath the posturing and the rhetoric, the artificiality of language and style, there it remains: the elegiac note which so often characterizes a great epic poem, the lament for an age, a civilization that is passing, for the old way and the old way's order, which the present is destroying.[3]

In Margaret Laurence's work, however, this reference to Ossian indicates far more than nostalgia and regret. As her Manawaka heroines come to know that they carry their place and their past with them always, so it is one of Laurence's deepest beliefs that this is inevitable for everyone. The point of the past is its active function in our present, not a vanished reference point on which to focus fond nostalgia, resentment or regret. The book of Ossian in *The Diviners* thus signifies a printed authority that by itself is simply an artifact of the past. Transmitted through Christie to Morag, however, the work becomes a dynamic factor in Morag's search for her own identity. The sight of the books of Ossian, the mystery of their Gaelic and Christie's reading of the passage describing the great chariot of Cuchullin unlock Morag's imagination to a far, mysterious horizon and bring a proud community of the past right into her present. When, later, she writes in her scribbler about the chariot built by Piper Gunn's woman, she patriates it into her own setting:

the front shaped like a ship and a bird
birch bark scrolls around the sides
carvings of deer and foxes and bears
carvings of meadowlarks
carvings of tall grasses
carvings of spruce trees and spruce cones
[p. 86].

This chariot, developing in Morag's imagination from the Chariot of Cuchullin, is now part of her myth – and we, the readers, have been offered a lesson in myth's on-going dynamic function in the development of the individual.

From the very first of Christie's tales, their function and power as myth are signalled in the text of *The Diviners.* Like all folk-literature, these stories, in the beginning, are orally transmitted; only *some* folk-literature, however, moves into the category of myth, and this depends on the need and belief of the listener. The tales of Piper Gunn are told to Morag to explain and illuminate her background and to engage and support her belief in her family's and her own pride and honour. When she accepts them they become, for her, powerful myths. She bases her identity on them and she acts out of her trust that they are a part of her.

Structurally, Margaret Laurence achieves her purpose with precision and finesse. There are three mythic sets woven into *The Diviners:* Christie's tales, which give Morag her distant past and also make her own father a hero and which she later passes on to Pique with the addition of Christie's own story; Jules (Skinner) Tonnerre's tales, told to Morag by Skinner, later passed on to their daughter with the addition of the songs that Jules personally passes on to Pique and of Pique's own song; and the adult Morag's half-playful, half-serious myth-making of Catharine Parr Traill.

The sequences in which Morag hears Christie's tales and then Jules' tales begin with the child's own need. The first tale of Piper Gunn is featured in Morag's Memory Bank Movies when she is nine, though she knows that Christie had told her the tale before that. He is drinking red biddy and declaiming the valour of his Logan ancestors. *The Clans and Tartans of Scotland,* one of his four treasured books, is printed evidence of his ancestors' greatness, but there is nothing in it about the Gunns to give Morag pride: "When she first looked it up, she showed it to Christie, and he read it and then he laughed and asked her if she had not been told the tales about the most famous Gunn of all, and so he told her" (p. 48). This first tale is the story of the great Piper and his woman, Morag, who inspired the displaced Sutherlanders with his music and gave them the courage to endure and survive:

> What happened then, to all of them people there homeless on the rocks? They rose and followed! Yes, they rose then and they followed, for Piper Gunn's music could put the heart into them and they would have followed him all the way to hell or to heaven with the sound of the pipes in their ears.
>
> And that was how they all come to this country, all that bunch, and they ended up at the Red River, and that is another story [p. 51].

When she goes to bed after this first story, Morag tells herself her own tale of Piper Gunn's woman, Morag, and falls asleep comforted by a bravery that she begins to identify with herself: *"Forests cannot hurt me because I have the power and the second sight and the good eye and the strength of conviction"* (p. 52).

Morag is twelve when Christie reads to her from the book of Ossian and they look at the Gaelic, "the strange words, unknown now, lost, as it seems to all men" (p. 65). Shortly after, she and Skinner meet in the Nuisance Grounds and she begins to see that brushing him out of her mind with "he isn't anybody" was wrong. He too has a tradition behind him. It includes two hero-ancestors from long ago, his grandfather, Jules, and Chevalier "Rider" Tonnerre, and his tradition too involves a strange language. When she boasts of Piper Gunn he retaliates with some brief references to his two heroes, but he won't tell her his stories.

Christie's *Tale of Piper Gunn and the Long March* is next recorded. Morag is still in public school and as Christie talks she interrupts with questions and she also begins to doubt "(They walked? A *thousand* miles? They couldn't Christie)" (p. 85). This tale tells of the march of the Sutherlanders, led by Piper Gunn and inspired by Morag, his woman: "if we must live here in this almighty godforsaken land, dreadful with all manner of beasts and ice and the rocks harsher than them we left, says Gunn's woman, at least let's be piped onto it" (p. 85). This story is about Manitoba and Morag is curious about its details, especially out of her dawning respect for Skinner Tonnerre, about the halfbreeds:

(Did they fight the halfbreeds and Indians, Christie?)
Did they ever. Slew them in their dozens, girl. In their scores.
(Were they bad, the breeds and them?)
What? [p. 86].

Christie's first two tales have given Morag two heroic ancestors, Piper Gunn and his wife, Morag. It is after this second one, set in Manitoba, that Morag writes down her description of the chariot, built in the woods by the Red River, that the first Morag built for Piper, their child and herself. At this time, too, Morag starts a story about Clowny Macpherson, "a little scrawny guy" who was really very tough. She is intuitively and imaginatively beginning to fuse Christie's bardic role with the ancient bard's in Ossian.

At this time also Christie brings the tales of her ancestry right down to her own father and his heroism at the Battle of Bourlon Wood in World War I. This is set off by his accidental finding of his regimental book, *The 60th Canadian Field Artillery Book.* Again, this story answers Morag's need. Christie cannot identify her father's picture in the group and his memories of the action cannot tally with the book's bare prose: "Oh Jesus, don't they make it sound like a Sunday School picnic? ... well, d'you see, it was like the book says, but it wasn't like that also. That is the strangeness" (p. 90). What Christie can do and does do is to make her father, Colin, into a hero for her: "Your dad saved my life that one time then" (p. 89).

This is a hard story for Christie to tell and he only goes on with it as Morag urges him. She would like to have the book for herself but Christie keeps that. Instead he gives her the hunting knife that "some young twirp of a kid" had traded him for a package of cigarettes. Margaret Laurence has symbolically joined Morag to the Tonnerres by that knife. A reader who knows *The Stone Angel* knows that John Shipley traded his mother's plaid pin to Lazarus Tonnerre for the knife.

In the textual sequence of *The Diviners,* the adult Morag's first conversation with Catharine Parr Traill comes next. This is myth-making with a difference. Where the child, Morag, needed ancestors to admire, trust and function as her models, the adult Morag needs a kind of friendly adversary against whom to test the strength of her own identity and resolve. Beyond this, Morag's communings with Catharine Parr Traill are humorous in their tone, providing a leavener for Morag's anxieties and a periodic lightening to the tone of her anxious self-examination. In terms of Margaret Laurence's illumination of the functions of history and myth, oral literature and written literature, however, the Traill-Morag episodes offer another level of instruction to the reader. Laurence is keenly aware of the authority invested in the printed word; she has already shown herself to be equally aware of its limitations ("It was like the book says, but it wasn't like that also. That is the strangeness").

To Margaret Laurence as to many of us, Catharine Parr Traill stands as the epitome of the benign, pioneer matriarch, "drawing and naming wild flowers –, writing a guide for settlers with one hand, whilst rearing a brace of young and working like a galley slave – with the other" (p. 95). Our evidence for Mrs. Traill's all-encompassing serenity and competence rests on her own printed books. When Morag, desperately anxious about Pique, finds "the pertinent text," she reads: "In case of emergency, it is folly to fold one's hands and sit down to bewail in abject terror. It is better to be up and doing" (p. 97). In their ensuing dialogue, Morag honours the achievement of Catharine Traill, but she also argues the difference in her own situation: "*You* try having your only child disappear you know not where Mrs. Traill. Also, with no strong or even feeble shoulder upon which to lean, on occasion" (p. 97). The printed word, Laurence is saying – *any* printed word – must not be taken as authority in itself. It can be inspiration, it can also provide example, but in itself it must be recognized as inert. Only through translation into the needs and actions of its recipient can it become a dynamic and positive force. Therefore, Mrs. Traill is Morag's "lady of blessed memory" and subsequently her "St. Catharine," but her canonization is granted by Morag with affectionate and knowing irony: Morag's problems are ultimately to be resolved out of her own and no one else's strength.

There is another factor active in Catharine Traill's intermittent presence in the text of *The Diviners*. The adult Morag has moved to McConnell's Landing in Ontario and there she intends to stay. It is part of Margaret Laurence's own belief that to become truly a part of the place – any place – it is necessary to assimilate that place's history into one's own consciousness. This Morag does through the person of Catharine Traill and the pioneer tradition that she represents. It is a far different tradition from the Manitoba past that Christie's and Skinner's tales represent, but it is equally necessary to the process of Morag's new patriation.

Christie tells his third and last tale, "Piper Gunn and the Rebels," to Morag when she is fifteen, troubled and sexually frustrated by her meeting with Skinner in the valley and in need of comfort. Christie is surprised when she asks him for one of the stories he used to tell her: "great jumping jesus, Morag, I thought you would have been past all that" (p. 129), and Morag has gone beyond questioning to correcting his facts. This is the story of how the Sutherlanders were roused by Piper Gunn's music to take the fort and save their farmland from "Reel and his gang of half-breeds." The story has lost its authority for her and she defends Riel and the Métis. Her thanks to Christie is a token only – he was right, she really is "past all that."

Morag hears Skinner's stories after they have fumblingly come together in his shack down in the valley: "But he puts an arm around her, and they walk the chill mud-carpeted streets beside the empty trees and the quiet half-dark houses, and he tells her. Stories for children" (p. 142). The next day, Skinner goes overseas with the Cameron Highlanders. After Dieppe, when Morag does not find his name among the long list of casualties from Manawaka, she tells herself his stories. It is here in the text that Lazarus' "Tale of Rider Tonnerre," "Rider Tonnerre and the Prophets," and "Old Jules and the War Out West" are recorded. The sequence ends with a fourth heading, "Skinner's Tale of Dieppe?," but no story follows. Now, when she is eighteen and ready to leave Manawaka for university, Morag possesses the tales of the two traditions. At this time, on the brink of adulthood, she also violently rejects them all.

Morag's passage from innocence to experience is, in one sense, gradually marked in the text, with her recollection of many incidents which hurt her and forced her growth ("Morag is twelve and is she ever tough"), and a few incidents, such as Christie's story-telling, which were a benign support to her growth. But her violent propulsion into the adult world comes with her experience of reporting the fire in the valley for Lachlan and the Manawaka *Banner.* After seeing the pitiful ruins of the shack where Piquette and her children died and watching the men, including Lazarus, carry out their charred remains, the world is all tragic cruelty for Morag: "She put her head down on the desk and cries in a way she does not remember having done before, as though pain were the only condition of human life" (p. 161). When next Christie starts ranting about his family and their proud past she rejects it all, not with rage, but with a weary, cynical hopelessness. All that is meaningless, she thinks, in the face of the awful reality she has seen and she stops Christie when he begins to explain to her why he used to tell her the old tales:

> "What does it matter, Christie? It was all so long ago."
>
> The Gunns have no crest, no motto, no war cry, at least according to what it says in the old book Christie still hauls out from time to time. Just as well. It's all a load of old manure [p. 162].

This is Morag's *non serviam.* She is going to leave Manawaka "and I'm never coming back." All the past, her life with Christie and Prin, her life in the town, the tales of her ancestors, are being shed like an old skin and the new Morag will be free. Through the years of her adult life, however, she will, reluctantly at first and then thankfully, come to realize that she is not free, nor can she be, nor does she want to be. And the past – all of it, including both her tales and Jules' tales – she will come to accept for what it must be to her if she is to grow and if she is to give her daughter, Pique, the myths she needs in order to grow.

So far the story of the young Morag as recalled by the adult Morag has been faithful to the basic conventions of the initiation-novel. In *The Diviners,* however, the second part of the novel is as carefully and explicitly charted as the first. Morag's reconstruction of her past affirms a step-by-step growth to integration and acceptance of herself and her place that is a world away from Huck Finn's lighting out for the territories or *Lady Oracle*'s compulsive escape-artistry, or even Dunstan Ramsay's restless avoidance of social commitment and responsibility until very late in his life.[4] She had to leave Manawaka in order to grow and, eventually, to understand where she had been. She had to reject, temporarily, the myths that had strengthened her childhood growth in order to learn to understand them in a new way. After ten years of marriage, she has to leave Brooke and the deepest reason for this is that she has already grown in her understanding beyond the point at which he first found her – the stage in which he needs and wishes her to remain. Even before her marriage, when she had gone back to Manawaka for a few days, Prin had told her another version of what happened to Colin and Christie at Bourlon Wood and she had begun to understand what Christie had done for her:

> Colin Gunn. Christie's tale of Gunner Gunn and the Great War. How Colin saved Christie, staved off his dying, that time away out there, on that corner of a foreign field that is forever nowhere. It hadn't happened that way, then, or probably not. It had happened the way Prin said. Christie holding Colin in his arms. Colin probably eighteen. Eighteen. Amid the shellfire and the barb wire and the mud, crying [p. 206].

As Christie and Morag talk later, Christie adds another element of puzzle to be considered in her journey towards recovery from the total rejection of all the past that she had vowed:

> "Look here, it's a bloody good thing you got away from this dump. So just shut your Goddam trap and thank your lucky stars."
>
> "Do you really think that, Christie?"
>
> "I do," Christie says, knocking back the whiskey. "And also I don't. That's the way it goes. It'll all go along with you, too. That goes without saying."

> But it has been said. *The way it goes – it'll all go – that goes.* Does Christie bring in these echoes knowingly, or does it just happen naturally with him? She has never known [p. 207].

Though at this point Morag denies that Christie is right, she has already taken a step towards acceptance and understanding. When she goes home to Prin's funeral she wants to ask Christie to tell all the old tales to her but cannot, and when she goes back to Brooke she rebels against the child-woman role that she has played with him:

> "It's too bad you had to go back to the town this last time," Brooke said. "You had effectively forgotten it. Now it's all risen up and it's only upsetting you, Morag. Can't you simply put it from your mind?"
>
> "I never forgot any of it. It was always there."
>
> "When you first came to me," Brooke says, "You said you had no past. I liked that. It was as though everything was starting for you, right then, that moment [p. 257].

Morag gradually comes to understand that Christie had made a world of innocence for her and peopled it with heroes to answer her needs. Her painful passage to experience began a complementary process in which initial rejection of the heroes was only a clearing of the ground before moving towards an adult's acceptance, understanding and positive use of the past. She moves from the need for heroes to the recognition that endurance and community of spirit are the true legacies of the past on which present generations must build. Christie's comforting of Colin Gunn and his care for Morag; Lazarus' indomitable "I'm going in, they're mine, there, them," at the time of the fire, do not eradicate the heroic figure of Piper Gunn. That she will always possess too. But her understanding, both of the past and its continuing presence and of her own responsibilities to it, to her present and to the future, modulates and broadens.

With the advent of Pique, the pattern begins to repeat itself, this time with a double heritage for the child and with Morag conscious of her function as a selector and shaper of the past for her daughter:

> Lazarus at the fire, Lazarus, snarling his pain, a stranger in the place where he lived his whole life. Lazarus, dead at 51.

> Will Morag tell Pique all she knows of Lazarus, or of Christie, for that matter? How will the tales change in the telling? [p. 338].

Jules visits Morag and Pique when Pique is five and again when she is fifteen. On the first occasion, he sings his ballad for his grandfather, Jules, and on the second, his songs for his father, Lazarus, and for Piquette, his sister. Meanwhile, Morag has told her Christie's and Lazarus' stories as well as the stories of Piper Gunn. Pique has her mythic inheritance by the time she is fifteen. Because of the patterning of the text, the alternating rhythm beween Morag's present situation and her memories, and because in the present time of the text Pique is a young adult, we are shown her movement from childish acceptance to questioning as a parallel movement to Morag's own remembered development. At twenty-one Pique has it all but, like her mother at the same stage, she questions its meaning to her:

> "I never know what really happened. There was only that one time when my Dad was here – when I was fifteen, eh? And he said a lot of things. And the songs – I've got those. And he said some more, when I saw him in Toronto, this time. But some of those stories you used to tell me when I was a kid – I never knew if they happened like that or not."
>
> "Some did and some didn't, I guess. It doesn't matter a damn. Don't you see?"
>
> "No," Pique said, "I don't see. I want to know what really happened" [p. 350].

Morag comes into full, final adult understanding of the importance of the myths to her and of Christie's dynamic part in giving them to her when she and Pique visit Dan McRaith in Scotland. As she looks across the sea to Sutherland, where she has always dreamed of going to find her people, she knows, finally, that her own place is "Christie's real country" (p. 391). Before Christie dies she is able to tell him that he has been her father to her, to hear his reply, "Well – I'm blessed" (p. 396), and to give him the funeral that draws together all that he has given her both as father and as bard, the source of her ancestral inheritance:

> He swings the pipes up, and there is the low mutter of the drones. Then he begins, pacing the hillside as he plays. And Morag sees, with the strength of conviction, that this is Christie's true burial.

> *And Piper Gunn, he was a great tall man, with the voice of drums and the heart of a child, and the gall of a thousand, and the strength of conviction.*
>
> The piper plays "The Flowers of the Forest," the long-ago pibroch, the lament for the dead, over Christie Logan's grave. And only now is Morag released into her mourning [p. 403].

Immediately after this in the sequence of the text, Morag releases herself from her half-humourous, half-serious connection with Catharine Parr Traill. She recognizes and claims her house and garden as her own, listing and naming its weeds and finally repudiating her imagined inferiority to the archetypal lady-pioneer:

> "I'm going to stop feeling guilty that I'll never be as hard-working or knowledgeable or all-round terrific as you were.... This place is some kind of a garden, nonetheless, even though it may be only a wild flower garden. It's needed, and not only by me. I'm about to quit worrying about not being either an old or a new pioneer. So farewell, sweet saint – henceforth I summon you not" [p. 407].

Margaret Laurence has demonstrated that, for Morag, the functions of myth have been to give her strength to develop into her own person, to find her own place and, finally, to rest easy in it. For Pique, as the book ends, her inheritance is sending her back to Galloping Mountain to find out whether or not her place is there with Jules' brother Jacques and the family commune of the Tonnerres. Pique has achieved a greater degree of maturity at this stage than Morag had known at a similar age. Pique is without the bitterness that Morag carried with her from Manawaka; unlike the young Morag in Winnipeg, Pique does not hide her heritage but is eager to explore it; most important of all, at this early age Pique has already reconciled her heritage and put it into her own song:

> There's a valley holds my name, now I know
> In the tales they used to tell it seemed so low
> There's a valley way down there
> I used to dream it like a prayer
> And my fathers they lived there long ago
>
> ....
>
> I came to taste the dust out on a prairie road
> My childhood thoughts were heavy on me like a load

> But I left behind my fear
> When I found those ghosts were near
> Leadin' me back to that home I never knowed [p. 441].

In the text of *The Diviners* Margaret Laurence has, of course, written down the stories that were orally transmitted by Christie and Jules to Morag and by Morag to Pique, as well as the songs that Jules sang to Pique and Pique to Morag. Through Morag's writing as well as through her own, Margaret Laurence also demonstrates the carrying of the past into the present through literature. *Shadow of Eden,* Morag's fourth novel, is finished after she and Pique have come to McConnell's Landing and it too is the story of the highland clearances and the emigration of the Sutherlanders to the Red River. Writing to Ella Gerson after her book is finished, Morag indicates the intertwining of her myth and the facts of history into her fiction:

> The man who led them on that march, and on the trip by water to Red River was young Archie MacDonald, but in my mind the piper who played them on will always be that giant of a man, Piper Gunn, who probably never lived in so-called real life, but who lives forever [p. 418].

The passing on of the authentic heritage of their people is a central preoccupation of writers of today, particularly of writers of the post-colonial nations. Laurence of Canada, Walcott of the West Indies, Soyinka and Achebe of Nigeria – these are preeminent among writers who accept a strong social and political, as well as artistic, responsibility in writing out of their own culture and primarily for their own people. Among contemporary Canadian novelists, Rudy Wiebe and Dave Godfrey are probably closest to Laurence in their interpretation of this challenge and responsibility. For Laurence, as for the others, a native, Canadian literary tradition in no sense negates or ignores the total and continuing stream of all literature in the past and in the present. Margaret Laurence's work is markedly "literary" in the conventional sense – *The Diviners,* for instance, is permeated with references to and resonances of *Paradise Lost, Paradise Regained* and *Samson Agonistes.* All of her work is also, of course, enriched by the spirit, the language and the rhythms of the Bible. But she is predominantly engaged in writing out of the experience of Canadians and in their accustomed speech patterns.

For her this begins in Manitoba. Until *The Diviners* it was possible to miss the uniquely Manitoban element in her work, for the town of Manawaka was not as relentlessly regionalized as was, for instance, Sinclair Ross's Saskatchewan town of Horizon. With the background of the Sutherlanders and the Métis, however, Morag's youth is unmistakably set in a Manitoba that has been given historical – and in Laurence's hand mythological – depth. She is very close to the historian, W.L. Morton, in what she has tried to do for her native province, beginning with the local and ultimately transcending it in her work.

There are many congruences between the works of W.L. Morton and Margaret Laurence, not only in the ideal towards which they write, but also in the circumstances of their careers. Professor Morton left the University of Manitoba to become Master of Champlain College at Trent University in Peterborough; and while there he wrote an epilogue to his earlier *Manitoba: A History* (1957). Margaret Laurence returned from ten years in England to settle in Lakefield near Peterborough, and in *The Diviners,* set on the Otonabee nearby, Morag recalls and reconstructs her youth in Manitoba. In his *Manitoba: A History* Morton wrote of the Selkirk Settlers and the Métis society with a passion of understanding and sympathy that Laurence shares and develops in her personalized treatment of the Sutherlanders and the Tonnerres. To Morton, the historian and the novelist each has a myth-making function and responsibility and their most basic problem is identical:

> The difficulty was to reconcile a landscape actually seen and realistically experienced with an internal landscape formed by reading. How could these be brought into a single, authentic vision in which neither would deny, but rather clarify the other?... I wanted, I think, that as the wilderness landscape had been remade by axe and plough into a cultivated landscape, that raw new landscape should be made into a human landscape of heightened tone and enriched association. I desired it to be seen not only as it could be seen, but as it might be seen.[5]

Margaret Laurence has expressed her sense of a common aim with Morton's in these words:

> I did in fact read, for the first time, Morton's *Manitoba: A History,* the summer that I began writing the first draft of *The Diviners.* I had, of course, read quite alot of prairie history

> previously, but Morton's history gave me not only a great many facts that I needed (although few of these were actually used in the novel) but also a sense of the sweep of history, the overview which I think I share. I found this to be especially true of those parts of the history which deal with the Métis people. I subsequently had many conversations with him about the nature of writing history and fiction. I believe ... as I think he does, too ... that the two disciplines are very much related. The historian, like the novelist, must be selective and must necessarily write his own interpretation of the historical era with which he is dealing. The novelist (at least, this is true in my own case) seeks to bring characters to life as much as possible and to place these individuals within the historical context of their time and place. What I think I share, most of all, with Morton is the sense of my *place,* the prairies, and of my *people* (meaning all prairie peoples) within the context of their many and varied histories, and the desire to make all these things come alive in the reader's mind [Correspondence with Clara Thomas, October 27, 1977].

Carl Berger speaks of Morton's wish "for a history of the West written with such fidelity to the inner texture of experience and so evocative of the sense of place that it would immediately trigger a recognition in those who had been molded by that history."[6] In *Manitoba: A History* Morton achieved the goal and the resolution that he strove for; in *The Diviners,* Margaret Laurence assimilated Morton's work with her own experience and the past of her people to achieve her goal. They are the writers who, more than any others, have given Manitoba a powerful historic and mythic identity.

NOTES

1. "A Conversation about Literature: An Interview with Margaret Laurence and Irving Layton," *Journal of Canadian Fiction,* vol. 1, no. 1, Winter 1972, pp. 65-8.
2. Margaret Laurence, *The Diviners,* Bantam edition, 1975. All page references are to this edition.
3. Andrew Hook, *Scotland and America 1750-1835,* Glasgow, Blackie, 1975, p. 119.
4. Wilfred Cude, "'False as Harlots' Oaths': Dunny Ramsay Looks At Huck Finn," *Studies in Canadian Literature,* vol. II, no. 2, Summer 1977, pp. 164-87.
5. W.L. Morton, "Seeing an Unliterary Landscape," *Mosaic* 33, 1970, pp. 7-8.
6. Carl Berger, *The Writing of Canadian History,* Oxford University Press, 1976, p. 246.

Steps to the Mythic: ***The Diviners*** *and* ***A Bird in the House***

MARIAN ENGEL

When *The Diviners* came out, I was delighted to be asked to review it by *Chatelaine*: no matter what one thinks of women's magazines, they reach a wide market and the people who read them are likely to read books by women. I had heard the novel was a big one, and I was interested in finding out if this were true, and promulgating the word if I agreed with it. I did.

I am a reviewer, not a critic. I review books sometimes badly, sometimes well. I do it because I like writing about books. I don't have any doctrine, though I try to avoid being influenced by friendship; I try to do the oldfashioned thing, relate the work to its genre, and to the rest of its author's work, before making a judgment. Sometimes, also, I can vent some other concern I have no forum for. I don't remember doing this with *The Diviners*. I remember trying to convey the excitement of reading a major work in proof. I had stayed up all night reading it, as if I were having a childish midnight feast.

So I did my job, enjoyed it and passed on to other things. Slowly, however, I became aware that there was another undercurrent in Toronto. The phone kept ringing with requests that I review the book for many, many other publications. In all these cases I knew I was not first choice, and I knew enough about the rules of the game to understand that the first-choice people hadn't liked the book and didn't want to say so. I began tackling them at Toronto literary parties, and as I am not a delicate tackler I elicited some embarrassment. Finally, I tackled one critic head-on. "Frankly," he said, "I didn't like it. I thought *A Bird in the House* was marvellous, an almost perfect book. Beside it, *The Diviners* looked big and sloppy."

Mon dieu. So that was it.

I had not, until I was asked to write this article, re-read *The Diviners,* though I had kept up with its reputation among women, literati, film-makers and Pentecostals. I opened it again with

* First published in the *Journal of Canadian Studies,* Vol. 13, No. 3 (Fall 1978).

trepidation. There are no absolutes. Critical theories are useful as can-openers but whether a book is good or bad ... with minor works only God and one's own taste can tell, and one's taste buds can go off; and it's only the hairs on the back of one's neck that tell that a book is major; perhaps after four years the *frisson* is gone?

It is not. I re-read the book with the same galloping eagerness and enjoyment and admiration. And the thought, how do I *dare* know this woman, she's too good to be speakable to; and small twitches of recognition. Some things bothered me about it still, some things impressed me, but its greatness was there like an object; it's as solid as a pound of cooking chocolate.

Then, to satisfy a desire for completeness, I re-read *A Bird in the House*. It's very, very good. I had not remembered it as well. It contains, also, the seeds of some of the concerns in *The Diviners,* though it is complete in itself. There is, however, a difference in scale between the two books that tells me something important about the Toronto critics I questioned: they are terrified of the monumental, particularly in the works of women.

Well, I can see that. I myself am exceedingly fond of the Regency, a period that handles grand stresses by guying them. Small things are easier to live with. The polite Canadian surface was surely invented to minimize tension. If you like Mozart you tend to shy away from Wagner. Even in the course of the Reputation Stakes.

The Reputation Stakes are being run more and more frequently in this country, so perhaps it is time to speak up. It would be a pity if *The Diviners* slipped through the net again.

Although it is improper to deal with the Manawaka novels as a progress, and *A Bird in the House,* obviously written over a period of time, as a step in this progress, there are useful comparisons to make between these books, and I shall make them in terms of *The Diviners*. The early life of Morag Gunn is the underside of the early life of Vanessa McLeod. Morag has not been endowed with an enduring (unendurable) family. Propriety, all her life and however she seeks it, escapes her. Though she and Vanessa have a number of things in common, writing is the only element in their lives that places them on a comparable level, and one has no doubt that the misspelt utterances of the child-outsider are more powerful than those of Vanessa, who, although she is a profoundly nice child, has inherited the smugness of her family's place in Manawaka society. A different spirit emerges from a household where the emotions are polished with beeswax every day.

And it is this flight from propriety, this decision to deal with the underbelly of Manawaka, that allows Laurence to rise above neat banality in *The Diviners.* Some of Morag's situation is outrageous to the point of seeming unreal: Prin and her doughnuts, Christie and the Nuisance Grounds: they are grotesque. They hark back not to good United Church realism but to Joe Gargary, Mr. and Mrs. Micawber and Mr. Bumble, though it is interesting that Laurence has chosen to cast Prin as a vegetable cipher rather than a termagant: proof of her understanding of women's lives.

All novelists have what I call "their sets," their casts of imaginary characters, stereotypes imposed by their early experience. The Mother, fierce or distant and gentle, warm or sharp; the Father, present or absent, stern or loving; siblings are often cast aside to simplify the progress of the adventuring hero; aunts, uncles, grandparents, substitute parents, teachers have their roles to play. I noticed when I was about twelve that the basic requirement for children's adventure stories was the absence of parents; permissive aunts were allowed but there was no adventuring while watchful Mums and Dads stood by; genres have their sets too.

In *A Bird in the House* the cast is familiar; loving Mother; Father well remembered after an early death; demanding grandparents; rebellious aunts. Familiar because we have met a woman as demanding as Grandma McLeod in Mrs. Cameron and a father like Grandfather Connor in *The Stone Angel.* The siblings are isolated from each other by age; the real drama is in the relationship of child and mother, of child and what she can intuit from the loaded atmosphere of her household.

In *The Diviners* the pattern changes. Laurence frees herself by freeing Morag; after the terrible moment when Mrs. Pearl tells the child that her parents are dead she becomes independent of narrow family constraints, thus capable of heroism. With Christie, she invents a background: the heroic Piper Gunn and his woman, battling for homes of their own against all odds, establish themselves in her spirit unhampered by adults ready to shout "balderdash". Christie, above all people, understands the need for dreams and he encourages in Morag these dreams that will lift her beyond and, though not until middle age, above the common lot.

In order to accomplish the depiction of a childhood that is delineated by dreams rather than conventions, Laurence has used, successfully in my view, a number of techniques that were not as apparent in her other works, where a good deal of art is disguised by craft. The 'memory-bank movies' were not at first universally approved. It might have been more sophisticated to set them off as bits of stream-of-consciousness, but it would not have been Laurence, who is above all a revealer of universals. Ballads and war stories and interior film are what we are all about, and she makes this clear.

Dreamer Morag, freed by story and song from a sordid childhood, must, however, endure the banalities of growing up like the rest of us. For a long time, she struggles to live down Prin and Christie, rise above nuisance and doughnuts (Did I ever bring Margaret a bag of doughnuts? Gawd!) to the heights of respectability. She does not enjoy respectability. That is not what respectability is for. Eventually she is led by her own nature and the songs inside her to the life of an outsider once more. She leaves her respectable husband for a brief and gritty liaison with the Métis Skinner Tonnerre, leaves Skinner for the life of an apprentice writer in Vancouver. It does not seem a coincidence that her second landlady is a skin-dancer with a snake.

The conflict in *The Diviners* is between an intense desire to belong to a rejecting and constricting society, and a desire for a life of one's own. This theme could have not been handled through the lives of the Camerons and McLeods on the other side of the tracks. In Morag, Laurence has created an arrant outsider, and stripped her of the solid family ties that gave Canadians, like good ships, the steadying characteristic know as "bottom". Morag has to find her own steadiness and she does this by never quite participating fully in the conventional situations her life offers her; she wants desperately to be a good wife, but her husband Brooke's terms deny her womanhood; one feels she has given Pique a bad moment or two as a mother; her attempts at casual sex are disastrous because she is not casual; like any orphan, she wants to worm in, she wants to belong too much; yet, at the same time, the watcher in her holds back. All her relationships with men, except for Skinner, are disastrous.

By having Skinner's child, she incorporates his mythology with her own. His accounts of his background are as sketchy as hers; like her, he has risen above pain and sordidness with songs and dreams. Through him, she achieves some kind of serenity, living in the present, living beside a river with a water diviner for a friend.

The great and the gothic are narrowly separated. It is easy for an author to slide from grand emotions into mawkishness. But Laurence keeps her balance. Morag's footing, however, is never sure; she makes mistakes, like the marriage to Brooke, but she is not a romantic; when she goes to Scotland she avoids mythic Sutherland, knowing painfully this time the difference between reality and dream. And it seems to me that this streak of harsh, gritty realism in Morag is what lifts the novel into the mythic. She is one of the few heroines who achieves the apocalypse of knowing what her life has been about, not through the agency of a man, but through her own experience.

Vanessa would have had the courage, but not the chance. Rachel and Stacey would have quailed. Morag is cognate perhaps only with Hagar, but Morag has dealt with her world where Hagar fled. And raised Laurence's work to a higher level through her incorporation with myth, memory and dream.

It is not, it is true, as neat a book as *A Bird in the House*. There are signs in the text of blots and erasures, spilled ink, thumbprints and tears. Tut, tut, Ms. Laurence, girls should be neat. It is unladylike to achieve apocalypse.

A Portrait of the Artist as Laurence Hero

SHERRILL GRACE

Phyllis Grosskurth was right when she said that in *The Diviners* we have "a looser, more complex, more sexually uninhibited Laurence. And never an Atwood victim."[1] None of Laurence's heroines is simply an Atwood victim; Morag Gunn is a full-fledged 'hero'. The fact that Morag is an artist contributes immensely to her role as hero, but she is also part of a larger Canadian pattern. Contrary to Ronald Sutherland who has announced the arrival of a "new" hero in Canadian fiction, I do not believe that the hero he describes as always "lurking in the work of Margaret Laurence [and] coming ... to full bloom in ... *The Diviners*" is new.[2] Within Morag's artistic identity lie many of the qualities that are present in Canadian heroes through the twentieth century beginning with Connor's *The Man from Glengarry* (1901) and Duncan's *The Imperialist* (1904).

In this paper, I consider the nature of the Laurence heroine both in and of herself and as one type of Canadian hero. One can best appreciate an artist-hero like Morag Gunn by understanding not only the literary tradition of the artist as hero but, more importantly, the specific Canadian literary tradition to which she belongs. In order to do this I have divided my study into two parts. First, I briefly discuss the 'problem' of the Canadian hero. Recent criticism has been too quick to describe this century's fiction as strewn with victims, failures, and alienated or lost selves. Second, I analyse at greater length the nature of the Laurence hero, more particularly, Morag Gunn.

I

The Canadian hero is not new, not necessarily a victim, and should not be discussed as if invented by novelists circa 1920. The danger in a cut-off date when trying to isolate a tradition, as Margaret Atwood does in *Survival,* is the implication that nothing came before. If one needs to set time limits, then 1900 is preferable

* First published in the *Journal of Canadian Studies,* Vol. 13, No. 3 (Fall 1978).

because it at least includes Connor and Duncan, both significant figures in the novel tradition who look back, in many ways, to nineteenth-century fictional forms. Many of our heroes are not victims or miserable failures. Ranald MacDonald, Lorne Murchison, Abe Spalding, Daniel Ainslie, Isabel Jardine, James Potter or Felix Prosper, Dunstan Ramsay, and Morag Gunn, to name a few, are successful heroes of a specific type. That a group of Canadian heroes are failures is hardly deniable. There is also a small number who have affinities with the traditional rebellious, asocial, self-reliant American hero. In *Butterfly on Rock,* Doug Jones offers the Adamic myth (following Lewis' *The American Adam*) as a way out of the confines of a garrison mentality. But D.J. Dooley, in a sharp critique of Jones' idea, points out that this myth embodies a fundamental revolt against convention, and that it is "illusory to see the Canadian as a new-born infant," that is, as an Adam.[3] If we can believe our literature and our institutions, conventions are important to Canadians; therefore, it comes as no great surprise that there are relatively few Canadian Adams.

What is the Canadian hero? Frequently he is a failure or a victim, a Philip Bentley or a David Canaan (both failed artists); occasionally he is an Adam, a Duddy Kravitz or a Noman; often he is a hero, in Clara Thomas' words, a Hero and Builder.[4] The factors that condition the type of hero found in a given novel are many. To some extent the characters in a novel reflect the accepted social mores of the particular historical period. At the same time, changes in literary form or mode, especially the shift from romance conventions to those of realism, dictate inevitable shifts in character portrayal. The nature of fictional heroes also reflects the national matrix from which the novel springs. Taken together, these heroes embody aspects of what Sutherland, in *The New Hero,* calls a "sphere of consciousness." One essential conditioning factor of the Canadian "sphere of consciousness" is puritanism; another is the land itself; still another is our social and political history.

The interesting fact is that there is a remarkable consistency in the nature of our heroes throughout the twentieth century, in spite of *formal* shifts from the romance of Connor to the realism of Margaret Laurence. These characters share at least five basic qualities, the first being their ability to work – there is more work done in Canadian fiction than on a chain gang. Following logically from this work ethic is the fact that these heroes are makers and builders devoted to the creation of a nation. Ranald MacDonald works to build Canada; Abe Spalding labours to civilize the prairie; Daniel Ainslie strives to maintain rational enlightenment and human betterment in a world of irrationality and darkness. Morag Gunn works too; in fact, she is pleased when Royland and the Smiths learn to speak of her writing as work, the only activity she honours with the title. She is also a maker and builder, forging in her work, to borrow Stephen Dedalus' words, the uncreated conscience of her race. These heroes are fundamentally conservative and it is for this reason that I cannot accept Sutherland's description of the "new" hero as a character for whom "traditional values mean nothing at all."[5] To speak of this type of hero as "coming finally to full bloom" in *The Diviners,* is to equate the observance of social forms with a deeper devotion to the conservation and continuity of human values. The type of Canadian hero being considered here is conservative in his reverence for the past, for traditions, for his 'home' and tribe. He achieves fulfillment of self *through* history, carried within him in the form of memory; he does not seek to destroy traditional ties, to wipe out his past, as do many of his American counterparts, because he is evolutionary, not revolutionary. This is, once again, the attitude of Morag and she describes the position very well:

> You Can't Go Home Again, said Thomas Wolfe. Morag wonders now if it may be the reverse which is true. You have to go home again, in some way or another.[6]

This type of hero has a highly developed moral consciousness which finds its expression in the acceptance of social values and/or an active sense of personal guilt. As we move from romance heroes to realist heroes, the focus for the moral concerns shifts as well: instead of embodying moral choices in external action or accepting external models for 'right' behaviour, the struggle is internalized. The characters' priorities, however, often seem to be much the same – work, conservatism, creation (of nation or conscience) and, the last quality I wish to discuss, loyalty to community. These heroes are morally concerned with the nature of their society and their own relationship to that society. This moral consciousness, inextricable from a social context, is less emphatic in many contemporary American novels, such as, for example, those of Vonnegut, Barth, Pynchon, or Dickey. Dickey's *Deliverance* is a case in point. His middle-aged would-be outdoorsmen bring nothing back when they return from their terrifying ordeal to the comfort of their homes – a comfort originally perceived as debilitating. Indeed, there seems to be no compulsion for them to incorporate their river experience into their 'normal' lives. In a book like *Surfacing,* however, the narrator, who is in many respects the conservative hero I am describing, is driven by her moral sense. She will return to the city with her new-found insights.[7]

The Canadian hero embodies a deep loyalty to community, as opposed to the individual self. Some very powerful scenes come immediately to mind: Abe Spalding looming in the entrance to the school at the end of *Fruits of the Earth* – "He had lived to himself and had had to learn that it could not be done..." – or Isabel Jardine returning to serve Marina and her husband at the conclusion of *The Nymph and the Lamp.* In *Survival,* Margaret Atwood suggests that the community itself, "the collective hero," might be a positive embodiment of the Canadian hero.[8] This group hero appeared as long ago as Goldsmith's "The Rising Village" and Howe's "Acadia", and as recently as Watson's *The Double Hook.* In *The Diviners,* the sense of community as a collective hero is very strong – the book, after all, is called *The Diviners.*

II

In Laurence's five Manawaka books, *The Stone Angel* (1964), *A Jest of God* (1966), *The Fire-Dwellers* (1969), *A Bird in the House* (1970) and *The Diviners* (1974), Hagar, Rachel, Stacey, Vanessa and Morag are very much alike, yet Morag clearly embodies a spiritual advance or a development in consciousness over her predecessors. To some extent, this can be explained by Laurence's developing technical expertise. For my present purpose, I must limit the comparison of the texts to the heroines' relative progress towards inner freedom and a fully satisfying spiritual development. In Laurence's words, one can "almost equate inner freedom with growth."[9]

While Hagar fails to reach this inner freedom, she is never a pathetic victim. Although she is too old and obdurate to change, she does come to understand herself – her pride, fear, loneliness, her lack of freedom.[10] Imprisoned in her own nature, she performs only two truly free acts in her life. Significantly, these two acts, finding a bedpan and offering a word of love to her son, are altruistic, directed outwards in the effort to comfort another person; freedom, for Laurence, is a moral and socially responsible condition. If we can speak of Hagar in Atwood's terms at all, we would have to say that she falls into Victim Position Three by acknowledging her situation and the aspects of her character that contribute to it.

Both Rachel and Stacey Cameron seem to be less vigorous, their lives less hopeful. For Rachel the future is an open book which she reads with a realistic eye:

> Where I'm going, anything may happen. Nothing may happen.... I will be different. I will remain the same.[11]

The most that can be said is that she sees more clearly by the end of the book, and she is up and moving. Stacey is not afforded even this problematic consolation. She remains trapped in her situation, redeemed only by her sardonic sense of humour. That she "may mutate into a matriarch" like Hagar in another forty years is not encouraging. Of all Laurence's women Rachel and Stacey are closest to Atwood victims, unable to break out of self-defeating postures. Vanessa has, however, broken free and is, in many ways, a prototype of the more complex Morag.[12] Vanessa is also an artist (*A Bird in the House* gives us a portrait of the artist as a young woman). More important, she defines her freedom by returning to her roots in order to celebrate her past.

This is precisely what occurs in *The Diviners* on a larger scale, implying that the status and nature of the hero is inextricable from the necessary *process* of growth through return. In order to explore the growth of the hero, one must examine the narrative voice (including certain techniques contained within that voice), the role of language, and the overall structure of the book. In her chapter on the artist in *Survival,* "The Paralysed Artist," Atwood points out that most of our failed artists appear in books in which they are written about, that is where the writer, using the third person, writes about the impossibility of being a Canadian artist. The characters choose either to stay within the culture and be crippled or to escape into another incomplete cultural identity.[13] The assumption is that the successful artist must be able to speak from within his own culture, preferably in his own voice.

Although Morag does not technically speak in her own voice, the third-person narrating voice, in the past tense for the fictional present and in the present tense for remembered sequences, is always extremely close to her, presenting events through her eyes, constantly adopting her mannerisms until we feel we are listening to her thoughts. Laurence uses this third-person voice brilliantly. Because this voice is so close to Morag the reader does not experience an abrupt shifting of gears when brief first-person passages are interjected. The third person allows a minimal distance from Morag creating, in addition, the sense that there are two Morags, one who experiences and remembers while the other writes, a doubling phenomenon quite common in artist-hero novels.[14] The narrative moves, not so much in two separate directions as it would if two distinct points of view were present (for example, *The Fire-Dwellers*), as in and out of Morag herself. At the same time, the third person provides an emotional control that safeguards Morag from sentimentality; her personality emerges as she talks about herself to herself in a calm, ironic tone. The third-person voice underlines the fact that this is not exclusively Morag's story, but the story of many people, of a country, of the past.

Morag's stories (in the case of Christie and Jules, stories within stories), and her Memory-bank Movies contribute an immediacy and authenticity to her memories, dramatizing Laurence's belief that the past is always present.[15] It is largely through Laurence's fusion of voice and *present* tense with the devices of story and movie that we perceive Morag's growth and development during three distinct phases of her life. It is memory which creates the self and the past in the act of remembering. Dramatic and oral devices, such as the songs and conversations with "C.P.T.," also make significant contributions to the narrative texture of the book – and hence to Morag. As a contrast to the main narrative they provide variety and vitality. They further dramatize the presentness of events, as in the "Conversation Overheard from the Teachers' Room" (50), or the chats with "C.P.T." They are evidence of a total enactment of life; where the main narrative communicates cerebrally, like Morag herself, these expressive modes communicate a felt reality. The implication for the heroine is that she is in touch with the full force of life; she is fully, sensuously, alive.

Equally central to the hero-as-artist novel and to *The Diviners,* is the unique importance of language. Morag has always been a "Wordsmith." Near the beginning of the book she remarks: "I used to think words could do anything. Magic. Sorcery. Even miracle" (4). She is compelled to flesh out in words a life for the stark snapshots of her parents, knowing full well that,

> *All this is crazy, of course, and quite untrue. Or maybe true and maybe not. I am remembering myself composing this interpretation, in Christie and Prin's house.* (7)

Through language we grasp the nature of fact and fiction, as well as our perception and understanding of ourselves and of the physical world. At one point she calls her work a "daft profession" for "weaving fabrications" (21). As a schoolchild who could not spell "Egypt," she knew that, "If she could've written it down she could've got it. Always the same" (55).

Language is more than a love or an obsession for Morag; it is reality, the only way she can know reality. Furthermore, it conveys the individuality of each of us; through our speech we are. Christie, for example, *is* his ranting. When Morag returns to Manawaka as Prin is dying she quickly finds herself slipping into Christie and Prin's speech:

> *The* both of them. As soon as she got back to Manawaka, she even began thinking in the old phraseology. Extraneous *the*, yet somehow giving more existence, more recognition to them than correct speech could have. Escapist. Wordsmith, forging screens. (203)

Moments like this promote the gradual realization of who she is. Christie and his speech are a part of her which she had tried to deny. Back in Toronto after Prin's funeral, Morag rebels openly against Brooke by expressing a hitherto hidden part of herself he has never wanted to know. Significantly, it is his words she rejects; by calling her "little one," he denies her complex adult reality:

> *Little one.* Brooke, I am twenty-eight years old, and I am five feet eight inches tall, which has always seemed too bloody christly tall to me but there it is, and by judas priest and all the sodden saints in fucking Beulah Land, I am stuck with it.... (210)

It is a delightful, familiar outburst echoing, of course, Christie.

In her review of *The Diviners* for the New York Times, Marge Piercy remarks that "why Morag is a writer is not apparent," and goes on to suggest that Morag might as well have been a dressmaker.[16] That she has so seriously misread *The Diviners* can be explained, perhaps, by the fact that there are two main traditions of artist-hero novels which Maurice Beebe describes as "Sacred Fount and Ivory Tower." Ivory Tower novels are those in which the artist-hero withdraws from life to write *about* the art of writing. In Sacred Fount novels, on the other hand, the artist-hero views art as the expression, not the imitation, of life:

> The Sacred Fount tradition tends to equate art with experience and assumes that the true artist is one who lives not less, but more fully and intensely than others. Within this tradition art is essentially the recreation of experience.[17]

The Diviners emphasizes art as the expression of life while Morag draws upon the Sacred Fount of life in order to write. From her early childhood, Morag loved stories and writing. She kept a scribbler full of her efforts and even attempted a poem on Jesus. She was writing stories in high school and again in University. During the course of the book she writes three novels, *Spear of Innocence, Jonah,* and *Shadow of Eden,* as well as a collection of stories, *Presences.* (It is tempting to draw the analogy with Laurence who wrote three novels and one book of stories set in Canada prior to *The Diviners.*)

To miss the centrality of the artist role is to miss two crucial features of the book, if not the entire point. For Morag, who is not an Ivory Tower artist, art and life are synonymous; hence, there is a richness of experience and a variety of narrative technique used to enact and dramatize the process of memory, the vitality of living. Still more important, there are many indications that the book we read is the book Morag is writing. One brief example should illustrate this level of the narrative. At the beginning of "Halls of Sion," Morag remembers a dream from the previous night after which she jotted down the words "*Jerusalem. Jerusalem*" (137). She is anxious to know what she meant because these words are the key to scenes she will write in the novel she is presently working on. The answer comes, not from retrospective exposition but from the enactment of the past. The words occur again on pages 137, 207, and 221. The quotation of the hymn sung at Prin's funeral gives us the necessary context:

> Jerusalem the golden
> With milk and honey blest –
> They stand those halls of Sion
> All jubilant with song,... (207)

The word "Jerusalem" relates not only to Morag's living memory of Prin's funeral, but to her recreation of her married life with Brooke Skelton. With great irony and sadness, then, Morag titles this period in her life and part III of her novel, "Halls of Sion."

This sense of *The Diviners* as the fourth novel Morag writes, arises from the structure of the book. It is the structure, as well, that embodies the development of Morag from child to artist-hero, one full step further than Laurence's previous heroines. The novel has five main structural units. The middle three, "The Nuisance Grounds," "Halls of Sion" and "Rites of Passage," develop three main stages in Morag's life moving chronologically towards her present as a middle-aged author working on her fourth novel. The first and fifth parts, "River of Now and Then" and "The Diviners," comprise the fourth stage in her life and the fictional present of the book; the two parts comprise a framing unit with Morag in her log house by the river during the summer months when she writes the story contained in parts II, III, and IV. The novel ends with these words – "Morag returned to the house, to write the remaining private and fictional words, and to set down her title" – "The Diviners," of course.

Ronald Sutherland's tripartite thematic paradigm of the Canadian novel, outlined in *Second Image,* is useful in describing the three main stages in Morag's life. He characterizes the first theme as "The Land and Divine Order" wherein the characters experience the dictates of hierarchical authority and rural values. In the next stage, "The Breakup of the Old Order," the characters struggle to escape both the land and traditional values, often by moving to cities. However, their lives are circumscribed by their inability to forget the old values or to accept new ones. The third stage, Sutherland describes as "The Search for Vital Truth":

> The search for meaning, of course, can be found in a large number of books, but the kind of search I have in mind here is in a special category – it begins at the zero point. All values have been discarded or cannot be genuinely accepted, and the protagonist attempts from his experience of life to formulate

an approach to reality which can supply him with a *raison d'être*.[18]

As I mentioned in the first part of this discussion, I feel that Professor Sutherland's description of the fourth theme, the new hero, fails to account for the heroine of *The Diviners*. There are other possible outcomes for the character who passes through the three preceding stages.

In part two of *The Diviners*, "The Nuisance Grounds," we return to Morag's roots on the land, first the parental farm and then the Logan house in the town of Manawaka. The ever-present prairie pervades the stories of Christie and Jules. The garbage dump (or nuisance grounds) represents the land as the source of Christie's texts ("by their garbage shall ye know them") and the unofficial burial ground. In addition to this image of the dump, part two offers a full topography of Manawaka. It provides a clear picture of the established order of the town with Christie and Prin near the bottom, only one rung above the Tonnerres. Morag quickly learns to despise Christie and what he stands for; she emulates the middle class. "The Nuisance Grounds" ends with Morag on the point of leaving Manawaka, for good, as she thinks; she believes that she and Jules "inhabit the same world no longer" (134).

Part III, "Halls of Sion," takes her from town to city, but not from entrapment to freedom. The process of breaking up the old order has only begun because she replaces one set of established values for another in her search for security. In order to win Brooke's love, she must follow his rules. Above all she must pretend she has no past and no fully mature future. Ironically, Morag is not happy in the Halls of Sion with her Prince because life there is static. She cannot accept the decorum of hairdressers, verstile black dresses, and evenings of worshipful students. She leaves once more, this time to return West. She has separated from her husband. She is pregnant by Jules, who has freed her to move in time (he is from her past; his child is her future). She is without funds and without any immediate means of livelihood. She is also homeless. To use Sutherland's words – her renewed search for meaning begins "at the zero point."

Part IV is appropriately titled, "Rites of Passage." It suggests the ordeals that the initiate must go through in order to reach maturity or understanding. It encompasses Morag's ordeals as a professional writer, her various sexual encounters, and the continuation of her journey in search of her past. Not until she gazes across the firth from Crombruach to Sutherland does she realize where she belongs:

> "It's a deep land here, all right," Morag says. "But it's not mine, except a long long way back. I always thought it was the land of my ancestors, but it is not."
>
> "What is, then?"
>
> "Christie's real country. Where I was born." (319)

This realization is crucial because only by returning to her own roots can Morag fully possess herself. The climax of her search comes as she buries Christie while Scotty Grant plays "the long-ago pibroch, the lament for the dead, over Christie Logan's grave" (329). Christie's burial fuses the ancient Scots heritage with Canadian soil to reveal Morag's ancestral place.

By the end of "Rites of Passage," Morag has enjoyed three deep relationships with men. Brooke, Jules, and Dan, while their portrayal is adequate, are more important as symbols of Morag's development than as individual characters. Laurence has used the men in her novel much as male writers use women in their artist-hero novels of the Sacred Fount tradition; they embody aspects of life for the protagonist.[19] Brooke represents a denial of life and growth, thereby blocking Morag's progress towards inner freedom. By turning to Jules, she breaks free from the stultifying demands of a superficial existence and the meaningless role of child-wife. Moreover, through her love for Jules she embraces not only her immediate Manawaka past, but the historical Indian and French roots of Canada. She learns her final personal and cultural lesson through Dan, the Scot. When she understands that he has a home, a place in which she does not belong, she can return to Canada and to the heritage she shares with Jules. Significantly, she does not wed herself to life in the form of any one of these men; as an artist she must fully experience life without enmeshing herself in it to the extent that she cannot withdraw sufficiently to write. The split between life and art, between the Sacred Fount and the Ivory Tower, is not absolute with Morag as it is with Dan (who *lives* in Crombruach and creates in London), but the tension between them is always present. Pique is, perhaps, a more debatable presence in the book. Clearly Morag has wanted a child and worries about whether she is a good Mother. However, like the men, Pique's major role seems to me to be a symbolic one; she embodies Morag's urge to grow into full maturity, she completes Morag's existence as a woman in a way a man cannot, and in the final scenes of the novel she embodies Morag's understanding and acceptance of the future – she will repeat Morag's quest and Morag must allow her to do so.

Parts I and V portray a Morag who has completed her search for meaning. Not only does she know who she is, she knows where she is. She has arrived home and accepted the fact that the past lives within her. In a brief interlude from the fictional present in "Rites of Passage," Morag admits that her "quest for islands had ended some time ago, and her need to make pilgrimages had led her back here" (293). Furthermore, she has relinquished much of her guilt, especially with regard to Pique, and received her inheritance – the Currie plaid pin. Most important, she can use her past as the material for her work. Instead of being crippled by her cultural heritage like Philip Bentley or Aquin's nameless narrator in *Prochaine Episode,* she is enriched. Like Christie, Jules, and Royland, she is a diviner, divining not only her own past, but also "the past of a collective cultural memory,"[20] and finding the water of inspiration, the "Strength of Conviction."

III

Morag Gunn is a middle-aged hero, a woman, Mother, wife, child, lover, friend. She is a successful quester in an age that disbelieves in quests, an inheritor, an ancestor, a diviner. She is an artist creating out of the very centre of her experience, celebrating the richness of life. She is an excellent example of the Canadian hero-as-builder. Her constant work is her way of living. She is highly introspective and troubled by feelings of guilt. And yet, because of her strength and determination, she comes to acknowledge the sacredness of her past and her deep loyalty to community and tradition. As long as she cuts herself off from her roots she is incomplete; her final victory is a function of her ability to embrace the totality of her experience. In writing *The Diviners* Morag (like Laurence) recognizes her position within something larger than self – the Canadian "sphere of consciousness," or a series of inheritors from whom the "gift, or portion of grace...

[will be] finally withdrawn, to be given to someone else" (369).

Laurence, herself, has called *The Diviners* "a very Canadian book."[21] Some Canadians, however, have found it an unsettling mirror image, attributable, in part, to the fact that Morag is a woman who succeeds without a man. This is the extent of her iconoclasm; she is a Hester Prynne who defies social decorum in order to express more fully the totality of her community. She is representative of a major type of Canadian hero, neither a victim nor an Adam, but one of a long line of hero-builders. Where Ranald MacDonald forged a country, Morag Gunn forges the uncreated conscience of her race.

NOTES

1. Review of *The Diviners* in *The Globe and Mail,* May 4, 1974.
2. Ronald Sutherland, *The New Hero* (Toronto: Macmillan Co., 1977), p. 16. In addition to Sutherland's *The New Hero,* the Canadian hero is discussed in his first book *Second Image,* in Atwood's *Survival* and in Doug Jones' *Butterfly on Rock.* Articles of interest in this connection are those by D.J. Dooley and Clara Thomas both cited below, as well as Warren Tallman's "Wolf in the Snow" and Robert McDougall's "The Dodo and the Cruising Auk" both of which appear in *Contexts of Canadian Criticism,* ed. Eli Mandel (Chicago: University of Chicago Press, 1971).
3. D.J. Dooley, "The Canadian Adam," *English Studies in Canada,* I, 3 (Fall 1975), p. 351. Dooley's purpose seems to be less a refutation of Jones' claim that there *are* Adamic heroes in our literature than a criticism of Jones' positive liberating claims for this hero.
4. Clara Thomas, "Canadian Social Mythologies in Sara Jeanette Duncan's *The Imperialist,*" *Journal of Canadian Studies,* 12, 2 (Spring 1977), p. 47.
5. *The New Hero,* p. 7.
6. Margaret Laurence, *The Diviners* (Toronto: McClelland and Stewart, 1974), p. 248. All references are to this edition and are included parenthetically in the text.
7. For further discussion of this question, see Rosemary Sullivan's convincing comparison, "*Surfacing* and *Deliverance,*" *Canadian Literature* No. 67 (Winter 1976), pp. 6-20.
8. Margaret Atwood, *Survival* (Toronto: Anansi, 1972), p. 245.
9. This quote is taken from the Canadian Writers on Tape interview, Ontario Institute for Studies in Education (Toronto: Van Nostrand Reinhold Ltd., 1971).
10. See *The Stone Angel* (Toronto: McClelland and Stewart, 1968), pages 292, 293, 307.
11. *A Jest of God* (Toronto: McClelland and Stewart, 1972), p. 201.
12. I have discussed the relationship of *A Bird in the House* and *The Diviners* in "Crossing Jordan: Time and Memory in the fiction of Margaret Laurence," *World Literature Written in English,* XVI, 2 (November, 1977), pp. 328-39. I suggest that Laurence's command of technique enables her to dramatize the growth of Vanessa and Morag thereby freeing them, on the narrative level, from the stasis that threatens the other women.
13. *Survival,* pp. 189-93.
14. Maurice Beebe, *Ivory Towers and Sacred Founts: The Artist as Hero in Fiction from Goethe to Joyce* (New York: New York University Press, 1964), see Chapter I, "The Divided Self."

15. "Time and the Narrative Voice," in *Margaret Laurence,* ed. William New (Toronto: McGraw-Hill Ryerson Ltd., 1977).
16. Marge Piercy, "Gritty Places and Strong Women," in *Margaret Laurence,* ed. William New (Toronto: McGraw-Hill Ryerson Ltd., 1977), p. 213.
17. Maurice Beebe, p. 13. Professor Beebe's thesis is that artist-hero fiction either portrays an artist who writes his life and lives his art or, at the opposite extreme, an artist who must withdraw from life completely in order to create. The tension between these poles is present but resolved in the best examples of artist-hero novels. Morag appears to have resolved the tension by embracing the belief that art is life.
18. *Second Image* (Don Mills, Ontario: New Press, 1971), p. 16.
19. Beebe, pp. 17-18.
20. "Time and the Narrative Voice," *Margaret Laurence,* p. 156.
21. "Literature and Canadian Culture: An Interview with Margaret Laurence," in *Margaret Laurence,* ed. William New, p. 29.

The Unity of the Manawaka Cycle

DAVID BLEWETT

With the publication in 1974 of *The Diviners* it became clear that Margaret Laurence's series of Manawaka novels was intended to possess a cohesion that went beyond the mere coincidence of place or the occasional reappearance of a character from an earlier novel. *The Diviners,* a work deeply concerned with the transmission of the values of the past through the generations, reaches back to complete a story begun in *The Stone Angel.* And if there were links of this kind, was it not possible that each of the separate works might be seen, from this perspective, as parts of a whole?[1] In this essay I argue that the Manawaka cycle is unified not only by the centripetal pull of the home town itself, but by the development over the four novels of a vision of the human condition which is not fully rendered until the cycle is completed.[2] This development imparts to the cycle a rhythm of reconciliation in which the fragmentariness of ordinary life, explored in the separate works, is seen against, and so continually absorbed into, a sense of design and purpose in the universe. My intention here is not to examine all the means by which that vision is worked out (that is beyond the scope of a single essay), but to consider three ways which seem to me to be important: the meaning of Manawaka; the continuity of a major device, that of contrasted pairs of individuals and images; and an elaborate parallel with T.S. Eliot's symbolism of the four elements in *The Wasteland.*

I

The primary unifying feature is Manawaka itself, the home town of all the narrators and many other characters, and the imaginative centre of the cycle. We derive our knowledge of the town from the accounts of the troubled women who are the protagonists, each of whom offers us a highly personal, retrospective, and frequently bitter perspective, such that at first the recurrence of Manawaka in their backgrounds appears fortuitous. Later, as we put together their separate narratives, we build up a picture of the social struc-

* First published in *Journal of Canadian Studies,* Vol 13, No. 3 (Fall 1978).

tures and physical features of the town. As we do so, we come to a deeper understanding of the meaning of Manawaka, which is not only a fictional town in southern Manitoba, but is also the embodiment of Margaret Laurence's vision of the human lot.

What chiefly strikes us about Manawaka is its social and physical divisions. The social structure of Manawaka is a rigid – if somewhat rickety – hierarchy, based on money and race. There are three main groups. First, the original settlers and their descendants, largely Scottish Presbyterians, proud, tough, hard-working, and, by and large, prosperous. There are subtle gradations of social degree within this group, but it is united against the rest of the town by its respectability. Outside respectable society there are various kinds of people who do not count socially – the Ukrainians (such as Nestor Kazlik and his family), unsuccessful farmers (such as Bram Shipley), and ne'er-do-wells (such as Christie Logan). Finally, outside the town and its social order altogether there are the Métis, the descendants of the original inhabitants of the land, but now dispossessed.

The geography of Manawaka and the country around it reflects and reinforces the social structure. Its main areas are the quiet, residential streets lined with brick houses inhabited by the well-to-do; a commercial centre of office buildings and stores owned by the wealthy businessmen and merchants; and an area of poorer houses near the CPR tracks, which cut across and further divide the town. Outside the town lie the farms, isolated, particularly in winter, and increasingly cut off as the Depression makes transportation expensive. And beyond the farms in the valley are the shacks of the Métis.

Manawaka is an emblem of human divisiveness. Its inhabitants are cut off from one another by pride, timidity, and the awareness of social differences, and as a result are largely unable to communicate their feelings, or even to recognize their emotional isolation and imprisonment. Like the speakers in the first section of Eliot's *Wasteland,* they are spiritually dead and if they live in Manawaka long enough, like Rachel Cameron's mother, they prefer not to be disturbed. Above all, they fear to make fools of themselves, which is their term for expressing their deepest wants and emotions. When at last Rachel partially overcomes her emotional and sexual inhibitions she sees herself as the "victim" of a jest of God, but the act which makes her a fool liberates her, and is seen as positive and God-given. Hence, too, the importance of Christie Logan, one of the greatest fools in modern literature, but for that reason a channel and an image of divine grace.

As an emblem of human separateness Manawaka renders Margaret Laurence's vision of the conditions of modern life, and perhaps of all human life, which is why it ultimately proves impossible to get away from. Manawaka, as Morag discovers, is within.[3] Each of the protagonists struggles to get away from the town, to break through its inhibiting confines into a new life somewhere else, and at one level that is what they achieve. But of course it is not Manawaka by itself which confines; rather the town is an expression of the forces within human beings that lead to alienation and separation. The struggle to break through those confines is necessary for spiritual growth, but with a greater maturity that the struggle brings comes the recognition that such forces are a permanent part of the human lot, always threatening and never completely subdued. To put this in another way, running away from Manawaka is like running away from oneself. The achievement of each of the protagonists is that, finally, she stands and faces, and so triumphs over, the Manawaka within.

II

The contrast between emotional inhibition and an open expression of affection is fundamental to Margaret Laurence's vision, and is conveyed through a series of contrasting pairs of individuals and images. These contrasting pairs, collectively a major organizing and unifying device in the novel cycle, reflect an habitual cast of mind, Margaret Laurence's sense of the contrasts and contradictions that spring up in life to divide human beings and which, unless overcome or reconciled, lead to isolation and deadness.

One of the earliest, and ultimately one of the most important, of the paired contrasts is the symbolic opposition of the town's cemetery and its garbage dump. Neat, orderly, and enclosed, like the lives of the respectable, the cemetery epitomizes Manawakan pomposity, aridity, and social superiority. For respectable families, like the Curries, the cemetery is a means of proclaiming their family pride and asserting their dynastic aspirations. But these values – while they may, when properly held,[4] be a means of strength, unity, and endurance – can and do become forces of snobbery and cruelty that lead to the severance and destruction of families and individuals. The extension of the cemetery and the values it suggests is Currie Memorial Park, a monument to family hatred, misunderstanding, and division. The false values of men like Jason Currie are suggestively conveyed not only by the cemetery's most imposing monument, the stone angel – symbol of the Currie hardness and blindness, which Hagar inherits – but by the description of the cemetery itself with which the first novel in the cycle opens. Its atmosphere is heavy, prim, constricted, like that of a funeral parlour, and its manicured appearance is a false assertion of the "clearly civilized" against the natural and indigenous: "the things that grew untended" as well as the "Cree with enigmatic faces and greasy hair."[5] The prairies, with their "scrub oak," "coarse couchgrass," and "faint, musky, dust-tinged smell" (p. 5), represent a naturalness and freedom that the pioneers despise and attempt to suppress (p. 15). Throughout the cycle, untended, open country is associated with liberated desires and is a source of spiritual renewal. When it is forgotten or ignored the land tends to become either a cemetery or a garbage dump.

The town dump, although "only a short way" from the cemetery, is its polar opposite. The dump represents the awkward and embarrassing, but actual disorderliness of much of human life, which we try to forget or conceal – "the unrecognized effluvia of our lives," not even worth "a decent concealment in earth" (*Stone Angel,* p. 26). In *The Diviners* we learn how the dump (now with fine irony called the "Nuisance Grounds") becomes the burial place, on at least two occasions, for aborted foetuses. The dump only too literally becomes "the town's unofficial cemetery" (*Diviners,* p. 124), receiving the unwanted evidence of passions that "respectability" attempts to deny and destroy. For children of the genteel families, like the fastidious Hagar Currie, innocently imagining that "life had been created only to celebrate tidiness" (p. 5), the dump reveals yet another side of life – the stark and sickening reality of filth, disease, mutilation, suffering, and the necessity of death – the facts of death which funeral parlours and cemeteries are designed to conceal. As a girl Hagar finds such horrors, even the sight of the newly-hatched, but dying, chicks, unbearable; later she learns the degree to which such things are part of human life.

That the two pieces of land set aside for disposal, the cemetery and the dump, should be not only vivid images of different kinds of death, but also represent different attitudes towards life is highly appropriate to the "nightmare life in death" vision of *Manawaka.* The Currie code of values, so aptly suggested by the cemetery – pride, neatness, emotional restraint, and granite-like stubbornness – is as life-destroying as the Shipley casualness and recklessness (associated with the dump), which leads to John's death and to the utter squalor and failure of Bram Shipley's farm. Neither set of attitudes offers more than a half life. What is desperately needed is a breaking down of the barriers of pride, which prevent the healthful contact of dissimilar values, attitudes and emotions. Hagar is attracted to Bram because, instinctively, she realizes that the Currie virtues of discipline and hard work must be enlarged and humanized by the Shipley virtues of spontaneity and freedom. The defeat of Hagar is the triumph of Manawaka divisiveness. The enduring image of that defeat is, suitably, a tombstone bearing the two names, Currie and Shipley, back to back, a monument not to union but to a perpetual divide.

The two attitudes to life and death suggested by the wasteland images of cemetery and garbage dump are further explored in the two middle novels of the cycle, the contrasting stories of the Cameron sisters, daughters, appropriately, of a funeral parlour owner. Rachel's death life, the result of her excessive self-restraint which leads her into an unwanted, emotionally-inhibited spinsterhood, is emphasized by images of punishment, confinement, infertility, sickness, terminal illness, and burial. Rachel's characteristic situation is confinement within doors looking out; she clings to the security of orderly and familiar interiors, protecting herself from the threatening outside world – other people and the forces of nature – while at the same time yearning for a more open life. The contrast between the grave (or, her buried sexual desire) and the out-of-doors (with its Edenic overtones of liberated desire) is established early in the novel when Rachel, out for a walk "just beyond the cemetery," comes across two teenage children making love.[6] The ultimate place of emotionless confinement is the grave, as Rachel, recalling Marvell's famous couplet, reminds herself just before she first makes love to Nick, significantly, out-of-doors (p. 90). When she makes love to Nick for the third and last time, and again out-of-doors, he asks her whether she had "realized you could see the cemetery so well from here" (p. 149). Her acknowledgement – "Yes. I don't like it much, though" – is a portent of the end of the affair, but also a sign that she has moved away from her life in death into a new life of greater freedom and awareness.

Rachel not only escapes from an emotional graveyard, but from the deadening social constrictions also associated in the cycle with the cemetery. And, as often in Margaret Laurence, emotional and social barriers topple together. Like Hagar, Rachel is attracted to someone who possesses a liveliness and boldness which sharply contrast with her own restrained, but "respectable," family background. At "your end of town," she confesses to Nick (who is the son of a Ukrainian milkman), people "always seemed more ... free ... and not so boxed-in.... In my family you didn't get emotional. It was frowned upon" (pp. 87-8). The degree of Rachel's liberation from social conventionality is marked by the two difficult decisions she comes to. First, she resolves, if pregnant, to have and to keep an illegitimate child. (She is not, and fuller consideration of such a defiance of social norms is deferred to *The Diviners.*) Secondly, she decides, despite her mother's protests that the move will kill her, to leave their funeral apartment and go to Vancouver, that is, to the city and to a new freedom.

The nightmare existence of Stacey MacAindra, differing in almost every respect from that of her sister, Rachel, furnishes one of the cycle's most strongly drawn contrasts. For Stacey, extroverted and popular as a child and now married with four children, life in the modern city of noise, confusion, fear, and sudden death demands an almost impossible discipline and control in order to ward off the threatened disintegration of her world. In *The Stone Angel* the image of that disintegration was the garbage dump; in this novel it expands to become the city itself, especially the waterfront and skid-row with its human "trash," which Stacey impulsively visits as the novel opens. Even the back lanes where her children play, "the alleys where garbage tins teeter and lean castaway cats scrounge,"[7] takes on the appearance of the garbage dump, but down by the harbour the image darkens. She encounters the meths drinkers, and whores, and "granite-eyed youngsters looking for a fix," and overhead she sees the gulls, which "scavenge from the city" and live on "sea-sodden bread crusts and water-logged orange peel" (p. 9). In her worst moments of torment and guilt she has a vision of the city collapsing, like Hiroshima, in an apocalyptic conflagration, incinerating her family – the buildings "charred, open to the impersonal winds, glass and steel broken like vulnerable live bones, shadows of people frog-splayed on the stone like in that other city" (p. 11).

Stacey's is a view of life from an urban wasteland of physical and moral decomposition; Rachel's from the neat and imprisoning rows of the well-kept graveyard. But in one important way the lives of the two sisters are alike; both are able to find a way out of the living death. It is in this context that the significance of the interior monologues, the major narrative mode of the cycle, should be understood. The real hell of the lives of the protagonists is within. Stacey, like Rachel, has become separated from genuine human contact; she is no longer able to communicate openly with those around her, including her husband, and she has no close friends of her own sex. An exaggerated fear for her children's lives and a sense both of her own inadequacies and of her body's decay have lead her to retreat into the false security of incipient alcoholism. The cure for her condition, as for Rachel, is to come out of herself, to come out, as Luke says to her, "From wherever you're hiding yourself" (p. 181). At the height of her crisis and on the edge of a breakdown, she seeks out, in the night, away from the noise and glare of the city, the stillness of a more natural environment. Her encounter there with Luke, and the brief affair that follows, is curative. She returns to a world that is as difficult as before, but her regained contact with a life outside herself now enables her to face such major domestic crises as the death of Buckle Fenwick and the near-drowning of Duncan. Indeed, these events now draw her closer to Mac, with whom contact, both sexual and emotional, is renewed.

In the final novel of the cycle the image of the garbage dump, and its connexion with the cemetery, is changed and developed. In the earlier novels the dump (or, by extension, the city, particularly its seamy side) suggested the stark, unlovely realities of life, which threaten the civilized orderliness that we try to create for ourselves, while the cemetery suggested the quality of lives where orderliness, exalted into a code of exclusiveness called respectability, leads to a denial of life. In *The Diviners* both images retain these basic meanings, but a new dimension is added, particularly to the dump, by virtue of the fact that Morag is the adopted daughter of Christie Logan, the town's scavenger. For the first time in the cycle, the narrative perspective is not that of the respectable middle-class, but that of the socially disreputable. And from this changed viewpoint we realize that the contrast of the cemetery with the garbage dump, and the attitudes to life that they suggest, is not as considerable as it earlier appeared, and is, in fact, largely a middle-class conception and concern. Both places are set aside for what is, after all, a similar purpose: "All the dead stuff together there on the same hill," as Morag observes, "Except that the cemetery is decent and respectable" (p. 57).

Christie, with his gift of "garbage-telling," knows the degree to which the lives of most men and women are made up of sham, false pride, and petty self-deception; the degree to which families with plots in the cemetery may be more truly disreputable, morally, than the social rejects like Christie and Prin; and the degree to which their attitudes towards people like himself are a prime cause of human divisiveness. It is this bitter knowledge that Christie expresses at Prin's funeral when he grimly asserts that he would have preferred to bury "her my own self... In the Nuisance Grounds" (p. 208). And later, at his own death, Morag, sharing his painful vision of human heartlessness and hypocrisy, and understanding his true dignity and decency despite his job and social position, knows that the Nuisance Grounds are "where Christie really should be buried" (p. 326). Paradoxically, the garbage dump, for all its sordid associations, by the end of the cycle stands for an humanity, which we see in Christie Logan, and which is the very reverse of the inhumanity earlier associated with Jason Currie, the cemetery, and Currie Memorial Park. The two men form one of the most important contrasts in the cycle, one which exemplifies the pervasive opposition of graveyard and garbage dump. Jason Currie, although rich, denies his own daughter and spitefully deprives her of his fortune. Christie, although poor, adopts and loves the orphan, Morag, giving her, in material things, little more than the shelter of his house, furnished, tellingly, with objects from the dump. The compassion of Christie (his name is, of course, significant) is a life-giving force, a means of grace which offers the only true alternative to the spiritual death of Jason Currie and the world he represents.

The forces of social prejudice of that world, which make Prin and Christie the sort of people who "ought" to be buried in the town's unofficial cemetery, are responsible for denying burial in the cemetery altogether to Lazarus Tonnerre, descendant of "The Métis, once lords of the prairies [but] now refused burial space in their own land" (p. 219). Jules, listening to excuses, is under no illusion about the real reason: "I guess I know why they really wouldn't have him. His halfbreed bones spoiling their cemetery." The Métis, and the Tonnerre family in particular, are victims of a social injustice and maltreatment far greater than the indifference, however callous, shown to Prin and Christie.

The effect upon individuals of this historical mistreatment is one of the lessons Morag learns, and it makes her relationship with Jules central not only to *The Diviners* but to the moral vision of the cycle as a whole. At first, as schoolchildren, then once as lovers, Jules and Morag meet as equals, a condition that is underlined by their accidental encounter in the Nuisance Grounds, where Jules, like Christie, collects things for his shack. But, inevitably, forces of divisiveness still beyond Morag's awareness drive them apart, as Jules perceives when Morag leaves for college: "To him, she is now on the other side of the fence. They inhabit the same world no longer" (p. 134). Her upward social mobility (she fulfills Jules' taunt that she will "Go to college and marry a rich professor," p. 133) means that she is soon in a different world from Christie too, as her reluctance to return home, even for her wedding, emphasizes. In the terms of the two polar images I have been tracing, Morag has moved from the garbage dump to the cemetery, that is, her rise in social class is attained at the price of emotionally dying, as her married name perhaps suggests. But Morag does not die, though she goes underground for a time, and her return to vitality is indicated in two ways – by her reborn artistic creativity and by the return of Jules.

Morag's decision to leave her husband and then to have a child by Jules, subversive though it is of conventional morality, is seen as right because it is a defiant, and deeply-felt, assertion of a moral principle that is at the heart of Margaret Laurence's vision, namely, that being true to oneself (which is at least the first step in not being false to others) is a moral imperative. Another way of putting this is to say that individuals matter more, infinitely more, than the collective abstractions to which people bind themselves, such as race, or class, or "family." Often, of course, the decision to be true to oneself will make the individual who decides to violate conventional codes and loyalties appear a fool, sometimes even in his own eyes. Morag gives up "everything" in order to possess the only thing that really matters; but in this way, by becoming a fool, she finally learns Christie's lesson. The rightness of Morag's decision is confirmed in a scene near the end of the novel in which the Currie plaid pin (given by Hagar to John Shipley in *The Stone Angel*) and Lazarus Tonnerre's knife are discovered, recognized, and exchanged. Pique, the illegitimate daughter of the adopted daughter of the town's garbage collector and the granddaughter of Lazarus Tonnerre, denied burial in his own lands, will become the heir to both the Curries and the Tonnerres. Pique is thus the sign and hope of the possibility of reconciliation.

III

The note of quiet optimism on which *The Diviners* ends, the closing suggestion of reconciliation and of the defeat of many of the devisive forces that deaden and destroy human life, is the final and culminating repetition in a pattern that gradually emerges in the Manawaka cycle. The movement of the cycle, like that of Eliot's *Wasteland,* which it resembles in this as in other ways, is from dryness to water, from spiritual barrenness to rebirth, from separation to reconciliation. And this pattern of diversity reconciled, of a universal design composed from separate elements, is fashioned by an elaborate imagery of the four elements, one of which predominates in each of the four novels.

In *The Stone Angel* earth, in the form of land and property, but also as wasteland and wilderness, is the foremost element. For the early settlers, "fledgling pharaohs in an uncouth land" (p. 3), the prairies presented an opportunity to acquire property, to establish a dynasty, and finally to commemorate themselves in stone monuments. But spiritually, as their pharaonic obsession with "The Burial of the Dead" suggests, theirs is a "dead land,"[8] and it becomes so physically when the drought and the Depression turn the prairies into a desert wilderness (pp. 168-9). The correspondence between the spiritual and physical symbolism of the earth is reinforced by Hagar's acknowledgement that "Pride was my wilderness" (p. 292). She sees herself as a wanderer in a spiritual wasteland of her own creation, even on one occasion comparing herself to "Napoleon or Lucifer" (p. 191). The main source of allusion to wandering in the wilderness is, of course, biblical. Hagar, the daughter of a prairie "pharaoh," calls herself "the Egyptian" (p. 40), and is fully aware of the story of her namesake, the Egyptian concubine of Abraham, who was driven out into the wilderness with her son. Like her biblical counterpart, Hagar, dying, is shown a well of water in the wilderness (p. 187), and the story ends with her seizing a drink of water. Hagar, like the speakers in the first section of *The Wasteland* and for much the same reason, has needed but feared water (pp. 224-5), the means of renewal in either a physical or a spiritual wasteland, but now at the end of her life, having at last performed two "truly free" acts, she is finally able to accept it.

Air, in the form of wind and voices, is the dominant element in *A Jest of God,* as it is in the "A Game of Chess" section of *The Wasteland.* And, like the other elements, air has both a good and a bad aspect. Rachel finds the wind and the voices of those who speak in tongues threatening since they represent the same thing: escape from her prim, restricted existence into a freer expression of her innermost desires. The novel opens with the chanting of the girls in the schoolyard:

The wind blows low, the wind blows high
The snow comes falling from the sky,
Rachel Cameron says she'll die
For the want of the golden city.

Rachel, at 34, is already dying emotionally, because she cannot let herself go, cannot, so to speak, give herself up to the wind, that is, to the forces of natural desire. She complains that the wind is becoming colder (p. 11), but what she really means, as the rest of the paragraph makes clear, is that escape is increasingly difficult. When she does escape, through her affair with Nick, the wind looses its threatening force; she happily scatters the ashes of her reputation "to the wind" (p. 92). And, as the story closes, she yields herself to the wind like a feather: "The wind will bear me, and I will drift and settle, and drift and settle. Anything may happen, where I'm going" (p. 201).

Similarly, glossalalia, which for Calla is an ecstatic utterance she yearns for, appears to Rachel a menacing and "sinister foolery" (p. 35). Calla believes that "We hold ourselves too tightly these days" (pp. 26-7), and that this inhibition cuts us off from older sources of religious inspiration and expression, but Rachel is merely horrified by the "Dionysian" (p. 36) surrender to impulse and instinct: "How can anyone bear to make a public spectacle of themselves? How can anyone display so openly?" (p. 35). Rachel's fear of religious exhibitionism is a symptom of her more serious repression, which is emotional and sexual, as the words of some of the hymns sung at the Tabernacle suggest (e.g. "In full and glad surrender, I give myself to thee," p. 34). Calla recognizes that Rachel's speaking in tongues "wasn't ... a religious experience" (p. 37), though she can have little idea of the real significance of that extraordinary occurrence in which, horrified, Rachel listens to her own voice:

> *That voice:*
>
> Chattering, crying, ululating, the forbidden transformed cryptically to nonsense, dragged from the crypt, stolen and shouted, the shuddering of it, the fear, the breaking, the release, the grieving –
>
> Not Calla's voice. Mine. Oh my God. Mine. The voice of Rachel. (p. 36)

The pun on crypt (a greek word meaning hidden, hence a burial vault, as well as something secret) is our key to the passage. The voice that Rachel hears is the voice of her long suppressed desires, buried in an emotional crypt but now dragged forth (as if by a grave robber), though still incomprehensible, that is, cryptic, to others. But this traumatic episode is the beginning of Rachel's discovery that giving voice to one's emotions, that is, being a fool, is healthier than the decorous stifling of expression that Manawakan respectability encourages. By the end of her story Rachel has learned the meaning of her "other voice" which cried out in the Tabernacle "wordless and terrible, the voice of some woman mourning for her children" (p. 181). Like the biblical Rachel, this one also mourns for her children, recognizing the fact that her children will "always be temporary." But her ordeal has taught her a more important truth: "But so are everyone's" (p. 201). Her plight, she discovers, is universal.

In “A Game of Chess” the sterility of modern sexual relations is contrasted with the richness and sensuousness of one of the greatest of all love stories. In *A Jest of God* modern life, including sexual relations, is seen not merely in the cold and abstract terms of a chess game, but as a cosmic hollow laugh: “If I believed, I would have to detest God for the brutal joker He would be if He existed” (p. 42). But the lesson Rachel learns is that God appears a jester only to those who are afraid of being thought a fool. In realizing that she would “be honoured to be of that company [of fools]” (p. 198), that is, among those who are true to themselves and to others, without regard to appearance, Rachel learns the supreme lesson of the cycle.

The Fire-Dwellers is Margaret Laurence’s fire sermon. The wasteland atmosphere is now located, as in Eliot’s poem, in the “Unreal city,” and the dominant element is, of course, fire. In the sermons of Buddha and Augustine, to which Eliot alludes, fire is the sterile burning of lust which prevents the ascent to spirituality. In *The Fire-Dwellers* Stacey takes her text instead from St. Paul: “Better to marry than burn ... but he didn’t say what to do if you married *and* burned” (p. 211). Fire symbolizes Stacey’s hellfire existence in which everything burns with tormenting fires: her lust, her alcoholism, visions of destruction and death, the city itself. The fire prevents her achieving not a heightened spirituality, but contact with reality. Her life becomes a burning hell of inner torment and self-imprisonment.

We need not pause long over the many fire references, which are among the most easily apprehended symbols in the novel cycle, but it is important to notice that fire, like the other elements, has both a positive and a negative aspect. The novel opens with the nursery rhyme: “Ladybird, ladybird, Fly away home,” and it recurs as a refrain suggesting Stacey’s deepest anxieties: “Your house is on fire, Your children are gone.” At the very end of the novel, when Stacey has won a measure of peace, the rhyme is quoted for the last time, but it has at least partially lost its threatening force. She wonders: “Will the fires go on, inside and out?” But she is resigned to what she knows is the answer: “Until the moment when they go out for me, the end of the world.” Fire, in a word, is also life itself: hope, warmth, civilization, sex. Stacey no longer fears the fire; she has come to terms with it.

The Diviners, the culmination of the cycle and its most technically accomplished novel, makes elaborate use of all four elements, though water, as the title suggests, is now the most important. In this sense it corresponds to the last two sections of *The Wasteland,* "Death by Water" and "What the Thunder Said."

Earth acquires a new value for a generation of city-dwellers who return to the land "with caring," and, unlike the prairie farmers of *The Stone Angel,* see it "as a gift and not an affliction" (p. 335). Air, as in *A Jest of God,* takes the form both of wind, which ripples the river surface making it appear to flow both ways, and voices, above all, in the great declamations of Christie and the songs of Jules. Fire retains its destructiveness as a symbol of religious fanaticism (p. 196), and as the agent of the death of Jules' sister and her children. Water, however, as in *The Wasteland,* bears the greatest significance for it is the symbol of cyclical renewal and hence of the mystery of life.

Water occurs in two major forms in *The Diviners.* As the river, "flowing both ways" (p. 370), which opens and closes the novel, it is an emblem of a great paradox, the permanence and flux of existence, that is, of the endurance of human kind through the ever-changing generations. One of the major themes of *The Diviners* and, as we now may see, of the Manawaka cycle, is the relationship of the generations, of the relationship of past, present, and future. The story of Manawaka, which begins with the dynastic aspirations of Jason Currie and then traces the diverging lives of its inhabitants over four generations, ends with a tale of "The inheritors" (p. 369), that is, with the way in which those aspirations are fulfilled, not certainly as Jason Currie wished or intended, but more generously and splendidly, in the Manawaka cycle itself. A greater monument to human struggle, sorrow, endurance, and ultimate victory than the stone angel has been erected; it is the vision of the artist, comparable to the gift of the diviner, that creates that monument. And the vision of the artist is the ability to see into the river of life. Morag knows that it is not given, even to the artist, to see very far into the river: "Near shore, in the shallows the water was clear.... Only slightly further out, the water deepened and kept its life from sight" (p. 370). But what she has seen she records, and the cycle ends as she returns from the river "to write the remaining private and fictional words, and to set down the title."

A second symbolic use of water is suggested by the title, and is closely related to the water symbolism of the river. On the morning on which the novel opens Morag catches sight of Royland, the water diviner: "Morag always felt she was about to learn something of great significance from him, something which would explain everything. But things remained mysterious, his work, her own, the generations,the river" (p. 4). The inexplicable power of the diviner, his ability to find the vital sources of water, on which all life ultimately depends, is the cycle's most powerful image for what in religious terms is called grace and in art is called vision. It is the gift possessed by Calla when she speaks in tongues and by Christie when he tells the tales of Piper Gunn. The two figures in *The Diviners* who possess the gift of grace and insight to the greatest degree (other than Morag and the largely symbolic figure of Royland himself) are Christie and Jules. The figures of the scavenger and the *shaman* (p. 223), Christie and Jules, are specifically linked with that of the diviner (pp. 173, 236, 337) and all three become part of the artist. In an important sense *The Diviners* is a novel about writing a novel, that is, about finding the mysterious sources of artistic creativity. This question – "What in hell was she divining for?" (p. 83) – is one that hangs over the novel from the beginning and is only answered, and then not conclusively, in the final pages. What Morag realizes she "had to learn from the old man," Royland, is again: "The inheritors." Morag's search, like Royland's (pp. 196-7), has been for her true self. Though much of the process and the result remain mysterious, she perceives that she has been guided in her search by Christie and by Jules, both now dead, and to whose gifts she is heir. Her inheritance, "the gift, or portion of grace, or whatever it was" (p. 369), allows her to become an artist, and so to write the tale of the generations, which is the Manawaka cycle.

Water symbolizes not only the re-entry into life (physical revival, spiritual awakening, artistic inspiration), but also, ambiguously, the way into death. For example, at the beginning of *The Diviners* Pique leaves a note for Morag saying that her relationship with Gord is finished: "tell him I've drowned and gone floating down the river." And death by water is a motif throughout the cycle. Significantly, both Stacey and Morag, at moments of intense despair, are reminded of the psalmist's cry: "Save me, O God, for the waters are come into my soul" (p. 337; *The Fire-Dwellers,* p. 164). The first stage in the process of spiritual renewal is the recognition of need, so that death by water may become the means, paradoxically, of rebirth.

In *The Wasteland* the coming of revitalizing rain is preceded by the fearsome sound of thunder. In the Manawaka cycle there are two thunder gods, the phoney Thor Thorlakson, who is frightening only for a time, and Jules Tonnerre, whose "voice like distant thunder" (p. 225) warns of his angry hatred for all white men. The voice of thunder carries a terrifying and universal message, for Jules expresses the anguish of all who suffer from the forces of human cruelty, indifference and divisiveness. Through her love-hate relationship with Jules, Morag learns, indeed, what the thunder says, and that relationship is part of the means by which she severs the "inner chains which had kept her bound and separated from part of herself" (p. 222). Her compassionate understanding of Jules' suffering, and her attainment of self-knowledge, provide the vision which *The Diviners* renders.

The symbolism of the four elements and the parallel with *The Wasteland,* the continuity of major paired images, the interplay of character, and the recurrence of Manawaka, are means to an end. Together they reinforce our growing sense throughout the cycle that the inner lives of individuals, the relationship between human beings, the passing of the generations, and the ordering of society are profoundly interconnected. The source of the Manawaka cycle's impressive unity is Margaret Laurence's vision that the fragments of experience are part of a larger, universal design.

NOTES

1. In her fine study of *The Manawaka World of Margaret Laurence* (Toronto, 1975), Clara Thomas tells us that Margaret Laurence wants the works to be read "essentially, as one work" (p. 131) and also that *The Diviners* "culminates and closes the circle of the Manawaka novels" (p. 168). Dr. Thomas explores the unity of the cycle along rather different lines from the ones I take.
2. Margaret Laurence's collection of short stories about Manawaka, *A Bird in the House,* provides us with further details about Manawaka and pursues some of the themes we find in the novels, but we are much less concerned with the present life and difficulties of the narrator than is the case in the novels. For this reason the book was not cast in novel form, and for this reason I have not included it in my discussion.

3. *The Diviners* (Toronto, 1974), p. 290. Subsequent references are given in the text.
4. Cf. the heroic pride of Piper Gunn and the importance attached to the discovery of the plaid pin and the clasp knife in *The Diviners.*
5. *The Stone Angel* (Toronto, 1968), p. 5. Subsequent references are given in the text.
6. *A Jest of God* (Toronto, 1974), p. 79. Subsequent references are given in the text.
7. *The Fire-Dwellers* (Toronto, 1973), p. 9. Subsequent references are given in the text.
8. T.S. Eliot, *The Wasteland,* l. 2.

Manawaka and Deptford: Place and Voice

JOHN LENNOX

Margaret Laurence and Robertson Davies have created Canadian settings in and against which characterization and intrigue can be measured. Their Canadian worlds – Manawaka and Deptford – bring to mind Del Jordan's description in *Lives of Girls and Women* of the people she knows in her own town: "People's lives, in Jubilee as elsewhere, were dull, simple, amazing and unfathomable – deep caves paved with kitchen linoleum."[1] This description is evoked in different ways throughout the Manawaka and Deptford works. Hagar Shipley remarks, "I know, I know. How long have I known? Or have I always known, in some far crevice of my heart, some cave too deeply buried, too concealed?"[2] In *A Jest of God,* Rachel Cameron notices how the painted walls of the Tabernacle of the Risen and Reborn are "dense and murky, the way the sea must be fathoms under."[3] The place is "like some crypt, dead air and staleness, deadness, silence" (p. 31). Stacey MacAindra asks herself when it was that her husband "started to go underground, living in his own caves?"[4] Whenever Vanessa MacLeod's Grandfather Connor – "The Great Bear" – is angry, he retreats wordlessly to the basement where "from his cave, however, the angry crunching of the wooden rockers against the cement floor would reverberate throughout the house."[5] To Morag Gunn, her memory is the cave where the shadows of her parents move, "two sepia shadows on an old snapshot, two barely moving shadows in my head, shadows whose few remaining words and acts I have invented."[6] Manawaka's caves are places of concealment, retreat, menace, revelation.

Caves are also an important part of Deptford as the town's name suggests. Dunstan Ramsay tells about how Percy Boyd Staunton's stubborn refusal to accept any responsibility for Mary Dempster's misfortune "seemed to deepen my own guilt, which had now become the guilt of concealment as well as action."[7] In *The Manticore,* David Staunton is taken back through the Jungian arche-

* First published in *Journal of Canadian Studies,* Vol. 13, No. 3 (Fall 1978).

types until he encounters in the primeval caves of Switzerland the sanctuaries of man's bear-worshipping ancestors and discovers that he has been "reborn, by the terror of the cave."[8] Magnus Eisengrim (Paul Dempster) describes how, after being sodomized as a boy, he remembered his father's reading "about Lot and his daughters, though I had never followed what it was they did in that cave."[9] Next he tells how Willard "pushed me into a place that was entirely dark, and confined.... Then a door below me was closed, and snapped from the outside, and I was in utter darkness" (p. 36). Soon afterward, as Paul begins to work with the carnival mechanical effigy, he talks of feeling that "inside Abdullah I had entered into my kingdom" (p. 57). Thus, caves in the Deptford cycle are also associated with agony, ordeal and revelation which are usually and intimately linked with the forces of Deptford from which the protagonist attempts to free himself.

Against Del Jordan's description of lives in Jubilee, Laurence's and Davies' created worlds can be importantly differentiated from one another. Davies deals literally and figuratively with "deep caves" which become the mystery and experience and knowledge of the esoteric and the unusual – hagiography, Jungian psychology and countless worlds of wonders. In Laurence, one finds both deep caves *and* kitchen linoleum for she illuminates the mystery and experience and knowledge of the familiar and the commonplace. Through an examination of the Manawaka and Deptford fiction, and through more particular examination of *The Stone Angel* and *Fifth Business,* place and voice in the fiction take on an intriguing significance.

Setting is one example of this differentiation. While the social mythology of the small town is recognizably North American, the social mythology of the small town Scots – mercantile, practical, aggressive and proud – is distinctively Canadian. In a language true to his time and place, Jason Currie tells his children, "Nobody's going to hand you anything on a silver platter. It's up to you, nobody else. You've got to have stick-to-itiveness if you want to get ahead. You've got to use a little elbow grease" (*The Stone Angel,* p. 13). The role of contributors to the new Presbyterian church is an abbreviated inventory of Manawaka's values: "Luke McVitie, lawyer. Jason Currie, businessman. Freeman McKendrick, bank manager. Burns MacIntosh, farmer. Rab Fraser, farmer" (p. 16). Rachel

Cameron, describing Manawaka, observes that "half the town is Scots descent and the other half is Ukrainian.... The Ukrainians knew how to be the better grain farmers, but the Scots knew how to be almightier than anyone but God" (*A Jest of God,* p. 65). In his description of Deptford in *Fifth Business,* Dunstan Ramsay outlines the town's geographical situation, religious denominations and occupations of distinction – one lawyer, one banker, two doctors, one dentist, one veterinarian. The town's industries consist of a canning factory, a sawmill, and a few shops. Being of Scots descent, Dunstan confesses that until he was twenty-five, he believed that the Scots were "the salt of the earth" (*Fifth Business,* p. 17) and that, as Scots, the Ramsay family was esteemed "for common sense, prudence, and right opinions on virtually everything" (p. 17). Manawaka and Deptford thus share in a material and moral commonwealth. Nancy Bjerring capsulizes the Anglo-Saxon mentality as Dunstan perceives it in Deptford. By extension, the same characteristics are indigenous to Manawaka: "It is the sort of mentality which, with its severe unemotional empiricism, rejects any notion of spirituality or the mystical."[10] This mentality distinguishes Dunstan's parents, but "it is shared too, by most of the town of Deptford, Davies' microcosm of Canada."[11] Bjerring adds that "the nature and character of Deptford (and Canada) are firmly rooted in practical common sense and a solid reliance on material, down-to-earth reality."[12] It is out of this setting that Davies' protoganists move to Europe or elsewhere as if anticipating Liesl's question to Dunstan about "how you are going to get the infant Magnus Eisengrim out of that dreadful Canada and into a country where big spiritual adventures are possible" (*Fifth Business,* p. 194). As a result, Davies' settings in the Deptford trilogy are very often European or international because they seem to offer narrative distance, greater imaginative possibilities and more unusual knowledge. Apart from a section of *The Diviners,* Laurence's settings are Canadian. In them, knowledge and spiritual adventures take place in what often appears to be an agonizing parochialism of place and mind. Place in the Deptford trilogy exposes the reader either to the pedestrian life of small town Canada with its solid citizens and its freaks or to the extraordinary mysteries and people of older cultures imbued with a thoroughgoing aesthetic sense. Place in the Manawaka cycle discovers the extraordinary within the pedestrian.

Intimately connected with place in these two fictional cycles is voice – the actual speech and personalities of the narrators. An examination of the opening passages of the first work of each cycle provides an initial means of examining voice:

> Above the town, on the hill brow, the stone angel used to stand. I wonder if she stands there yet, in memory of her who relinquished her feeble ghost as I gained my stubborn one, my mother's angel that my father bought in pride to mark her bones and proclaim his dynasty, as he fancied, forever and a day.
>
> Summer and winter she viewed the town with sightless eyes. She was doubly blind, not only stone but unendowed with even a pretense of sight. Whoever carved her had left the eyeballs blank. It seemed strange to me that she should stand above the town, harking us all to heaven without knowing who we were at all. But I was too young then to know her purpose, although my father often told me she had been brought from Italy at a terrible expense and was pure white marble. I think now she must have been carved in that distant sun by stone masons who were the cynical descendants of Bernini, gouging out her like by the score, gauging with admirable accuracy the needs of fledgling pharaohs in an uncouth land.
>
> (*The Stone Angel,* p. 3)
>
> My lifelong involvement with Mrs. Dempster began at 5:58 o'clock p.m. on the 27th of December, 1908, at which time I was ten years and seven months old.
>
> I am able to date the occasion with complete certainty because that afternoon I had been sledding with my lifelong friend and enemy Percy Boyd Staunton, and we had quarrelled, because his fine new Christmas sled would not go as fast as my old one. Snow was never heavy in our part of the world, but this Christmas it had been plentiful enough almost to cover the tallest spears of dried grass in the fields; in such snow his sled with its tall runners and foolish steering apparatus was clumsy and apt to stick, whereas my low-slung old affair would almost have slid on grass without snow.
>
> (*Fifth Business,* p. 9)

For all Hagar's blunt directness, *The Stone Angel* begins metaphorically with the dominating symbol of the novel. The opening passages link Hagar and the angel inextricably and point to a correspondence which will bind just as inextricably the blindness of the angel to the heedless and unwitting confession by which Hagar gropes her way to revelation. *Fifth Business,* however, begins with precise information that is meant to establish immediately a sense of the narrator's accuracy and veracity. Dunstan's *apologia* is witting and self-conscious as his first words focus on himself and on specific data. The contrast between confession and document will be a hallmark separating the voices of Manawaka and Deptford.

In the subsequent paragraphs of the first sections of *The Stone Angel* and *Fifth Business,* the initial distinctions hold. Hagar's allusive language mirrors the density of her experience. Dunstan's objective language is a reflection of his need to exercise control over complexity. Hagar's voice spans ages and civilizations through metaphor, alliteration and a Scots deprecation. Dunstan sticks to facts and his account is initially barren of any figurative language. Ironically, the aesthetic sense, whose lack in Deptford Dunstan laments, preponderates in the first section of *The Stone Angel* as it does not in *Fifth Business.*

The second section of each first chapter sustains the established points of view. Hagar notes, "Now I am rampant with memory" (*The Stone Angel*, p. 5) and Dunstan writes, "In making this report to you, my dear Headmaster, I have purposely begun with the birth of Paul Dempster, because this is the cause of so much that is to follow" (*Fifth Business,* p. 12). Hagar is overwhelmed by her past, and what follows is a torrent of unedited confession in which she cannot make a case either for or against herself. With Dunstan's account is continued a sense of selected, controlled documentation examining cause and effect in the interest of self-justification as he presents his case against "that ineffable jackass Lorne Packer, M.A. and aspirant to a Ph.D." (*Fifth Business,* p. 14).

Selection, control and distance are germane to setting and characterization in *Fifth Business.* Although Dunstan appears to be writing a serious autobiographical document, there is often in his voice a deliberate and imaginative play of wit and erudition in the interest of comic fabrication. The reader frequently encounters a narrator who is jesting with him, testing the reader's credulity, thereby prompting the reader to question Dunstan's credibility. Cast in the role of Headmaster, the reader comes to realize that questions of narrative truthfulness are central to the use of voice, Dunstan remembers, for example, that Deptford "was dominated by a family called Athelstan, who had done well out of lumber early in the nineteenth century" (*Fifth Business,* p. 16). The parallel with the young St. Dunstan in the household of King Athelstan calls into question the trustworthiness of the narrator. Further, the catalogue of Dunstan's early women – "Agnes Day, who yearned to take upon herself the sins of the whole world ... Gloria Mundy, the good-time girl ... Libby Doe, who thought sex was the one great, true and apostolic key and cure" (*Fifth Business,* p. 106) – involves play, wit and manipulation on the part of a narrator who is selecting, arranging and creating from an ironic distance, however outraged and passionate he may be. The larger ongoing sense of documentation is not designed to foster a sense of objective, historical or case-book truth, but it is contrived to lend the aura and authority of that kind of truth to Dunstan's account.

Unlike Dunstan's, Hagar's voice animates the unselfconscious and obsessive reconstruction of her past. Her account dissolves distance by drawing the reader immediately into the visual and sensual surround of her world. Her story is told without the intellectual *legerdemain* or playful erudition of Dunstan Ramsay. When she remembers, "How anxious I was to be neat and orderly, imagining life had been created only to celebrate tidiness, like prissy Pippa as she passed" (*The Stone Angel,* p. 5), her irony is in dead earnest, not in sport. Her wit and learning do not raise her above her milieu, however fervently she may wish it, but position her most emphatically in the centre of it. For Hagar, her story *is* her life relived and re-evaluated; for Dunstan, his story is lifelike. Morag Gunn is the one Manawaka narrator involved in a dynamic and compulsive reconstruction of her life who initially acknowledges her necessary fabrication of setting and character: "I don't recall when I invented that one. I can remember it, though, very clearly. Looking at the picture and knowing what was hidden in it. I must've made it up much later on, long long after something terrible had happened" (*The Diviners,* p. 9). Nevertheless, these fabrications are neither comic nor ironic. The distance between them and Morag is only apparent. Her totems and legends are the snapshots from which she constructs her childhood identities. Christie's legends – the stories of Piper Gunn – captivate Morag as a child and then temporarily fail her as her awareness of historical facts grows. Finally, though, they are reborn with their truth immediate, intact and unassailable in Morag who herself has grown to embrace them fully. In a letter, she writes about "Piper Gunn, who probably never lived in so-called real life but who lives forever. Christie knew things about inner truths that I am only just beginning to understand" (*The Diviners,* p. 418). Appearance and reality are, in the end, reconciled precisely through Morag's awareness of the distance between them.

In an article entitled "Notes on an Unfinished Novel," John Fowles notes how "the most difficult task for a writer is to get the right 'voice' for his material; by voice I mean the overall impression one has of the creator behind what he creates."[13] Fowles goes on to talk about his admiration for "the ironic voice that the line of great nineteenth-century novelists, from Austen through to Conrad, all used so naturally."[14] He argues that "irony needs the assumption of superiority in the ironist. Such an assumption must be anathema to a democratic, egalitarian century like our own. We suspect people who pretend to be omniscient; and that is why so many of us twentieth-century novelists feel driven into first-person narration."[15] The voices of the Deptford trilogy conflate the three elements of Fowles' discussion – first-person narration, irony and omniscience. In the narrations of Dunstan Ramsay, David Staunton and Magnus Eisengrim, there is a consistent "assumption of superiority" which also marks other characters like Padre Blazon, Liesl and Johanna von Haller. First-person narration does not make us aware of the limits of what can be known so much as of the impressive range of knowledge possessed by the different characters. Dunstan, in his magisterial role of teacher, hagiographer and writer uses irony to engage and school the reader in a kind of playful but instructive test of narrative truthfulness. In his turn, David Staunton is the brilliant criminal lawyer also accustomed to assume in public and private life an imperious stance. He views his world with a defensive and patronizing detachment often conveyed through the same kind of sententious play with vocabulary and figurative language as Dunstan. David describes the congregation at his father's funeral as they listen to the eulogy "with that stuporous receptivity which is common to Canadians awash in oratory" (*The Manticore,* p. 42). Later, he wonders whether the tax men taking inventory of Boy Staunton's fortune, envied and hated him: "Were they glorying in their authority? Were they conscious of putting down the mighty from their seat and exalting the humble and meek?" (*The Manticore,* p. 51). The satiric hyperbole in the first quotation and the comic evocation of the Anglican "Magnificat" in the second establish the narrator's conscious distancing of himself, both in vocabulary and attitude, from what he is describing. In fact, the purpose of David's analysis is to make him realize that he cannot control his life and to bring him closer to integration and acceptance of himself and his world. As the novel moves from *mise-en-scène* to case-brief to diary, David moves toward self-knowledge. Through this narrative structure and through the use of Jungian archetypes as organizing principles, however, even David's "cure" and reconciliation seem formulistic and remote. Distance and omniscience are also germane to the voice of Magnus Eisengrim who can paraphrase the first verse of Psalm 42 and, in so doing, make an artifact of his past: "As the hart pants after the water brooks, even so my blasphemous soul panted after the Wizard" (*World of Wonders,* p. 26). This use of figurative Biblical language is no doubt the result of Magnus' early exposure to Happy Hannah in Wanless's World of Wonders, but it also confirms a characteristic of the voices heard throughout the Deptford trilogy. They are measured, refined, assured, professorial because each of the books is ostensibly concerned with being some kind of document. As such, a tone of precision, learning and magisterial authority must be established early.

Margaret Laurence uses voice in a different way. Those of her protagonists who consistently or occasionally assume a kind of authority – and one thinks primarily of Hagar Shipley – quickly reveal themselves as unwittingly self-deceptive. And those voices which express a wider knowledge, such as Vanessa MacLeod's, have been made so through a tolerance and a wider understanding which the years have brought. On the whole, the Manawaka protagonists are plagued with questions, tormented by them, finally humanized by them. In addition, their questions are as immediate as their language. Margaret Laurence said that in writing *The Stone Angel,* she felt "an enormous conviction of the authenticity of

Hagar's voice, and I experienced a strange pleasure in rediscovering an idiom I hardly knew I knew, as phrases from my grandparents kept coming back to me."[16] In *The Stone Angel,* the reader recognizes this authenticity too in phrases like "the funniest wee things." "every man jack of them," "I'll tell the world," "for mercy's sake," "that's their look-out." He hears it in Rachel's idiom – "Thanks ever so much. You shouldn't have," "I'll phone you, eh?," "I'm out of my mind" – and in Stacey's "Got it on the brain," "the automatic kiss bit," "they damn near killed themselves laughing." And when Rachel says "But it's her lookout," her language betrays both the extent to which her life is still tied to that of her mother's generation and the distance which separates her from a life of her own.

In Laurence's fiction, the language of colloquial speech is often the language of description. In *The Fire-Dwellers,* the reader is told that "the MacAindra residence on Bluejay Crescent is not classy, but it is not rundown either" (p. 31). In *The Diviners,* the brown paper envelope Christie has given Morag for her photographs smells "faintly shitlike, faintly the sweetish ether smell of spoiled fruit" (p. 6). The swallows around Morag's house fly "zinging across the water, swooping and scooping up insects to feed their newly hatched fledglings" (p. 53). The voices of speech and description unite to forge a unity of tone which works most effectively in the Manawaka novels. Sometimes different levels of speech are orchestrated to describe an atmosphere of moving pathos:

> Tom, don't you worry none –
> Mother of God, pray for us now and at the hour of –
> Mein Gott, erlöse mich –
> You mind that time, Tom? I mind it so well –
> I am sorry for having offended Thee, because I love –
> Erloöse mich von meinen Schmerzen –
> Bram!
>
> (*The Stone Angel,* p. 275)

Sometimes the voice is effective in its brevity as when the voluble and blasphemous Christie reacts to Morag's expression of love with the terse "Well – I'm blessed" (*The Diviners,* p. 396).

In the use of voice in the Manawaka novels, there is not the same emphasis on intellectual precision through aphoristic, careful language as one finds in the voices of the Deptford trilogy. Dunstan Ramsay, David Staunton and Magnus Eisengrim, along with Padre Blazon, Liesl and Johanna von Haller, are skilled in the formulation and articulation of ideas because their language so directs them. The language of the Canadian protagonists is rather formal and academic. As a result their voices do not unite them to their native environment so much as raise them above and outside it. David Staunton who, in a fit of rage, calls his sister an "utter, vile, maggoty, stinking turd" (*The Manticore,* p. 129) does not speak (as he does not speak in the rest of the novel) in a voice or idiom authentic to his time and place. His language, in this moment of rage, is stagey, wooden, unconvincing. Those characters who do speak a recognizable idiom – Davies' localized Canadians – are most often presented as cretins or buffoons or grotesques through language humorously caricaturized by jargon, turns of speech, quirks of pronunciation and vulgarisms. For example, Milo Papple, the barber: "Jeez, Dunny, this is the first time I ever give you a haircut – you know that. Trimmed your Pa a coupla times after you went to the Front ... Jeez the war's made a difference in this little old burg.... He [Jerry Cullen] was always kinda stupid" (*Fifth Business,* p. 93-4). Dunstan's immediate, decorous gloss of Milo's conversation further heightens the burlesque effect of the barber's language and subject-matter: "The prurient, the humiliating, and the macabre were Milo's principal areas of enthusiasm, and we explored them all" (*Fifth Business,* p. 95). There are numerous other satiric renditions of various levels of colloquial speech. Boy Staunton on Leadbeater's Jesus: "But what kind of carpenter was He? Not making cowsheds, I'll bet.... He just wasn't bumming His way through Palestine; He was staying with people who knew Him as a man of substance who also had a great philosophy. You know, the way those Orientals make their pile before they go in for philosophy" (*Fifth Business,* p. 109). David Staunton: "In the Anglican church I nodded my head, as if to say 'Quite so,' or (in the slang of the day) 'Hot spit!" whenever Jesus was named in a hymn" (*The Manticore,* p. 88). Jimmy Veale, the killer, calls "Hiya, shit-heel!" (*The Manticore,* p. 246) and shouts to the chaplain, "Listen, I'm gonna piss when I can't whistle, and that's all there is to it, so don't give me none of your shit" (p. 246). In *World of Wonders,* Gus shouts, "Willard, you son-of-a-bitch, what the hell have you got us into now? Lemme look at this kid" (p. 47). And when Sir John Tresize asks the unlettered Paul Dempster, "M'boy, what does that gesture mean to you?," Paul replies, "Kiss my arse, Sir John" (p. 201). The different levels of language in Davies' novels are sharply contrasted and deftly manipulated to create humour through juxtaposition. This satiric use of the Canadian voice is skillful and its significance is fundamental to a discussion of point of view in the Deptford cycle. Nancy Bjerring argues that Davies' Salterton novels show how "Europeans are among the initiated, Canadians are 'rustic beyond redemption'.... Ultimately we can accuse Davies of having little respect for his Canadian characters, and enjoying them only inasmuch as they provide him with foils to his eminently amusing and often scathing wit."[17] She goes on to say that in *Fifth Business* "we get at last a truly realistic depiction of Canadian mores and morality, of psychological orientation and motivation. And finally his criticisms of the 'Canadian sensibility' are valid, sharp and thought-provoking. The easy laughs at the expense of the Canadian cultural wasteland have been replaced by real insights into the spiritual problem of Canada."[18] It seems to me, however, that the use of voice in the Deptford trilogy also sustains a continuity between it and the Salterton novels. One cannot deny the acuity of insights and criticisms in *Fifth Business* and in the other two works of the cycle. There is also in them, as in the Manawaka books, both an undeniable ability to dramatize our spiritual, moral and social dilemmas and a profound sense that, ultimately, life is to be trusted. Nevertheless, the careful, magisterial voices of Dunstan Ramsay, David Staunton and Magnus Eisengrim tacitly suggest that the other Canadian characters remain, in one way or another, "rustic beyond redemption." One suspects further that in the Deptford world, Hagar Shipley might very possibly figure as one of those Scots Canadians whose pretensions and errors invite epigrammatic portraiture or peremptory dismissal. Implicitly or explicitly, the vocabulary, idiom and tone of the Deptford narrators claim international citizenship rather than any specific patriation. As a consequence, their stories are inflected and deflected out of Canada to a country "where big spiritual adventures are possible." In dramatizing the division between the "homespun" or the plain speaker and the social civilized being, the Deptford novels perpetuate a traditional, graceless dichotomy in Canadians' view of themselves, a dichotomy which is so convincingly belied and bridged by the Manawaka voices.[19]

Davies' characters are noticeably extraordinary in one way or another. Dunstan is a war-hero and eccentric hagiographer; David Staunton is a brilliant and successful criminal lawyer; Magnus Eisengrim is an enigmatic and internationally famous illusionist. In one way or another, all bear proudly the stamp of their public and private uniqueness. By contrast, Laurence's characters are undistinguished – old ladies, spinster school teachers, housewives, small-town girls and, most different, writers. Laurence takes these apparently unexceptional people and renders them unique by showing their inner lives animated, tormented, enriched and deepened by their own unfathomed complexities. Through their characters, both Laurence and Davies powerfully acknowledge the mystery at life's core, but what for Davies is the mystery of the unusual and the esoteric, is for Laurence the mystery of the commonplace – not just deep caves, but kitchen linoleum as well.

The kinds of mythologies present in the Deptford and Manawaka works also help complement the different uses of place and voice. Deptford's mythologies are ecclesiastical, psychological, theatrical and folkloric. The story of St. Dunstan and the Jungian process in *Fifth Business,* the structural use of Jungian archetypes in *The Manticore,* the legends of Sir John Tresize and Merlin in *World of Wonders* are the mythologies of Europe, the country of "big spiritual adventures." Manawaka's mythologies are those of Scots-Irish Canada – the small town, mercantile Calvinism and the Old Testament world associated with both. They are the mythologies of heroes and self-made men like Jason Currie and Vanessa MacLeod's Grandfather Connor whose foot journey of one hundred miles eventually assumes epic meaning in her mind. They are the legends of dispossessed newcomers like Piper Gunn. They are the stories of another ancient, wandering people seeking deliverance in a new land: Hagar, Abraham, Jacob and the angel in *The Stone Angel*; Rachel and Jonah in *A Jest of God*; Jericho's walls in *A Bird in the House*; Sion in *The Diviners.* They are the history of the new land itself – Louis Riel and Batoche in *The Diviners.* There is a way in which Laurence works out from her particular place and its times to touch what they, and we, represent universally. Davies works the other way – from the outside in – and the effect is quite different. Within this distinction, place and voice identify some of the differences between the Deptford and Manawaka worlds.

At the end of *Lives of Girls and Women,* Del Jordan has lemonade and cake with the reclusive and eccentric Bobby Sherriff who has previously loomed large and grotesque in her gothic imagination. As she talks with him, he becomes quite ordinary and harmless. However, as Bobby Sherriff moves to take her empty plate into the house, he rises on his toes like a ballerina and, in Del's imagination, suddenly inhabits a world even more mysterious than the one she had earlier built around him. To her, his action seems to take on "a concise meaning, a stylized meaning – to be a letter, or a whole word, in an alphabet I did not know."[20] Out of this alphabet, she will eventually compose her story. Manawaka and Deptford are also like alphabets whose letters are linked and sounded by voices we hear as we read. These voices are compelling, endlessly fascinating and they recognize equally the mysteries of life. Given this special skill and perception, however, it is ultimately the Manawaka voices which articulate the accents and places of the Canadian imagination with the most authentic resonance.

NOTES

1. Alice Munro, *Lives of Girls and Women,* Signet Book (Scarborough, Ontario: New American Library of Canada, 1974), p. 210. All subsequent references will be taken from this edition.
2. Margaret Laurence, *The Stone Angel,* New Canadian Library (Toronto: McClelland and Stewart, 1968), p. 292. All subsequent references will be taken from this edition and will appear in the text of the essay.
3. Margaret Laurence, *A Jest of God,* New Canadian Library (Toronto: McClelland and Stewart, 1974), p. 30. All subsequent references will be taken from this edition and will appear in the text of the essay.
4. Margaret Laurence, *The Fire-Dwellers,* New Canadian Library (Toronto: McClelland and Stewart, 1973), p. 22. All subsequent references will be taken from this edition and will appear in the text of the essay.
5. Margaret Laurence, *A Bird in the House,* New Canadian Library (Toronto: McClelland and Stewart, 1974), p. 62. All subsequent references will be taken from this edition and will appear in the text of the essay.
6. Margaret Laurence, *The Diviners* (Toronto: Bantam Books, 1975), p. 18-19. All subsequent references will be taken from this edition and will appear in the text of the essay.
7. Robertson Davies, *Fifth Business,* Signet Book (New York: New American Library, 1970), p. 23. All subsequent references will be taken from this edition and will appear in the text of the essay.

8. Robertson Davies, *The Manticore* (New York: Viking Press, 1972), p. 306. All subsequent references will be taken from this edition and will appear in the text of the essay.
9. Robertson Davies, *World of Wonders* (Toronto: Macmillan, 1975), p. 32. All subsequent references will be taken from this edition and will appear in the text of the essay.
10. Nancy Bjerring, "Deep in the Old Man's Puzzle," *Canadian Literature,* Number 62 (Autumn 1974), p. 50.
11. *Ibid.*
12. *Ibid.*, p. 52.
13. John Fowles, "Notes on an Unfinished Novel," in *The Novel Today,* ed. Malcolm Bradbury, Fontana (Glasgow: Collins, 1977), p. 13.
14. *Ibid.*
15. *Ibid.*
16. Margaret Laurence, "Gadgetry or Growing? ... Form and Voice in the Novel," a lecture given at the University of Toronto, October, 1969.
17. Bjerring, "Deep in the Old Man's Puzzle," p. 49.
18. *Ibid.*, p. 50.
19. I am indebted to my colleague Clara Thomas whose observation I have paraphrased from her *Ryerson of Upper Canada* (Toronto: Ryerson, 1969), p. 85.
20. Alice Munro, *Lives of Girls and Women,* p. 211.

The Women of Margaret Laurence

ROBERT D. CHAMBERS

In modern Canadian fiction, the element of religion achieves an impressive variety of expressions. It can look outward beyond Canada to the catastrophe of European Jewry under Hitler, a tragedy which can be traced from Philip Child's moving novel, *Day of Wrath* (1945), through the fictional worlds of Henry Kreisel and Mordecai Richler, to the recent treatment of the theme in Hugh MacLennan's *Voices in Time*. Equally, the religious emphasis can be turned intensely inwards, depicting through that process the richly individual experience of sectarian religious life within Canada. Here examples abound: the genial satire on the pettiness of inter-denominational rivalry which one finds in Sara Jeannette Duncan and Stephen Leacock; the movement, in Robertson Davies' fiction, from the high-spirited assault on the Anglican Establishment in the Salterton trilogy to the profound Jungian humanism of the Deptford trilogy; the earnest and anguished exploration, in the early novels of Rudy Wiebe, of the purposeful web of Mennonite history.

In life and in literature, the mode of religious experience can be vividly experimental. Malcolm Lowry's brilliant novella, "The Forest Path to the Spring," applies to a Canadian setting the traditional ingredients of earlier religious allegories. In a similar way, Del Jordan's experience of "Baptizing" in Alice Munro's *Lives of Girls and Women* reveals a unique vision which is terror-struck by a satanic combination of sexual desire and fundamentalist belief. The note of extreme thematic radicalism emerges in a book such as Morley Callaghan's *The Loved and the Lost*; the attempt to act out the Christian Gospel in modern Canada is, Callaghan implies, simply to court martyrdom.

Some characters in modern Canadian fiction escape the wrath of God through a kind of cavalier eclecticism: one thinks of W.O. Mitchell's character, Archie Nicotine, who had been successively Methodist, Presbyterian, United, Baptist, Pentecostal, and Mormon and was, as the novel opens, once again "between

* First published in the *Journal of Canadian Studies*, Vol. 18, No. 2 (Summer 1983).

dogmas."[1] More typical are the tense, heart-locked Puritans of Hugh MacLennan's novels. They illustrate a thesis which has come to dominate our thinking about the place of religion in modern Canadian life:

> If God looked down on them that summer, the kind of God their ministers had told them about, He must have been well pleased, for by summer's end all of them ... were conscious of their sins. Longing to do their best, they had discovered there is no best in this world. Yearning for love, they had found loneliness. Eager to help one another, they had made each other wretched. Dreaming of better lives, they had become totally discontented with the lives they led.[2]

The thesis is clear enough: that Protestant Puritanism (or Catholic Jansenism in Quebec) produced in Canada an inhibited, guilt-ridden people who were thereby prevented from entering into the full joys of this life, and who also developed deep fears about access to the full joys of the afterlife. In books such as *The Precipice* and *Each Man's Son,* MacLennan traces this baneful curse of Calvinism from Geneva to the Scottish lowlands and hence, by infection, to the Highlanders who migrated to the New World; in characters such as Stephen Lassiter and Daniel Ainslie, he creates memorable portraits of modern Puritans who, austere and lonely, struggle to understand that the will of God cannot be done while they are frightened and ashamed of themselves.[3]

There is, however, amongst the riches of modern Canadian fiction, one world in which traditional aspects of religion are evoked and dramatized with particular brilliance. Faced by those moments in life when earthly solutions seem either inadequate or impossible, yet aware of "how utterly tremendous is the mystery our ancestors confidently called God,"[4] the women of Margaret Laurence often drift skywards, seeking something way out there. They meet these moments in very different ways: Vanessa wonders, Rachel panics, Stacey burbles, Morag divines, and Hagar haggles.[5]

At the outset, notice that for Laurence the secular church is never a satisfactory recourse. Laurence is apparently alienated from the wild irrationality and uncontrolled emotional indulgence of fundamentalism. Noreen's and Calla's Tabernacle of the Risen and Reborn gets some bad innings in the Manawaka novels. But the available alternatives are just as appalling:

> The wood in this church is beautifully finished. Nothing ornate – heaven forbid. The congregation has good taste. Simple furnishings, but the grain of the wood shows deeply brown-gold, and at the front, where the high altar would be if this had been a church which paid court to high altars, a stained-glass window shows a pretty and clean-cut Jesus expiring gently and with absolutely no inconvenience, no gore, no pain, just this nice and slightly effeminate insurance salesman who, somewhat incongruously, happens to be clad in a toga, holding his arms languidly up to something which might in other circumstances have been a cross.[6]

Whatever else true religion may be for Laurence, it is not a mindlessly ordered respectability. Mrs. Cameron – Rachel's and Stacey's mother – is the great prototype here. She would no doubt encounter the Great Day of Judgment itself by suggesting – albeit in a genteel but telling way – that St. Peter's robe needed dry-cleaning. As Vanessa asserts, and it is a cry which echoes into every corner of Laurence's house of fiction: "I could not really comprehend these things, but I sensed their strangeness, their disarray. I felt that whatever God might love in this world, it was certainly not order."[7]

Rachel, at thirty-four an unmarried Manawaka school teacher, worries about being moulded into a pattern of surface rigidity, her natural and life-giving impulses permanently repressed into eccentric behaviour: "I will grow too orderly, plumping up the chesterfield cushions just-so before I go to bed. I will rage in my insomnia like a prophetess."[8] Her frequent cry of despair – "*what will become of me?*" – grows particularly intense when she mistakenly believes that she is carrying Nick Kazlik's child. She turns to God for help, and the form her prayer takes is fascinating evidence of Laurence's concept of this very traditional form of recourse:

> We seem to have fought for a long time, I and You.
>
> The ones who do not have anyone else, turn to You – don't you think I know? All the nuts and oddballs turn to You. Last resort. Don't you think I know?
>
> My God, I know how suspect You are. I know how suspect I am.
>
> If You have spoken, I am not aware of having heard. If

You have a voice, it is not comprehensible to me. No omens. No burning bush, no pillar of sand by day or pillar of flame by night.

Rachel's attempt to differentiate herself from all the religious "nuts and oddballs" is here delicately touched with irony, for she is herself on her knees "where the floorboards are splintered [and] the rug doesn't reach." She, too, has turned to God only in extremity. Moreover, her demand for evidence of God's advice is no doubt Laurence's way of saying that Rachel is at once too literal and too pragmatic. Yet the solution to her anguish is her own, apparently not God's at all:

I don't know what I've done. I've been demented, probably. I know what I am going to do, though.

Look – it's my child, mine. And so I will have it. I will have it because I want it and because I cannot do anything else.[9]

When the imagined pregnancy turns out to be a benign tumor, Laurence does not lead us to believe that a divine hand has been at work.

It is Rachel's older sister Stacey – a school dropout who fled Manawaka to become an embattled housewife and mother of four in a middle-class Vancouver suburb – who chats away so wonderfully to the Deity:

At the Day of Judgement, God will say *Stacey MacAindra, what have you done with your life?* And I'll say, *Well, let's see, Sir, I think I loved my kids.* And He'll say, *Are you certain about that?* And I'll say, *God, I'm not certain about anything any more.* So He'll say, *To hell with you, then. We're all positive thinkers up here.* Then again, maybe He wouldn't. Maybe He'd say, *Don't worry, Stacey, I'm not all that certain either. Sometimes I wonder if I even exist.* And I'd say, *I know what you mean, Lord. I have the same trouble with myself.*[10]

Behind this kind of pleasantry, Stacey gropes for some pattern of meaning – some threads of purpose – amidst a life which seems to her "one unbroken series of trivialities."[11] Always between kids and husband and father-in-law, scrambling to find babysitters, rushing with lunches and shopping, her mind gyrates wildly: "I can't cope. I do cope."[12] When she is able to catch her breath, she generally lets God know exactly how frenzied her life is:

> Listen here, God, don't talk to me like that. You have no right. *You* try bringing up four kids. Don't tell me you've brought up countless millions because I don't buy that. We've brought our own selves up and precious little help we've had from you.[13]

Stacey's profound fear is that the little community of her family will be mortally fragmented against all her wishes and despite all her efforts. As the TV explodes pictures of dead children into her living room, Stacey prays for her family to survive intact, loving and caring for one another, communicating easily and creatively. But she is realistic enough to know that such simplicity – a life stripped down to its most fruitful essence – can never be. She somehow knows also that it is a sin not to hope for it to be so.

Like all of Laurence's women, Stacey is a true survivor; she weathers her mother, her husband's periodic disaffections, the near drowning of her son, even a love affair which brings her perilously close to destroying what she most hopes to protect. Frazer's *The Golden Bough* sits unread on her bedside table, just as it had when the novel opened. It is simply not important that Stacey know intellectually what she has so boisterously, and courageously, lived out through experience itself: "Give me another forty years, Lord, and I may mutate into a matriarch."[14]

Morag Gunn achieves what neither Rachel nor Stacey could ever contemplate: Morag dares to love across racial lines, and it may be this aspect, rather than anything else, which has made *The Diviners* so controversial within Canada.

Those familiar with the Manawaka novels are aware of the Tonnerres, the Métis family who lived in mere shacks even beyond the Nuisance Grounds. The name itself, which runs like an ominous warning through these books, translates exactly as "thunder bolt" and thus carries with it Laurence's conviction that buried within Canada's ongoing historical process is an immense bomb on a short fuse.

Vanessa MacLeod, for example, develops from books a highly romantic stereotype of Canadian Indian life which is smashed by the bitchy and alienated reality that is Piquette Tonnerre.[15] In *The Fire-Dwellers,* Stacey unexpectedly encounters Val Tonnerre on a Vancouver street:

> Even her presence is a reproach to me, for all I've got now

and have been given and still manage to bitch on and on about it. And a reproach for the sins of my fathers, maybe. The debts are inherited and how could the damage ever be undone or forgiven?[16]

Laurence sets about answering Stacey's question in *The Diviners*. Morag's love-making with Jules Tonnerre, which creates their daughter Pique, is touched throughout with a sense of historic restitution:

In her present state of mind, she doesn't expect to be aroused, and does not even care if she isn't, as though this joining is being done for other reasons, some debt or answer to the past, some severing of inner chains which have kept her bound and separated from part of herself.[17]

The movement of generations through history is the form that Laurence's resolution takes. By the end of the novel, Pique has been equipped culturally to move beyond the so-called civilization of Manawaka, which has been utterly tragic for the Tonnerres. Pique's decision, after Jules's death, to seek out her father's people in their natural habitat on Galloping Mountain becomes symbolically linked with Morag's obsession with the river which flows both ways. Inevitably, Pique moves with her generation into the future, but symbolically she moves backwards into her Canadian past to encounter her Métis set of cultural heroes. The other set came from Scotland:

Now Piper Gunn had a woman, and a strapping strong woman she was, with the courage of a falcon and the beauty of a deer and the warmth of a home and the faith of saints ... and she stood there beside her man on the rocky coast, and watched that ship come into the harbour in that place. And when the plank was down and the captain hailing the people there, Piper Gunn began to walk towards that ship and his woman Morag with him, and she with child, and he was still playing "The Gunns' Salute."[18]

That sheen of glory exists only in the epic past; the other Morag, obsessively watching the river flow both ways, lives in a very different present: "I am deficient in faith,"[19] she confides to the ghost of Catharine Parr Traill.

In history – or at least in Christie Logan's version of it – the Piper led off and the poor Scots immigrants followed; in the present, Morag turns inwards, divining uncertainly, probing amidst her huge accumulation of memories, trying to sort it all out, and wondering – especially wondering if Pique will be all right. And Pique meets her on that ground:

> "Ma—" she added, "you'll take care, eh? You'll be okay?"
>
> "Of course. I *am* okay."
>
> And in a profound sense, this was true.
>
> Pique put one thin brown arm around Morag's shoulders.
>
> "So long, then."
>
> "So long. Go with God, Pique."
>
> "Ma, you have some pretty funny expressions."
>
> "Now, then, don't I just?"
>
> She watched while Pique walked across the meadow to the river and the boat. Then she walked back inside the house.[20]

Now the river carries Pique – *"harbinger of my death, continuer of life."*[21]

Finally – and so that I may indulge in the paradox of putting first things last – Hagar and *The Stone Angel.* Published in 1964, the first in the sequence of Manawaka novels, *The Stone Angel* has been accepted as a modern Canadian version of certain central and traditional religious themes: spiritual pride leading to the aridity and lovelessness which accompanies any separation from God. Critics have explored Laurence's deliberate use of Old Testament analogies, and the point has been well made that Laurence resolves Hagar's spiritual isolation through New Testament acts – particularly two acts – of gratuitous and selfless love.[22]

Instead of adding refinements to these critical approaches, I wish to explore certain parallels between *The Stone Angel* and the much earlier world of John Milton's *Paradise Lost.* One can begin by noting that, like Milton's Satan, Hagar begins with a deliberate act of rebellion against her father. I am not of course suggesting that we think of Hagar as Satan or of Jason Currie as God, but the act of rebellion is crucial in both cases. Notice Laurence's early description of Jason:

> Auntie Doll was always telling us that Father was a God-fearing man. I never for a moment believed it, of course. I couldn't imagine Father fearing anyone, God included, especially when he didn't even owe his existence to the Almighty. God might have created heaven and earth and the

majority of people, but Father was a self-made man, as he himself had told us often enough.[23]

Beneath the humour here is the clear fact that Jason Currie is absolutely a law unto himself, and he commands the will of his daughter Hagar only until such time as she has developed a will equal to his. Laurence renders the battle between them in magnificent terms when Hagar announces to Jason that she intends to marry Bram Shipley:

Instead, I looked at him just as hard as he was looking at me.

"I've worked for you for three years."

"There's not a decent girl in this town would wed without her family's consent," he said. "It's not done."

"It'll be done by me," I said, drunk with exhilaration at my daring.

"I'm only thinking of you," Father said. "Of what's best for you. If you weren't so pig-headed maybe you could see that."

Then without warning, he reached out a hand like a lariat, caught my arm, held and bruised it, not even knowing he was doing so.

"Hagar—" he said. "You'll not go, Hagar."

The only time he ever called me by my name. To this day I couldn't say if it was a question or a command. I didn't argue with him. There never was any use in that. But I went when I was good and ready, all the same.[24]

Hagar's marriage to Bram causes a permanent separation from her family; she never again speaks to her father; her father never sees Hagar's children. Community of family is totally rent.

I find it useful to think of Hagar's long married life with Bram against a backdrop of Miltonic ideas. In the divorce tracts, Milton insists that the loss within marriage of mutual solicitude and compassion is in effect a divorce and should thus be one in fact and in law. Milton's words make this ideal clear: "when the minds are fitly dispos'd and enabl'd to maintain a cherfull conversation, to the solace and love of each other."[25] When that state no longer exists, Milton argues, God has departed from that marriage and its continuation is a blasphemy.

God never was, in Milton's terms, a part of Hagar's and Bram's marriage, for they withhold both friendship and love from each other. Even as a young girl, Hagar could not bring herself to respond selflessly; she failed, when asked, to warm her dying brother Dan; she was always cold and blind like the sightless stone angel in the Manawaka cemetery, an image which returns to haunt her even into her ninetieth year:

> My bed is cold as winter, and now it seems to me that I am lying as the children used to do, on fields of snow, and they would spread their arms and sweep them down to their sides, and when they rose, there would be the outline of an angel with spread wings.[26]

How different from those other angels who guarded the sleeping Adam and Eve in Paradise before the Fall.

Laurence understands, I think, that the disaffections in human relationships are something primal. Towards the close of the novel, when Hagar is wandering on the beach at Shadow Point, she overhears two young children, a boy and a girl:

> They're playing house – that much is obvious. The boy is searching for clam shells. He trots along the sand, head down, peering, stooping to pick one up here and there. He rinses them in the water, paddling in a short way in his bare feet, and then returns.
>
> "Here," he says. "These can be bowls."
>
> "No," she says. "They're plates. We've got enough bowls. Look, I've got them all fixed up, and here's our food."
>
> Everything has grown tidy and organized under her hands....
>
> "This is the cupboard," he says. "Let's say we keep the plates here, in a pile."
>
> "No, it's not the cupboard, Kennie," she says. "It's the dinner table, and we've got to put the plates all around, one for each. Here – gimme." Hagar mutters to herself: "Take warning, my girl. You'll be sorry."
>
> "See," she says smugly. "They go like this."
>
> How neatly she's set the table. He kicks at the log and the dinner service jitters and jumps. A platter falls, scattering its prime roast of moss.[27]

She is thus imaginatively linked with Eve in the Garden, just as the fall of a platter in the children's playhouse is linked in the tradition of religious literature with the Fall of Man. At the very end of the book, dying in hospital, Hagar is allowed to witness an example of true marriage when Tom comes to visit his wife Elva. Their surname, significantly, is Jardine.[28]

Hagar, it seems to me, stands as a summary of all the women of Margaret Laurence. What fate dealt to them in modern Canada is hardly prelapsarian. As Hagar says:

> I can't change what's happened to me in my life, or make what's not occurred take place. But I can't say I like it, or accept it, or believe it's for the best. I don't and never shall, not even if I'm damned for it.[29]

What remains for us as readers – we who have, like an omniscient God, gained insight through these novels far beyond the characters' own capacity (for such is the grace of literature) – we can begin to comprehend the immense potential always before us to redeem this tragedy of human waste. We live, as Germaine Greer reminds us, in an "age of conformism without community, of proximity without communication."[30] Margaret Laurence's novels leave open to us always the possibility of positive response. The unuttered and unheard pleas of her women (though overheard by us) require our empathy, our understanding, our forgiveness as they echo powerfully into our own lives:

Listen Nick–
Listen Mack–
Listen Bram–
Listen God.

NOTES

1. W.O. Mitchell, *The Vanishing Point* (Toronto: Macmillan, 1973), p. 17.
2. Hugh MacLennan, *Each Man's Son* (Toronto: Macmillan, 1951), p. 200.
3. This theme in MacLennan's novels is explored further in my article, "Hugh MacLennan and Religion: *The Precipice* Revisited," *Journal of Canadian Studies*, Vol. 14, No. 4 (Winter 1979-80), pp. 46-53.
4. I owe this phrase to MacLennan, *The Watch that Ends the Night* (Toronto: Macmillan, 1959), p. 324.
5. *The Women of Margaret Laurence* is also a piece for the theatre, created and acted by Norma Edwards, produced by Juliana Saxton, and directed by Frances Halpenny. It has toured widely in Canada, and its selections from the Manawaka novels are so arranged that one has the sense of listening to a series of monologues directed towards God.
6. Margaret Laurence, *A Jest of God*, New Canadian Library 111 (Toronto: McClelland and Stewart, 1974), p. 41. For the Tabernacle of the Risen and Reborn, see "A Bird in the House" (gathered in the volume of the same name) and Chapter Two of *A Jest of God.*
7. Laurence, "To Set Our House in Order," from *A Bird in the House* (Toronto: McClelland and Stewart-Bantam, 1978), p. 49.
8. Laurence, *A Jest of God,* p. 202.

9. *Ibid.*, p. 171.
10. Laurence, *The Fire-Dwellers,* New Canadian Library 87, (Toronto: McClelland and Stewart, 1973), pp. 10-11.
11. *Ibid.*, p. 95.
12. *Ibid.*, p. 141.
13. *Ibid.*, p. 168.
14. *Ibid.*, p. 308.
15. See the story called "The Loons" in *A Bird in the House,* pp. 96-108.
16. Laurence, *The Fire-Dwellers,* p. 265.
17. Laurence, *The Diviners* (Toronto: McClelland and Stewart-Bantam, 1975), p. 271. The years 1973-1975 produced a number of important novels which deal with the Indian and Métis problems: W.O. Mitchell's *The Vanishing Point* (1973), Rudy Wiebe's *The Temptations of Big Bear* (1973), Laurence's *The Diviners* (1974), and David Williams' *The Burning Wood* (1975).
18. Laurence, *The Diviners,* pp. 50-51.
19. *Ibid.*, p. 170.
20. *Ibid.*, p. 450.
21. *Ibid.*, p. 290.
22. For example, see two studies of *The Stone Angel:* Dennis Cooley, "Antimacassared in the Wilderness" and David L. Jeffrey, "Biblical Hermeneutic and Family History in Contemporary Canadian Fiction," both published in a special Post-War Canadian Fiction issue of *Mosaic,* Spring 1978.
23. Laurence, *The Stone Angel* (Toronto: McClelland and Stewart-Bantam, 1978), p. 13.
24. *Ibid.*, p. 42.
25. A recent discussion of Milton's place within the history of the theme of love and friendship within marriage is Jean H. Hagstrum, *Sex and Sensibility* (Chicago: University of Chicago Press, 1980). The quotation from Milton's divorce tracts is from Hagstrum, p. 33.
26. Laurence, *The Stone Angel,* p. 71.
27. *Ibid.*, pp. 167-68.
28. See the sequence in *The Stone Angel* on pp. 236-37. The concept of children in a playhouse (essentially a form of the Eden myth) is worked out in the novel in the relationship between Hagar's son, John, and Arlene.
29. *Ibid.*, p. 142.
30. I owe this quotation from Germaine Greer's *The Female Eunuch* to my daughter Leslie.

A Laurence Log

SUSAN J. WARWICK

A listing in chronological order of selected events in Margaret Laurence's life as a writer including her book and periodical publications. In listing short stories and articles, dates and locations are given only for the first appearance in print of the item listed. If a short story or article has been reprinted in one of Laurence's collections, this is noted in parentheses following initial entry. The book reviews listed represent only a small selection of those written by Laurence over the course of her career as a writer. A check list of selected books and articles, in chronological order, on her work is appended to the Log.

In listing bibliographic items the following abbreviations have been used:

TT *The Tomorrow-Tamer and Other Stories.*
BH *A Bird in the House; Stories.*
HS *Heart of a Stranger.*

1926

Jean Margaret Wemyss born July 18 in Neepawa, Manitoba; daughter of Robert Wemyss and Verna Simpson Wemyss. Robert Wemyss' family history is traced to the Scots family of Wemyss, sept of the Clan MacDuff of Burntisland in Fifeshire, Scotland. John Wemyss, father of Robert, came to join his family in Canada in 1881 and shortly thereafter established himself as a barrister in Neepawa. Robert, the eldest son, was born in 1896 to John Wemyss and Margaret Harrison Wemyss. After serving in France during World War I, returned to Neepawa and joined his father's law firm. Married Verna Simpson in 1922. Verna Simpson's family history is traced to County Tyrone, Ireland. John Simpson, father of Verna, was born in Milton, Ontario in 1856 and in 1886, after marrying Jane Bailey, moved to Neepawa where he became an undertaker. Verna was born in 1896 to John Simpson and Jane Bailey Simpson.

---

* Compiled by Susan J. Warwick (York University), January 1978 for the *Journal of Canadian Studies*, Vol. 13, No. 3 (Fall 1978). Updated by Susan J. Warwick, December 1987.

1930

Verna Simpson Wemyss died suddenly of an acute kidney infection; her older sister, Margaret Simpson, came to Neepawa to care for her niece, (Jean) Margaret Wemyss, then aged four. Before her return to Neepawa Margaret Simpson was a teacher in Calgary; was instrumental in the founding of the Neepawa Public Library.

1931

Margaret Simpson married Robert Wemyss.

1933

Robert Wemyss Jr., son of Robert Wemyss and Margaret Simpson Wemyss, half-brother to (Jean) Margaret Wemyss, born.

1935

Robert Wemyss Sr., Margaret Wemyss' father, died. Jane Bailey Simpson, Margaret Wemyss' maternal grandmother and Margaret Simpson Wemyss' mother, died.

1938

Margaret Simpson Wemyss moved, with her two children, Margaret and Robert, into the home of her father, John Simpson.

1939

Margaret Laurence's first story, "Pillars of the Nation," written for a *Winnipeg Free Press* Contest. Marks the beginning of the town of Manawaka: "The name of Manawaka comes from Indian words. Their meaning has been buried for so long that it can never be found, not even in the spring ploughing." Won an honourable mention.

1940-1944

Attended Neepawa Collegiate; editor of school newspaper, *The Annals of the Black and Gold*; awarded Governor-General's Medal in 1943.

1944

Entered United College in Winnipeg to study English on a scholarship. United College was an Arts and Theology College of about 750 students, an affiliate of the University of Manitoba. During period at United College began what was to be a lasting friendship with Adele Wiseman. During these years, as well as after, involved with "The Winnipeg Old Left," a group composed of members of the CCF, the CCP and their followers dedicated to social reform.

1945

Study at United College continued; published several poems in the college paper, *VOX,* as well as the short story "Calliope."

"Calliope," *VOX,* 18:3b, 10-12.

1946-1947

Assistant editor of *VOX* during final year at United College; published several poems, a short story and a study of Robinson Jeffers' poetry in *VOX.* Graduated with Honours in English in the spring of 1947.

"Tal des Waldes," *VOX,* 19:3, 3-5, 39-40, 54.

1947-1948

Worked as a reporter for *The Winnipeg Citizen.* Wrote book reviews, a daily radio column and covered labour news.

1948

Married Jack Laurence, a civil engineering graduate of the University of Manitoba.

1949

Jack and Margaret Laurence moved to England.

1950

Laurences moved to the British Protectorate of Somaliland (now Somalia) where Jack Laurence was in charge of a dam-building project. During time in Somalia Margaret Laurence collected and translated the folk tales and poetry that would be included in *A Tree for Poverty.* Was aided in this endeavour by Musa Galaal and B.W. Andrzejewski, both scholars and researchers into Somali literature.

1952

Jack Laurence left the final stages of the dam-building project in the hands of a Somali engineer; moved to the Gold Coast, now Ghana. Daughter Jocelyn born during leave in England.

1953

John Simpson, Margaret Laurence's maternal grandfather, died.

1954

Began writing the African short stories that later were collected and published under the title *The Tomorrow-Tamer.*

A TREE FOR POVERTY: SOMALI POETRY AND PROSE. Published for the British Protectorate of Somaliland. Nairobi: Eagle Press, 1954, pp. 146. Dublin: Irish University Press, 1970, pp. 146. Hamilton, Ontario: McMaster University Library Press, 1970, pp. 146.

1955

Son David born in Ghana. Began writing first novel, to be titled *This Side Jordan.* Completed this novel in Vancouver in 1960.

1956

Malcolm Ross, editor of *Queen's Quarterly,* accepted and published Margaret Laurence's first African short story.

"Drummer of All the World," *Queen's Quarterly,* Winter 1956, 487-504. (Included in *TT.*)

1957

Ghana achieved independence. Laurences returned to Canada and settled in Vancouver. Margaret Simpson Wemyss, Margaret Laurence's stepmother, died.

1958-1959

Continued writing African short stories and *This Side Jordan* in Vancouver.

"The Merchant of Heaven," *Prism International,* 1:1 (September 1959), 52-74. (Included in *TT.*)

1960

Completed final draft of *This Side Jordan.*

"The Perfume Sea" in *Winter's Tales* 6, ed. A.D. Maclean (London: Macmillan, 1960), 83-120. Excised version of "The Perfume Sea" appeared as "The Exiles," *Saturday Evening Post,* CCXXXIV (June 3, 1961), 28-29. (Included in *TT* as "The Perfume Sea.")

"Godman's Master," *Prism International,* 1:3 (Spring 1960), 46-64. (Included in *TT.*)

"A Gourdful of Glory," *Tamarack Review,* 17 (Autumn 1960), 5-20. (Included in *TT.*)

THIS SIDE JORDAN. Toronto: McClelland and Stewart, 1960, pp. 282. New York: St. Martin's Press, 1960, pp. 304. London: Macmillan, 1960, pp. 281.

1961

Began writing the first draft of *The Stone Angel.* Awarded President's Medal, University of Western Ontario, for "A Gourdful of Glory." Awarded Beta Sigma Phi First Novel Award for *This Side Jordan.*

"The Tomorrow-Tamer," *Prism International,* 3:1 (Fall 1961), 36-54. (Included in *TT.*)

1962

Completed first draft of *The Stone Angel* in Vancouver. Awarded President's Medal, University of Western Ontario, for "The Tomorrow-Tamer." Separated from Jack Laurence; moved with children, to England; took up residence in a flat in Hampstead. During ten years in England wrote numerous book reviews for journals and newspapers. Began writing the stories that later were collected and published under the title *A Bird in the House.*

"The Rain Child" in *Winter's Tales 8,* ed. A.D. Maclean (New York: St. Martin's Press, 1962), 105-142. (Included in *TT.*)

"The Spell of the Distant Drum," *Saturday Evening Post,* CCXXXV (May 1962), 24-25 (excised version). (Longer version included in *TT* under title "The Voices of Adamo.")

1963

Rewrote *The Stone Angel* while living in Hampstead flat.

"The Pure Diamond Man," *Tamarack Review,* 26 (Winter 1963), 3-21. (Included in *TT.*)

"Mask of Beaten Gold," *Tamarack Review,* 29 (Autumn 1963), 3-21.

"The Sound of the Singing" in *Winter's Tales 9,* ed. A.D. Maclean (New York: St. Martin's Press, 1963), 62-104. (Included in *BH.*)

THE TOMORROW-TAMER. Toronto: McClelland and Stewart, 1963, pp. 243. London: Macmillan, 1963, pp. 243. New York: Knopf, 1964, pp. 236. *Die Stimmen von Adamo.* Translation of *The Tomorrow-Tamer.* Munich; Zurich: Droemer Knaur, 1965. Reprinted as *The Tomorrow-Tamer and Other Stories.* Toronto: McClelland and Stewart, 1970 NCL N70, with "Introduction" by Clara Thomas, pp. 244.

THE PROPHET'S CAMEL BELL. Toronto: McClelland and Stewart, 1963, pp. 241. London: Macmillan, 1963, pp. 239. Published as *New Wind in a Dry Land.* New York: Knopf, 1964, pp. 295.

1964

Moved to Elm Cottage in Buckinghamshire, England. Began writing *A Jest of God.* Awarded President's Medal, University of Western Ontario, for "Mask of Beaten Gold."

"To Set Our House in Order," *Ladies Home Journal,* LXXXI (March 1964), 80-82 (excised version). (Longer version included in *BH.*)

"A Queen in Thebes," *Tamarack Review,* 32 (Summer 1964), 25-37.

"The Very Best Intentions," *Holiday,* 36 (November 1964), 107-108+. (Included in *HS.*)

"A Bird in the House," *Atlantic Monthly,* 214 (November 1964), 64-71. (Included in *BH.*)

"The Perfume Sea." Adapted by Max Shoub. Shoestring Theatre, CBC TV, Montreal, April, 1964.

THE STONE ANGEL. Toronto: McClelland and Stewart, 1964 (Winter), pp. 308. London: Macmillan, 1964 (Winter). New York: Knopf, 1964 (Winter), pp. 308. *Der Steinerne Engel.* Translation of *The Stone Angel.* Munich; Zurich: Droemer Knaur, 1965. Toronto: McClelland and Stewart, 1968 NCL N59, with "Introduction" by William H. New, pp. 308.

1965

Continued work on *A Jest of God* in Buckinghamshire. Vacationed in Greece.

"The Epic Love of Elmii Bonderii," *Holiday,* 38 (November 1965), 35+. (Included in *HS.*)

"The Mask of the Bear" in *Winter's Tales 11,* ed. A.D. Maclean (New York: St. Martin's Press, 1965), 37-61. (Included in *BH.*)

Excerpt from *The Stone Angel.* Adapted by George Ryga. CBC, *Sunday Night,* April 1965. CBC's FM Network, *FM Theatre,* October 1966.

1966

Began writing *The Fire-Dwellers* at Elm Cottage. Also began extensive research for and the writing of *Long Drums and Canons.* Travelled to Egypt in December, having been commissioned to write several articles on that country; these were not published upon her return to England as war had broken out in the Middle East, making travel there impossible; they were later published in *HS.*

"Sayonara, Agamemnon," *Holiday,* 39 (January 1966), 21-24+. (Included in *HS.*)

"Crying of the Loons," *Atlantic Advocate,* 56 (March 1966), 34-38. (Included in *BH* under title "The Loons.")

"In Pursuit of My Past on the Road From the Isles," *Maclean's,* 79 (May 2, 1966), 26a-26h. (Included in *HS* under title "Road From the Isles.")

"A Bird in the House." Adapted by Len Petersen. CBC, *Tuesday Night,* February 1966.

A JEST OF GOD. Toronto: McClelland and Stewart, 1966 (Summer), pp. 240. London: Macmillan, 1966 (Summer), pp. 202. New York: Knopf, 1966 (Summer), pp. 240. Published as *Now I Lay Me Down.* London: Panther Books, 1968, pp. 188. This edition was withdrawn shortly after it was released as film version of novel was released under title *Rachel, Rachel. Raquel, Raquel.* Translation of *A Jest of God* by Agustin Gil Lasierra. Barcelona: Ediciones Grijalbo, 1969. Reprinted as *A Jest of God.* Toronto: McClelland and Stewart, 1974 NCL N111, with "Introduction" by G.D. Killam, pp. 202.

1967

Awarded Governor-General's Medal for Fiction for *A Jest of God.* Made an Honorary Fellow of United College, the University of Winnipeg; the first woman and youngest person to be so honoured. Maintained residence in Buckinghamshire; writing of *The Fire-Dwellers* continued.

"Horses of the Night," *Chatelaine,* 40:7 (July 1967), 46, 70-77. (Included in *BH.*)

"The Half-Husky." CBC adaptation of "Nanuk." *CBC Anthology Series,* Autumn 1967.

"Nanuk," *Argosy,* 28:11 (November 1967). (Included in *BH* under title "The Half-Husky.")

1968

"Open Letter to the Mother of Joe Bass" in *The New Romans,* ed. A.W. Purdy (Edmonton: M.G. Hurtig Ltd., 1968), 34-37. (Included in *HS.*)

"Introduction," *The Lamp at Noon and Other Stories.* By Sinclair Ross. Toronto: McClelland and Stewart, 1968 NCL N62.

Film version of *A Jest of God* released as *Rachel, Rachel* by Warner Brothers.

LONG DRUMS AND CANONS: NIGERIAN NOVELISTS AND DRAMATISTS 1952-1966. London: Macmillan, 1968 (Autumn), pp. 209. New York: Praeger, 1969, pp. 209.

1969

Returned to Canada. Laurences divorced. Acquired cottage on the Otonabee River, near Peterborough, Ontario; from 1971-1973 spent summers in cottage where a large portion of *The Diviners* was written. Writer-in-Residence at Massey College, the University of Toronto, Autumn 1969-Spring 1970.

"Le bâtard," Translation of "The Half-Husky," *Liberté,* 11 (March-April 1969), 143-161.

"Ten Years' Sentences," *Canadian Literature,* 41 (Summer 1969), 10-16.

"Gadgetry or Growing ... Form and Voice in the Novel," Lecture delivered at the University of Toronto, Autumn 1969.

THE FIRE-DWELLERS. Toronto: McClelland and Stewart, 1969 (Spring), pp. 308. London: Macmillan, 1969 (Spring), pp. 308. New York: Knopf, 1969 (Spring), pp. 308. *Ta Maison est en Feu.* Translation of *The Fire-Dwellers* by Rosine Fitzgerald. Paris: Editions Stock, 1971. Montreal: H.M.H., 1971. Reprinted as *The Fire-Dwellers.* St. Albans, Herts: Panther Books, 1973. Toronto: McClelland and Stewart, 1973 NCL N87, with "Introduction" by Allan Bevan, pp. 308.

1970

Completed term as Writer-in-Residence at University of Toronto. Awarded D.Litt., McMaster University, Hamilton, Ontario. Returned to England. Began contributing to *Vancouver Sun.*

"Roses and Yew." Review of *Memoirs of Montparnasse* by John Glassco. *Tamarack Review,* 54 (Winter 1970), 77-80.

"I am a Taxi," *Vancouver Sun,* February 7, 1970, 6. Reprinted in *Vancouver Sun,* May 16, 1970, 6. (Included in *HS.*)

"Stubborn Pride." Review of *The Humback* by Mort Forer. *Tamarack Review,* 55 (Spring 1970), 77-79.

"Sources," *Mosaic,* 3:3 (1970, Centennial Issue), 80-84. (Included in *HS* under title "A Place to Stand On.")

"The Natives are Restless Tonight," *Vancouver Sun,* December 26, 1970, 6.

A BIRD IN THE HOUSE: STORIES. Toronto: McClelland and Stewart, 1970 (Winter), pp. 207. London: Macmillan, 1970 (Winter). New York: Knopf, 1970 (Winter), pp. 207. Toronto: McClelland and Stewart, 1974 NCL N96, with "Introduction" by Robert Gibbs, pp. 207.

JASON'S QUEST. Illustrated by Staffan Torell. Toronto: McClelland and Stewart, 1970 (Spring), pp. 211. London: Macmillan, 1970 (Spring). New York: Knopf, 1970 (Spring), pp. 211.

1971

Made a Companion of the Order of Canada. Spent summer in cottage on the Otonabee; remainder of year spent at Elm Cottage in England.

"Down East," *Vancouver Sun,* March 20, 1971, 6. (Included in *HS.*)

"Salute of the Swallows," *Vancouver Sun,* May 22, 1971, 6.

"The River Flows Both Ways," *Vancouver Sun,* December 11, 1971, 6.

1972

Awarded LL.D., Trent University, Peterborough, Ontario, May 26, 1972. Awarded LL.D., Dalhousie University, Halifax, Nova Scotia, May 1972. Awarded D.Litt., University of Toronto.

"African Experience." Review of *Farquharson's Physique and What It Did to His Mind* by David Knight. *Journal of Canadian Fiction,* 1:1 (Winter 1972), 77-78.

"Put Out One or Two More Flags," *Vancouver Sun,* February 25, 1972, 6. (Included in *HS*.)

"Voices From Future Places," *Vancouver Sun,* April 23, 1972, 6.

"Hello Aunt Nelly: I'm on the Telly," *Vancouver Sun,* June 17, 1972, 6. (Included in *HS* under title "Inside the Idiot Box.")

"Commentary," *Journal of Canadian Fiction,* 1:3 (Summer 1972), 74-75.

"Living Dangerously ... By Mail," *Vancouver Sun,* September 23, 1972, 6. (Included in *HS*.)

"Where the World Began: A Small Prairie Town as an Aspect of Myself," *Maclean's,* 85 (December 1972), 22-23, 80. (Included in *HS*.)

"Time and the Narrative Voice" in *The Narrative Voice,* ed. John Metcalf (Toronto: McGraw-Hill Ryerson Ltd., 1972), 126-130.

1973

Summer spent on the Otonabee writing *The Diviners*. Writer-in-Residence at the University of Western Ontario.

"The Wild Blue Yonder," *Vancouver Sun,* September 1, 1973, 6. (Included in *HS*.)

1974

Writer-in-Residence at Trent University. Returned permanently to Canada; acquired a home in Lakefield, Ontario. Awarded D.Litt., Carleton University, Ottawa, Ontario, November 1, 1974. Delivered convocation address at Carleton University, November

1, 1974. Divining Contest held at the Ontario Science Centre after *The Diviners* was published.

"Introduction," *Above Ground.* By Jack Ludwig. Toronto: McClelland and Stewart, 1974 NCL N100.

"Loneliness is Something that Doesn't Exist Here," *Globe and Mail Weekend Magazine,* May 11, 1974, 7. (Included in *HS* under title "The Shack.")

Review of *Crackpot* by Adele Wiseman. *Globe and Mail,* September 28, 1974, 33.

Review of *Alligator Pie* and *Nicholas Knock and Other People* by Dennis Lee. *Globe and Mail,* October 5, 1974, 35.

"The Greatest Gift of All," *Globe and Mail Weekend Magazine,* December 21, 1974, 2-4. (Included in *HS* under title "Upon a Midnight Clear.")

THE DIVINERS. Toronto: McClelland and Stewart, 1974 (Spring), pp. 380. London: Macmillan, 1974 (Spring). New York: Knopf, 1974 (Spring), pp. 380. Toronto: Bantam Books, 1975 (Spring), pp. 467.

1975

Awarded Governor-General's Medal for Fiction for *The Diviners.* Awarded D.Litt. *honoris causa,* Brandon University, Manitoba, May 1975. Delivered convocation address at Brandon University, May 1975. Awarded D.Litt., University of Western Ontario, London, Ontario. Awarded LL.D., Queen's University, Kingston, Ontario. Delivered convocation address at Queen's University. Awarded D.Litt., Mount Allison University, Sackville, New Brunswick, October 17, 1975. Delivered convocation address at Mount Allison University, October 17, 1975. Awarded Molson Prize for *The Diviners.*

Review of *Memoirs of a Survivor* by Doris Lessing. *Globe and Mail,* June 7, 1975, 37.

Review of *Theme for Diverse Instruments* by Jane Rule. *Globe and Mail,* June 25, 1975, 23.

Review of *Radclyffe Hall at the Well of Loneliness* by Lovat Dickson. *Globe and Mail,* August 30, 1975, 30.

Review of *Ross and Buckler* by Robert D. Chambers. *Globe and Mail,* November 8, 1975, 35.

"The Olden-Days Coat," *Globe and Mail Weekend Magazine,* December 20, 1975, 2-4.

1976

Woman of Year Award presented by B'nai B'rith Toronto Women's Branch. Controversy over the teaching of *The Diviners* in high schools in the Peterborough area developed.

"Introduction," *House of Hate.* By Percy Janes. Toronto: McClelland and Stewart, 1976 NCL N124.

"Man of Our People." Review of *Gabriel Dumont: The Métis Chief and His Lost World* by George Woodcock. *Canadian Forum,* December-January 1976, 28-29. (Longer version included in *HS*.)

HEART OF A STRANGER. Toronto: McClelland and Stewart, 1976, pp. 221.

1977

Awarded D.Litt., Simon Fraser University, British Columbia. Periodical Distributors' Award for mass paperback edition of *A Jest of God,* October 17, 1977.

"Listen. Just Listen" in *Divided We Stand,* ed. Gary Geddes (Toronto: Peter Martin, 1977), 25.

1978

Release of National Film Board's *Margaret Laurence, First Lady of Manawaka.*

"Column," *Maclean's,* 91 (April 17, 1978), 18.

"Ivory Tower or Grassroots?: The Novelist as Socio-Political Being" in *A Political Art: Essays and Images in Honour of George Woodcock,* ed. William H. New (Vancouver: University of British Columbia Press, 1978), 15-25.

"Introduction," *Crackpot.* By Adele Wiseman. Toronto: McClelland and Stewart, 1978 NCL N144.

1979

Talk given at Kingston United Church where her friend, Lois Wilson, was pastor.

The Olden Days Coat. Toronto: McClelland and Stewart, 1979.

Six Darn Cows. Toronto: James Lorimer, 1979.

1980

Wrote NDP election campaign letter which was mailed to 300,000 individuals on January 18, 1980. Awarded second prize, Canadian Library Association's Best Children's Books of 1979, for *The Olden Days Coat.* Awarded D.Litt., York University, Ontario, June 1980. Work on Energy Probe's Board of Directors.

"Gadgetry or Growing: Form and Voice in the Novel," *Journal of Canadian Fiction,* No. 27 (1980), 54-62.

The Christmas Birthday Story. Toronto: McClelland and Stewart, 1980.

1981

Began service as Chancellor of Trent University, Peterborough, Ontario. Co-host of visit to York University, Ontario by Chinese writer Ding Ling and her husband, Chen Ming. Sale of Otonabee River cottage. Release of Atlantis Films' *The Olden Days Coat,* directed by Bruce Pittman.

"A Friend's Tribute to Ethel Wilson," *Toronto Star,* January 24, 1981, F&.

"W.L. Morton: a personal tribute," *Journal of Canadian Studies,* 15 (Winter 1980-1981), 134.

1982

Chancellor of Trent University, Peterborough, Ontario. Continuing work with Energy Probe.

"Catcher in the Corn," *Books in Canada,* November 1982, 32-33.

1983

Chancellor of Trent University, Peterborough, Ontario. Work with Energy Probe, Third Track, Project Ploughshare, Operation Dismantle. Bronze portrait bust by sculptress Almuth Lutkenhaus installed in library at Trent University. "My Final Hour" address given at Trent University.

"A Statement of Faith" in *A Place to Stand On: Essays By and About Margaret Laurence,* ed. George Woodcock (Edmonton: NeWest Press, 1983), 56-60.

1984

Renewed controversy over the teaching of her works in high schools. Work on Lynn McDonald's election campaign. Delivered convocation address at Simon Fraser University, British Columbia, February 1984. Speech to Judges Conference on censorship, Spring 1984.

"My Final Hour," *Canadian Literature,* No. 100 (Spring 1984), 187-197.

"Clara Thomas: Biographer, Teacher, Critic – and Pioneer," *Essays on Canadian Writing,* No. 29 (Summer 1984), 7-10.

"The Greater Evil," *Toronto Life,* September 1984, 58-59, 92-96.

1985

Work on memoirs. Continuing controversy regarding teaching of works in high schools. Peterborough School Board gives approval to books, April 1985. Surgery for cataract in right eye, August 1985. Continued work with Energy Probe, Project Ploughshare, Operation Dismantle.

"When you were five and I was fourteen," *Quill & Quire,* 51 (April 1985), 24.

1986

Continued work on memoirs; first draft completed in early July. Led Energy Probe campaign on tritium. Celebrated sixtieth birthday with large gathering of family and friends, July 19, 1986. Admitted to hospital with breathing difficulties, August 22; cancer diagnosed. During September and October taped memoirs for transcription by Joan Johnston. Transcription completed in mid-October and editing begun.

"Prospects for Peace," *Homemaker's Magazine,* 21 (January-February 1986), 18, 22+.

"Hubert Evans: a great and valiant spirit," *Quill & Quire* 52 (September 1986), 72.

1987

Died January 5, 1987. Memorial service held at Bloor Street United Church, Toronto, presided over by Reverend Lois Wilson, January 9, 1987. Tributes to Laurence's life and work appeared throughout the year in all media. Editing of memoirs, *Dance on the Earth,* continued by her daughter, Jocelyn, in preparation for publication in 1988.

Books and Articles on Margaret Laurence

WISEMAN, ADELE. "Somali Literature," *Queen's Quarterly,* 62 (Winter 1956), 610-611.

DOBBS, KILDARE. "Outside Africa," *Canadian Literature,* 8 (Spring 1961), 62-63.

KREISEL, HENRY. "The African Stories of Margaret Laurence," *Canadian Forum,* 41 (April 1961), 8-10.

ANONYMOUS. Review of *This Side Jordan. University of Toronto Quarterly,* 30 (July 1961), 406-407.

ANONYMOUS. Review of *The Prophet's Camel Bell. Maclean's,* 76 (October 19, 1963), 81-82.

GODFREY, DAVE. "Figments of the Northern Mind," *Tamarack Review,* 31 (Spring 1964), 92-93.

DAVIES, ROBERTSON. "Self-Imprisoned to Keep the World at Bay," *New York Times Book Review,* June 14, 1964, 4-5, 33.

KIRKWOOD, HILDA. "The Compassionate Eye," *Canadian Forum,* 44 (July 1964), 94.

BLACKMAN, E.C. From "Letters in Canada: 1963" in *University of Toronto Quarterly,* 33 (July 1964), 431-432.

ROBERTSON, GEORGE. "An Artist's Progress," *Canadian Literature,* 21 (Summer 1964), 53-55.

GIRLING, H.K. "Travel," *Queen's Quarterly,* 71 (Autumn 1964), 456-457.

GODFREY, DAVE. "For Bonfires/For Burning," *Tamarack Review,* 33 (Autumn 1964), 92-94.

CALLAGHAN, BARRY. "The Writings of Margaret Laurence," *Tamarack Review,* 36 (Summer 1965), 45-51.

READ, S.E. "The Maze of Life: The Work of Margaret Laurence," *Canadian Literature,* 27 (Winter 1966), 5-14.

BANNERMAN, JAMES. "The Passion of a Prairie Spinster," *Maclean's,* 79 (October 1, 1966), 55.

DUFFY, DENNIS. "Critical Sympathies," *Tamarack Review,* 42 (Winter 1967), 80-82.

HARLOW, ROBERT. "Lack of Distance," *Canadian Literature,* 31 (Winter 1967), 71-72, 74-75.

ROSENGARTEN, H.J. "Inescapable Bonds," *Canadian Literature,* 35 (Winter 1968), 99-100.

ENGEL, MARIAN. "The Girl Who Escaped from Manawaka Is at the Core of Margaret Laurence's New Novel," *Saturday Night,* 84 (May 1969), 38-39.

BOXILL, ANTHONY. Review of *Long Drums and Canons. The Fiddlehead,* 80 (May-July 1969), 105-106.

GOTLIEB, PHYLLIS. "On Margaret Laurence," *Tamarack Review,* 52 (Summer 1969), 76-80.

THOMAS, CLARA. "Ascent and Agony," *Canadian Literature,* 42 (Autumn 1969), 91-93.

THOMPSON, KENT. Review of *The Fire-Dwellers. The Fiddlehead,* 82 (November-December 1969), 72-73.

SPETTIGUE, D.O. Review of *The Fire-Dwellers. Queen's Quarterly,* 76 (Winter 1969), 4, 722-24.

THOMAS, CLARA. *Margaret Laurence.* Toronto: McClelland and Stewart, 1969, pp. 64.

THOMPSON, KENT. Review of *A Bird in the House. The Fiddlehead,* 84 (March-April 1970), 108-111.

KREISEL, HENRY. "A Familiar Landscape," *Tamarack Review,* 55 (Spring 1970), 91-92, 94.

DOBBS, KILDARE. "A Certain Relish for Tears," *Saturday Night,* 85 (August 1970), 26-27.

WOODCOCK, GEORGE. "Jungle and Prairie," *Canadian Literature,* 45 (Summer 1970), 82-84.

KIRKWOOD, HILDA. Review of *A Bird in the House. Canadian Forum,* 50 (September 1970), 221-222.

JONES, D.G. *Butterfly on Rock: A Study of Themes and Images in Canadian Literature.* Toronto: University of Toronto Press, 1970, pp. 197. References to Laurence's work appear throughout the text.

THOMAS, CLARA. "Proud Lineage: Willa Cather and Margaret Laurence," *Canadian Review of American Studies,* 2 (Spring 1971), 1, 3-12.

CARROLL, DAVID. Review of *Long Drums and Canons. University of Toronto Quarterly,* 40 (Summer 1971), 359-360.

BOWERING, GEORGE. "That Fool of a Fear: Notes on *A Jest of God,*" *Canadian Literature,* 50 (Autumn 1971), 41-56.

MCLAY, C.M. "Everyman is an Island: Isolation in *A Jest of God,*" *Canadian Literature,* 50 (Autumn 1971), 57-68.

THOMAS, CLARA. "Bashing On," *Canadian Literature,* 50 (Autumn 1971), 88-90.

THOMAS, CLARA, transcriber. "A Conversation about Literature: An Interview with Margaret Laurence and Irving

Layton," *Journal of Canadian Fiction,* 1:1 (Winter 1972), 65-69.

FORMAN, DENYSE, and UMA PARAMESWARAN. "Echoes and Refrains in the Canadian Novels of Margaret Laurence," *Centennial Review* (Michigan State University), 16 (Summer 1972), 233-253.

DJWA, SANDRA. "False Gods and the True Covenant: Thematic Continuity between Margaret Laurence and Sinclair Ross," *Journal of Canadian Fiction,* 1:4 (Fall 1972), 43-50.

NEW, W.H. "Life and Time: Laurence's *The Stone Angel,*" in his *Articulating West; Essays on Purpose and Form in Modern Canadian Literature.* Toronto: New Press, 1972, 207-215.

PESANDRO, FRANK. "In a Nameless Land: the Use of Apocalyptic Mythology in the Writings of Margaret Laurence," *Journal of Canadian Fiction,* 2:1 (Winter 1973), 53-58.

RICOU, LAURENCE. *Vertical Man/Horizontal World.* Vancouver: University of British Columbia Press, 1973, 92, 116-120, 135.

GIBSON, GRAEME. "Margaret Laurence" in his *Eleven Canadian Novelists Interviewed by Graeme Gibson.* Toronto: Anansi, 1973, 181-208.

CAMERON, DONALD. "Margaret Laurence: The Black Celt Speaks of Freedom" in his *Conversations with Canadian Novelists.* Toronto: Macmillan of Canada, 1973, 96-115.

MINER, VALERIE. "Matriarch of Manawaka," *Saturday Night,* 89 (May 1974), cover, 17-20.

ATWOOD, MARGARET. "Face to Face: Margaret Laurence as Seen by Margaret Atwood," *Maclean's,* 87 (May 1974), 38-39, 43-46.

LEVER, BERNICE. "Manawaka Magic," *Journal of Canadian Fiction,* 3:3 (Summer 1974), 93-96.

BEVAN, ALLAN. Review of *The Diviners. Dalhousie Review,* 54 (Summer 1974), 360-363.

CAMERON, DONALD. "The Many Lives of Margaret Laurence," *Weekend Magazine,* July 20, 1974, 3-5.

THOMAS, AUDREY. "A Broken Wand?" *Canadian Literature,* 62 (Autumn 1974), 89-91.

KERTZER, J.M. "*The Stone Angel:* Time and Responsibility," *Dalhousie Review,* 54 (Autumn 1974), 499-509.

MOSS, JOHN. *Patterns of Isolation.* Toronto: McClelland and Stewart, 1974. References to Laurence's work appear throughout the text.

MICKELBURGH, BRITA. Review of *The Diviners. The Fiddlehead,* 104 (Winter 1975), 111-114.

ENGEL, MARIAN. "It's the Grit. Laurence is Unforgettable because She is Us," *Globe and Mail,* April 19, 1975, 37.

GOM, LEONA. "Margaret Laurence and the First Person," *Dalhousie Review,* 55 (Summer 1975), 236-251.

HIND-SMITH, JOAN. "Margaret Laurence" in her *Three Voices.* Toronto: Clarke Irwin, 1975, 3-60.

THOMAS, CLARA. *The Manawaka World of Margaret Laurence.* Toronto: McClelland and Stewart, 1975. illus. biblio. Reprinted Toronto: McClelland and Stewart, 1976 NCL N131. biblio.

GOM, LEONA. "Laurence and the Use of Memory," *Canadian Literature,* 71 (Winter 1976), 48-58.

THOMAS, CLARA. "The Wild Garden and the Manawaka World," *Modern Fiction Studies,* 22:3 (Autumn 1976), 401-411.

MORLEY, PATRICIA. "The Long Trek Home: Margaret Laurence's Stories," *Journal of Canadian Studies,* 11:4 (November 1976), 19-26.

MONK, PATRICIA. "Shadow Continent: The Image of Africa in Three Canadian Writers," *Ariel,* 8, No. 4 (October 1977), 3-25.

HEHNER, BARBARA. "River of Now and Then: Margaret Laurence's Narratives," *Canadian Literature,* 74 (Autumn 1977), 40-57.

GRACE, SHERRILL. "Crossing Jordan: Time and Memory in the Fiction of Margaret Laurence," *World Literature Written in English,* 16 (November 1977), 328-339.

DOMBROWSKI, THEO Q. "Who Is This You? Margaret Laurence and Identity," *The University of Windsor Review,* 13, No. 1 (Fall-Winter 1977), 21-38.

CARRINGTON, ILDIKO DE PAPP. "'Tales in the Telling': *The Diviners* as a Fiction about Fiction," *Essays on Canadian Writing,* No. 9 (Winter 1977-1978), 154-169.

NEW, WILLIAM H., ed. *Margaret Laurence: The Writer and Her Critics.* Toronto: McGraw-Hill Ryerson Ltd., 1977.

HARRISON, DICK. *Unnamed Country: The Struggle for a Canadian Prairie Fiction.* Edmonton: University of Alberta Press, 1977.

COOPER, CHERYL. "Images of Closure in *The Diviners,*" in *The Canadian Novel: Here and Now,* ed. John Moss. Toronto: NC Press, 1978, 93-102.

THOMAS, CLARA. "Women Writers and the New Land," in *The New Land: Studies in a Literary Theme,* eds. R. Chadbourne and H. Dahlie. Waterloo: Wilfrid Laurier University Press, 1978, 45-59.

COOLEY, DENNIS. "Antimacassared in the Wilderness: Art and Nature in *The Stone Angel,*" *Mosaic,* 11, No. 3 (Spring 1978), 29-46.

JEFFREY, DAVID L. "Biblical Hermeneutic and Family History in Contemporary Canadian Fiction: Wiebe and Laurence," *Mosaic,* 11, No. 3 (Spring 1978), 87-106.

JOHNSTON, ELEANOR. "The Quest of *The Diviners,*" *Mosaic,* 11, No. 3 (Spring 1978), 107-117.

HUTCHEON, LINDA. "Atwood and Laurence: Poet and Novelist," *Studies in Canadian Literature,* 3 (Summer 1978), 255-263.

WILLIAMS, D. "The Indian Our Ancestor: Three Modes of Vision in Recent Canadian Fiction," *Dalhousie Review,* 58 (Summer 1978), 309-328.

DAVIDSON, CATHY N. "Pats and Perspective in Margaret Laurence's *The Stone Angel,*" *The American Review of Canadian Studies,* 8, No. 2 (Autumn 1978), 61-69.

PETERMAN, MICHAEL, ed. and introd. *Journal of Canadian Studies,* 13, No. 3 (Fall 1978). Special Margaret Laurence Issue. Contains articles by George Woodcock, Patricia Morley, W.H. New, John Watt Lennox, David Blewett, Kenneth James Hughes, Clara Thomas, Sherrill Grace, Marian Engel, and Susan J. Warwick.

RUSSELL, KENNETH. "God and Church in the Fiction of Margaret Laurence," *Studies in Religion/Sciences Religieuses,* 7 (Fall 1978), 435-446.

DOMBROWSKI, THEO Q. "Word and Fact: Laurence and the Problem of Language," *Canadian Literature,* No. 80 (Spring 1979), 50-62.

OSACHOFF, M.G. "Moral Vision in *The Stone Angel,*" *Studies in Canadian Literature,* 4 (Winter 1979), 139-153.

WARWICK, SUSAN J. *Margaret Laurence: An Annotated Bibliography.* Downsview, Ontario: ECW Press, 1979.

SORFLEET, JOHN R., ed. *Journal of Canadian Fiction,* No. 27 (1980). Special Margaret Laurence Issue. Contains Articles by Patricia Morley, Miriam Packer, R.N. Labonte, A. Maeser, J. Coldwell, J. Leney, M. Mortlock, Leslie Monkman.

DAVIDSON, A.E. "Cages and Escapes in Margaret Laurence's *A Bird in the House*," *The University of Windsor Review*, 16 (Fall-Winter 1981), 92-101.

TWIGG, ALAN. "Margaret Laurence: Canadian Literature," in *For Openers: Conversations with Twenty-Four Canadian Writers*. Madeira Park, British Columbia: Harbour, 1981, 261-271.

FABRE, MICHEL, ed. *Etudes Canadiennes*, No. 11 (1981). Special Issue on *The Stone Angel*.

MORLEY, PATRICIA. *Margaret Laurence*. Twayne's World Author Series, No. 591. Boston: Twayne, 1981.

WAGNER, L.W. "Margaret Laurence's *The Diviners*," *The University of Windsor Review*, 16 (Spring-Summer 1982), 5-17.

ROOKE, CONSTANCE. "A Feminist Reading of *The Stone Angel*," *Canadian Literature*, No. 93 (Summer 1982), 26-41.

NEW, WILLIAM H. "Every Now and Then: Voice and Language in Laurence's *The Stone Angel*," *Canadian Literature*, No. 93 (Summer 1982), 79-96.

FABRE, MICHEL. "Words and the World: *The Diviners* as an Exploration of the Book of Life," *Canadian Literature*, No. 93 (Summer 1982), 60-78.

THOMAS, CLARA. "Pilgrims' Progress: Margaret Laurence and Hagar Shipley," *Journal of Canadian Studies*, 17 (Fall 1982), 110-116.

DEMETRAKOPOULOS, STEPHANIE A. "Laurence's Fiction: A Revisioning of Feminine Archetypes," *Canadian Literature*, No. 93 (Summer 1982), 42-57.

CHAMBERS, R.D. "Women of Margaret Laurence," *Journal of Canadian Studies*, 18 (Summer 1983), 18-26.

WOODCOCK, GEORGE, ed. *A Place to Stand On: Essays By and About Margaret Laurence*. Western Canadian Literary Documents, No. 4. Edmonton: NeWest Press, 1983.

COHEN, MATT. "Rebel Angel," *Books in Canada*, 13 (February 1984), 5-8.

DARLING, MICHAEL. "Undecipherable Signs: Margaret Laurence's 'To Set Our House in Order'," *Essays on Canadian Writing*, No. 29 (Summer 1984), 192-203.

HOWELLS, CORAL ANN. "Margaret Laurence: *The Diviners* and Audrey Thomas: *Latakia*," *Canadian Woman Studies*, 6 (Fall 1984), 98-100.

THOMAS, CLARA. "Towards Freedom: The Work of Margaret Laurence and Northrop Frye," *Essays on Canadian Writing*, No. 30 (Winter 1984-1985), 81-95.

BUSS, HELEN M. *Mother and Daughter Relationships in the Manawaka Novels of Margaret Laurence.* Victoria: University of Victoria Press, 1985.

BUSS, HELEN M. "Margaret Laurence's Dark Lovers: Sexual Metaphor, and The Movement Toward Individualization, Hierogamy and Mythic Narrative in Four Manawaka Books," *Atlantis* 11, No. 2, (Spring 1986), 97-107.

HINZ, E.J. and J.J. TEUNISSEN. "Milton, Whitman, Wolfe and Laurence: *The Stone Angel* as Elegy," *Dalhousie Review* 65, No. 4 (Winter 1986-1987), 474-491.

DENHAM, PAUL. "Come ye Before Him and Rejoice: The Contribution of Margaret Laurence," *NeWest Review* 12, No. 7 (March 1987), 3-4.

KEITH, W.J. "'Uncertain Flowering': An Overlooked Short Story by Margaret Laurence," *Canadian Literature,* No. 112 (Spring 1987), 202-205.

HINZ, E.J. "Religious Roots of the Feminine Identity Issue: Margaret Laurence's *The Stone Angel* and Margaret Atwood's *Surfacing*," *Journal of Canadian Studies* 22, No. 1 (Spring 1987), 17-31.

LEGENDRE, B.A. "Image Juxtaposition in *A Jest of God*," *Studies in Canadian Literature* 12, No. 1 (1987), 53-68.

KERTZER, J.M. *Margaret Laurence and Her Works.* Toronto: ECW Press, 1987.

BRADY, ELIZABETH and CLARA THOMAS, eds. *Canadian Woman Studies,* 8, No. 3 (Fall 1987). Special Laurence Issue subtitled *Margaret Laurence: A Celebration.* Contributions by Adele Wiseman, Timothy Findley, Rudy Wiebe, Hugh MacLennan, Miriam Waddington, Clara Thomas, Margaret Avison, Margaret Atwood, Al Purdy, Dorothy Livesay, and others.

Books That Mattered to Me

MARGARET LAURENCE

I confess that the subject of this talk – books that mattered to me – is a little daunting, to say the least. For those of us to whom books have been a major part of our lives, the books that mattered to us are legion. This is, of course, a blinding glimpse of the obvious. I do not need to say to *this* gathering that the books I'm about to mention are a *very* few of the very, very many that have influenced, enriched, disturbed and changed my life.

There is a family tale – perhaps apocryphal – that my mother and aunts were fond of telling me. Supposedly, on returning home from my first day at school, at the age of six, I gave as my considered opinion that I didn't think much of it – *one whole day* and I couldn't yet read. I have since tried to make up for that early slowness.

I was born in 1926 and grew up in the thirties. Like most people at that time, we had very little money, although we were much luckier than many. I was an insatiable reader – (when I *finally* learned, a little later than my first day at school!). There wasn't much money to buy books, although my family tried valiantly, and there was never a birthday or a Christmas when I wasn't given at least one book I'd wanted. There was no public library in my town until I was about 13 – my mother was one of the founders of that first small library, and one of its volunteer librarians. I did, however, have the immense good fortune to be born into a family of readers, and our house contained a great many books. One of the joys of my childhood was the complete set of Rudyard Kipling's books, most of which I read at a fairly tender age. Looking back now, it seems remarkable to me that although my reading of Kipling instilled in me a vast desire to travel to far places, his staunch British imperialism made very little impression, thank goodness. I think this is because Kipling – as many people now forget – had an enormous sympathy and even empathy with the peoples of India. It was, after all, his birthplace and remained his heart-place all his life. In any event, *Kim* was one of my best-

---

* This essay, prepared as a talk for the Friends of Bata Library, Trent University, appeared in the Friends' *Bulletin*, No. 4, 1981.

loved books when I was a child, as were, also, *The Jungle Books* and – with their English, historical, mythical and magical aspects – *Puck of Pook's Hill* and *Rewards and Fairies*. These books were among the many that helped to open my imagination to far-off places and long-ago people.

Two other books stand out in my memory of childhood reading. One is Robert Louis Stevenson's *Kidnapped* and the other is Arthur Conan Doyle's *The White Company*. The former, set just after Culloden, the tragic battle in which the Scots highland clans were finally broken and the fabric of their society torn forever, probably set me thinking about those historical events, but not in any conscious way at that time. Alan Breck, escaping through thc heather, was my ideal of bravery and adventure, and young David Balfour's triumph against his wicked uncle seemed to me to be just the sort of thing I myself would have been very good at, had the opportunity ever presented itself. Conan Doyle's book, with its – as I now see it – rather dreadful idealization of the English, and its marvellous evocation of Agincourt and the English bowmen, also had a hero, the lad Alain, with whom I identified totally. Does this seem strange to you? It seems strange to me, now; it did not seem so then. That book was in the Grade Seven library and I must have borrowed it three or four times that year, when I was twelve. That was the same year – this really dates me – that a young American singer first became popular, and the girls were pretending to swoon all over the place. His name was Frank Sinatra. I wasn't much of a swooner. On odds, I preferred Kim, Alan Breck, David Balfour and Alain. It was around this time that I began to perceive that I did not fit in with many of my contemporaries, although heaven knows I longed to do so.

Were there no women writers who spoke to my childhood? Not many. I don't recall ever wishing that I had been born a boy, which seems curious, considering that the boys in fiction were the ones who got to have all the exciting adventures. I suppose that because of my mother, who had been a high school teacher of English and who had once gone as a young woman on an exchange teachership for a year, to faraway Bermuda, and my aunts, two of whom were nurses, one a very distinguished nurse who had been for some years head of the Canadian Nurses Association – because of these strong independent-minded women, I always had the vague but powerful feeling that I, too, could participate in exciting events. There were, however, two women writers who were especially important to me, away back then. One was Nellie McClung and the other was L.M. Montgomery. Both, also, were Canadian writers, people who wrote out of territories not unlike my own, and this was not so usual at that time. Nellie McClung's personal history of strong feminism, the battles she had fought before I was born, to have women proclaimed 'persons', her fight for women's right to vote – these were not observed or known to me until I was much older. Only in my young adulthood did I realize how far-reaching was the victory of such women as Nellie McClung and Emily Murphy, to have women recognized as persons. They won in 1929. For the first three years of my life I was not a person, although I was, naturally, unaware of this fact at the time. But *Sowing Seeds in Danny,* sentimental and even positively treacly though it certainly was, in fact was a real influence in my life. The indomitable Pearl, holding the family together against vast difficulties, must have been to me what people now call a role model. Pearlie was young but she was brave and strong. She had humour and wit, and she put up with no nonsense from snobs. As far as L.M. Montgomery was concerned, my favourite of her books was her first, *Anne of Green Gables.* It remains, to my mind, a children's classic. My own daughter loved it when she was a child. The other of Montgomery's books that stirred me was *Emily of New Moon.* Both Anne and Emily were rebels – intelligent, talented girls who were not about to be put down. Emily had the added appeal of wanting to become a writer – *no,* of actually *being* a writer, as I myself was, even as a child, although I never dreamed I would someday be published. Of course, as was inevitable when those books were written, both Anne and Emily ended up – in sequels to those novels – by marrying the boy next door and becoming, if memory serves, somewhat more subdued. It is only fair to add, however, that the male characters, Gilbert and Teddie, did respect and acknowledge their wives' intelligence and talents. Those two fictional girls gave me, I think, the sense that a woman could be – and it was *all right* for her to be – an intelligent, independent-minded person who was determined to pursue her own vocation as well as being a wife and mother.

Now we move on to a few of the books that I recall as moments of Recognition and Revelation. I am leaving out, here, purposely, all the truly great and magnificent works of the past to which we all owe so much of our intellectual, emotional and spiritual development – the Bible, Shakespeare, Milton, John Donne, Melville, Hawthorne, and on and on and on. We can, I think, take those revelations for granted ... they must have happened in some way or another to all of us. I know they did to me, especially when I went to college in Winnipeg, at the age of 18, and discovered, quite literally, a whole new world. United College – now the University of Winnipeg – was at that time one of the small liberal arts colleges, not unlike Trent now, although much smaller. Those of us who were privileged to go there in the mid-forties will, I think, forever be grateful for the kind of caring, questioning, thoughtful educations we received there. Canadian writing, at that time, was not taught in any courses. But there were teachers – Arthur Phelps, among them, one of the great teachers in our land – who encouraged us to read Canadian writers. He was a personal friend of Frederick Philip Grove, and also of Morley Callaghan, who once visited – to our delight – a meeting of the English Club, a once-a-month event that took place at the Phelps' home, at which those of us who were devoted to English literature took turns in presenting our earnest, youthful but quite marvelously enthusiastic papers. Well, we *did* read Canadian books. We couldn't afford to buy them, and they weren't even greatly in evidence at the Public Library, but we read Gabrielle Roy, Hugh MacLennan, Morley Callaghan, and others, in the book department of the Hudson's Bay Company, just across the road from the college, a chapter at a time, hoping the sales clerks wouldn't notice us standing there, turning pages. A rather touching footnote to this story is that when I first met Dale Zieroth, the talented poet who was born in the same town as I was, just 20 years after myself, and who grew up on a farm near Glenella, Manitoba, he told me that when *he* was at United College, he couldn't afford to buy books, either, so he read my novel, *A Jest of God,* in the bookstore at the Bay, a chapter at a time, hoping the sales clerk wouldn't notice.

Recognition, Revelation. The first time this happened to me with great force was when I read Sinclair Ross's novel, *As For Me and My House*. It was published in 1941, and sank without a trace, for that was during the Second World War and people didn't want to be reminded of the so-called Dirty Thirties. It surfaced some years later as a Canadian classic and at last came into its own. I must have read it, however, in about 1942, because we got it for the Neepawa Library, my mother and a few others being very keen on acquiring Canadian books. I would have been 16 years old. I saw, reading it, that a writer *could* write out of a background similar to my own. You didn't need to live in London or New York. It was all *here.* Some five or six years later, W.O. Mitchell's novel, *Who Has Seen the Wind?* confirmed and strengthened this revelation. My fictional town of Manawaka is different in very many ways from the prairie towns of Ross and Mitchell. Nonetheless, it was these writers who showed me what I would ultimately have to do, namely to write out of my own place, my own time, my own people.

One of my contemporaries, Adele Wiseman, who is also a dear friend and has been so for more than 30 years, wrote a novel that I consider to be one of the finest written in the English language in the past 25 years or so. This was her first novel, *The Sacrifice,* published in 1956. It is an amazing piece of work. The vision of Abraham, his terrible anguish and his triumphs, the generations who followed him in this new land – all these spoke to me so deeply that it is impossible for me to honour them sufficiently in a few words. I have in my possession, incidentally, a letter that Adele found among her mother's things when Chaika Wiseman, the doll-maker, that beloved and wise woman, died just over a year ago. It is a letter I wrote from England, in 1950, to Adele's parents in Winnipeg. My husband and I were preparing to go to Somaliland, in East Africa, where Jack was to be in charge of a scheme to build *ballehs,* large earth dug-outs, to catch the once-yearly rainfall across the Haud Desert. Adele had not long before arrived in England, where she was working at the Stepney Jewish Girls' Hostel in London. She and I were carrying on the same discussions about writing that we had begun a few years before in North Winnipeg. In the letter, I described, somewhat touchingly, Jack's and my preparations to go to an unknown land, my hope that we had bought the right pots and pans, and that my one newly purchased – and very inexpensive – formal dress would prove suitable. I didn't know whether we were in for a giddy round of dances at Government House, or whether it would all be slogging through the desert. Anyway, I went on to say: "I was over at Adele's this afternoon. We read each other our manuscripts and told each other that we were going to write the two great novels of the century." Oh, young hopes! I was, of course, speaking in jest, and yet it is true that we both had, at that point, an undeniable sense of vocation. What manuscript of mine I showed to her that day, I can't recall – whatever it was, it came to nothing. But the manuscript of hers that I saw was part of the first draft of *The Sacrifice*. Adele and I had a joke in those days. We used to say to one another, "Just wait, kiddo, until we both win the Governor General's Award!" Of course we never dreamed that in the years to come, we both *would*.

I'm skipping many years and many books that made profound impressions on me. In 1960, my first novel, *This Side of Jordan,* set in West Africa, had just been published. I was working on a number of West African short stories, and also contemplating getting out my old diaries from Somaliland days, and trying to write an account of our experiences there. I was trying to *understand* our African experience, and it was at this point that quite by accident I came across the exact book I needed at the exact time I needed it. This was *Prospero and Caliban: The Psychology of Colonization,* by the French psychologist, O. Mannoni. In it, Mannoni describes his own anguished time in Madagascar, and his feeling that at last – terribly, frighteningly – he understood something of the Malagasy people's feelings, often inchoate, towards the French colonialists; the African people's rage, sense of spiritual violation, sense of powerlessness in the face of economic exploitation and social and psychological oppression, in the days before the independence movements were to become organized and politically effective, when the people's anguish expressed itself in unorganized and chaotic uprisings doomed to failure, at that point. To me, this book meant a real, literal revelation. It opened up to me an understanding of some of my own feelings and experiences in East and West Africa, and in the end, perhaps, taught me as much about my own land and the terrible injustices and outrages committed by imperialism against *our* native peoples, as it did about the peoples of Africa. I made use, I hope, of these insights in my West African stories, especially in a story called "The Voices of Adamo", and in my book on Somaliland,

The Prophet's Camel Bell. Much later, some of these insights were to return, informed this time with more knowledge of my own land and peoples, in my novel *The Diviners.*

Among the books relating to my own land, one that has meant the most to me is W.L. Morton's *Manitoba: A History.* I knew sadly little of the history of my own part of the country until relatively few years ago. When I was a child we were not taught a great deal of Canadian history, and what we *were* taught seemed to be mostly Acts of Parliament. It was standard practice to skim over the North-West Rebellions in very short order, and to present Louis Riel, Gabriel Dumont, Big Bear, Poundmaker and others as the bad guys who wanted to impede good old John A. Macdonald's grand design for Progress and the CPR. Yet I was born and grew up in a town called Neepawa, the Cree meaning of which is something like "Land of Plentiful Game". It was through these bluffs and valleys and open prairies that the bi-yearly buffalo hunts of the Métis and Cree swept along in bygone years. It was not far from here that the events of 1870 took place, when Riel sought to guarantee some rights for his people, and was finally driven into his 15-year exile, from which he returned in 1885, to Saskatchewan, to the heroic attempts made by the Indian and Métis peoples to save their land and their way of life, and to ultimate defeat and tragedy. Of these I knew nothing. My own grandfather had been the first lawyer in our town, and had incorporated the town, the name being interpreted then as Land of Plenty, and its symbol a cornucopia. A cornucopia! A European symbol having nothing to do with the history of the place. When I first read Morton's *Manitoba: A History,* it was with a tremendous sense of excitement, combined with an angry sense of having been deprived, when young, of my own heritage. I have since done a great deal of reading of prairie history, but it was Morton who first gave me the sense of my place's long and dramatic past.

One book I want to mention here, because of the depth of its perceptions and the scope of its vision, is F.R. Scott's *Essays on the Constitution.* Scott, our most distinguished constitutional lawyer and one of our finest poets, wrote these essays over some fifty years. They were collected in a single volume in 1977, and won the Governor-General's Award for non-fiction of that year. In these essays Scott discusses issues such as civil liberties, censorship, the rights of minorities, the need for due process of law as against the emotional hysteria of the vigilantes of any historical period. To me, Scott's book can be described in one word: *noble.* Here is one brief quote from an essay written in 1932, entitled *Freedom of Speech.*

> "*The time, it is to be hoped, has gone by,* wrote John Stuart Mill, *when any defense would be necessary for the principle of freedom of speech.* His hope was vain. The time for defending freedom never goes by. Freedom is a habit that must be kept alive by use."

These are words, I think, that we would do well to ponder deeply in our own times.

I want now to speak a little about a few more novels that have impressed, delighted and enlightened me, possibly to give you some further indication of my own tastes in reading and also of some of the standards to which I aspire as a novelist, those impossible standards that in our own self-assessment we never meet, those qualities in the writing of others that we instantly recognize.

The British novelist, Joyce Cary, has meant a very great deal to me. This is true of all his novels, but perhaps especially *The Horse's Mouth.* The artist Gulley Jimson and the immortal Sara Monday will inhabit my mind as long as I live. Here are characters who step right off the printed page and into the reader's mental and spiritual landscape. One of the most moving scenes in all fiction, to me, is the one in which Gulley Jimson, in the penultimate scene of this novel, is painting murals on war-wrecked walls that soon will be torn down.

Another novel that endures permanently within my mind, is *Arrow of God,* by the Nigerian writer Chinua Achebe. This is the story of Ezeulu, priest of his god Ulu, in post-colonial times in Nigeria, shortly after the British took over. At times, Achebe writes with rage and deep irony. Yet he does not write in any didactic way. He is speaking of humankind's dreadful misunderstandings of one another, of man's inhumanity to man, and he is speaking of individuals living within their own cultures and their own isolated skills and trying – often vainly – to communicate with one another. His character portrayals are nothing short of miraculous. If I may quote my own words, from a book of essays on contemporary Nigerian literature, *Long Drums and Cannons,* this is my conclusion about Ezeulu;

"Ezeulu, man and priest, god's man, like Oedipus and like Lear, has the power to reveal not only moving and terrifying aspects of himself, but moving and terrifying aspects of ourselves as well."

The word "great", as applied to writers, is a greatly abused word. There are very few writers, in any historical period, who can be called "great", and usually it is only the passage of time that confirms a writer in that status. However, I will go out on a limb and say that one writer now writing in the English language, whom I consider to be *great,* is Patrick White of Australia. When he was awarded the Nobel Prize, I rejoiced. All his novels have in some way changed my life, by the force of their characters, their sheer quality of alive-ness, their troubling and basically spiritual view of life. I would mention especially *The Tree of Man, Voss, Riders in the Chariot, The Solid Mandala, The Vivisector,* and *The Eye of the Storm.* How White can keep on writing novel after novel of such power, with such a huge assemblage of compelling characters, is something one can only marvel at, and give thanks for.

Of the large number of contemporary American works of fiction that have touched my life, I want to mention two – and my choice may seem strange, for these two writers are so different, so apparently far apart in subject matter, so totally unalike in style, that one might wonder how I could feel so strongly about both of them.

Kurt Vonnegut's novel, *Slaughterhouse Five,* I consider to be brilliant. His savage wit, his zaniness which is a cover for a perception so unremittingly honest that it is almost unbearable, his use of Science Fiction techniques to point up the lunacy of our times, his genuine rage against wars and human destruction – all these qualities in his writing I find quite stunning. Vonnegut has proclaimed himself a total pessimist – *Things are going to get worse,* he says, *and they are never going to get better.* And yet, there is a way in which he seems to be saying – it's up to us. To me, the act of writing is itself an act of faith. Vonnegut is totally concerned with human life, and he goes on speaking.

Tillie Olsen is an American writer with whom I feel a deep sense of empathy, tribal kinship, sisterhood. Her book, *Tell Me a Riddle,* consists of a novella and three short stories. She has written relatively little because of her personal circumstances. She married young, had four children and for many years had to work at a job outside her home. Her book, *Silences,* explores the circumstances that have prevented some writers, both female and male, from fulfilling their life's work. The Novella, *Tell Me a Riddle,* seems to me to be as close to perfection as any contemporary prose I have read. In just fifty printed pages – fifty! – Olsen communicates the story of a long marriage, an entire family, ancestral roots reaching back into a long ago past in other countries, the ways in which humans suffer and hurt one another and yet support and love one another. In my view, it is a small masterpiece.

I want to conclude by mentioning a few more Canadian novels that have moved and impressed me the most.

All of Gabrielle Roy's writing I admire and love. When I read *The Tin Flute* for the first time, I began to understand what a woman writer can do, in portraying women characters. I grew up reading books that had mostly been written by men. The women writers who spoke to my childhood were by no means able to tell all or most of their own truth. When I met the character of Rose Anna, the mother, in *The Tin Flute,* I was overwhelmed. I believed her to be one of the truly great characters in our literature.

The prairie writer Rudy Wiebe has written some tremendously good fiction. Of all his books, my favourite is *The Temptations of Big Bear,* which tells the story of the North-West rebellion of 1885, often from the viewpoint of Big Bear, the heroic leader of the Crees, who, tragically, lived to see his people defeated and dispossessed. When the Métis writer, Maria Campbell, author of an autobiographical book, *Halfbreed,* read *The Temptations of Big Bear,* she told Wiebe that she believed the spirit of Big Bear had guided him in the writing. She may well be right.

I could hardly conclude without speaking of Robertson Davies. Of all his writing, his novel *Fifth Business,* has meant the most to me. Dunstan Ramsay, who is so much more than the aging rather fussy schoolteacher that his students and colleagues perceive him to be, is a brilliantly portrayed character. This is, of course, in the broadest sense, a religious novel. I am not qualified to speak of the Jungian framework out of which Davies writes, but to me his are the great themes of good and evil, of humankind's need for grace.

One of the finest novels to have appeared in Canada in recent years, and indeed, one of our finest ever, is Timothy Findley's *The Wars.* This novel is written out of Ontario and the First World War, but Findley is in fact talking about *all* wars, those within the individual human being, those concealed but sometimes deadly ones that can occur within a family, and finally, those insane slaughterings that constitute wars between nations.

A very recent novel that also speaks powerfully to these issues is Hugh MacLennan's *Voices in Time.* This remarkable novel deals with the insanity of wars, the betrayal of one person by another, the miraculous power of the human spirit to survive.

What, if anything, do all these novelists – Canadian, English, American, West African, Australian – have in common? I think what they have in common is the ability to portray human individuals in all their complexity and ambiguity, in vitally alive terms, compassionately and caringly. They all have a strong sense of justice and of the possibility of human communication, even when these qualities, as so often happens, must be defined by their absence. In fact, the books, whether fiction, non-fiction or poetry, that have mattered the most to me throughout my adult life have been those that have a sense of our past and a belief that life itself is immeasurably valuable, to be worked for, hoped for, understood and proclaimed in whatever ways we are given to do.

My Final Hour

MARGARET LAURENCE

I am being given a unique opportunity. I will not have to postpone until my last gasp the imparting of the wisdom of my accumulated years to a breathlessly awaiting world. Just as well, as I have never been much of a believer in "famous last words". I suppose this is why King Lear's words, "Prithee, undo this button" seem infinitely more moving to me than any highflown rhetoric purportedly uttered by some well-known person when on the point of departing this vale of tears. Anyway, here I am, faced with the prospect of delivering the message of My Final Hour. I do not promise that it will be My Finest Hour, but I will do my best.

First, I would like to pass on one piece of advice. If, as you grow older, you feel you are also growing stupider, do not worry. This is normal, and usually occurs around the time when your children, now grown, are discovering the opposite – they now see that you aren't nearly as stupid as they had believed when they were young teenagers. Take heart from that. True, your newfound sense of stupidity will no doubt be partly due to the fact that the technology of the age has far outstripped any feeble knowledge of it that you may once have felt you had. It may, however, also be due to the fact that at last you may be learning a little healthy humility – humility in its true and indeed religious sense, which of course has nothing at all to do with self-effacement but with a recognition of your human limitations. I would not claim that I have learned that kind of humility – that struggle to learn will never cease. But at least I now can accept with some sort of equanimity that many things are beyond my power. I can try to help friends or family or strangers, but I can never "save" another in the profoundest sense. I can do what is within my human power, that is all. Anything else is delusion or spiritual pride, or so I believe. My limitations extend to many fields. I know now that I will never know an enormous amount about music or painting. My knowledge of science is likely to remain miniscule. I will never know as much as I would like to about the planets and their pat-

* "My Final Hour" was presented to the Trent Philosophy Society, March 29, 1983 and has appeared in *Canadian Literature*, No. 100.

terned courses. Even in my own area of so-called expertise, I will never read all the novels I would like to read, even though I read great numbers of them yearly. I will also never write a novel with which I am really satisfied. There is so much to do, so much to learn and experience, and one lifetime, however long it may be, is so short. I think of the verse from Psalms 39: "Hear my prayer, O Lord, and give ear unto my cry; hold not thy peace at my tears; for I am a stranger with thee, and a sojourner, as all my fathers were." Mothers, too, I feel compelled to add. Sojourner, yes, but this need not mean "tourist". My lifetime here is a short span, but I am not here as a visitor. Earth is my home. I have tried to read as widely as I can; I have always believed I had to live as well as write, to be a citizen and a person and a mother and a friend as well as a writer. But basically, I have spent a great part of my adult life in learning a profession – or, as I prefer to call it, a trade – that can never be mastered in its complexity and richness. I am fond of the story about the brain surgeon, who, meeting a novelist at a party, says "Oh ... you're a novelist, eh? When I retire, I plan to take up novel writing." "How interesting," the novelist replies. "When I retire, I plan to take up brain surgery."

Well, an acceptance of limitations does not mean that one is not constantly trying to extend the boundaries of knowledge and accomplishment. And it certainly does not mean an acceptance of defeat, in whatever fields our endeavors take place. It is my feeling that as we grow older we should become not *less* radical but *more* so. I do not, of course, mean this in any political-party sense, but in a willingness to struggle for those things in which we passionately believe. Social activism and the struggle for social justice are often thought of as natural activities of the young but not of the middle-aged or elderly. In fact, I don't think this was ever true, and certainly in our own era we are seeing an enormous upsurgence of people of all ages who are deeply and commitedly concerned about the state of our hurting and endangered world. There is a line from the old Anglo-Saxon poem, "The Battle of Maldon", that I think of frequently. It is this: "Mind must be the firmer, heart the more fierce, courage the greater, as our strength diminishes."

So the basic message of My Final Hour would have to be – do not despair. Act. Speak out. In the words of one of my heroines,

Catharine Parr Traill, "In cases of emergency, it is folly to fold one's hands and sit down to bewail in abject terror. It is better to be up and doing."

We are faced now with an emergency that concerns not only our own personal lives, but the lives of all people and all creatures on earth. Ours is a terrifying world. Injustice, suffering and fear are everywhere to be found. It is difficult to maintain hope in such a world, and yet I believe there must be hope. I want to proclaim my belief in the social gospel, as a Christian, a woman, a writer, a mother and a member of humanity, a sharer in a life that I believe in some way to be informed by the holy spirit. I do not think it is enough to hope and pray that our own lives and souls will know grace, even though my entire life as a writer has been concerned with my belief that all individual human beings matter, that no one is ordinary. The new commandment of the man of Nazareth speaks very clearly. "Thou shalt love thy neighbor as thyself."

The social gospel is no easier now that it ever was. My generation was the first in human history to come into young adulthood knowing that the human race now had the dreadful ability to destroy all life on earth and possibly the earth itself. Only later did we realize the full extent of the destruction of life, a continuing destruction passed on to the then-unborn children of survivors, but we did know that after Hiroshima, August 6th, 1945, the world would never be the same again. The annihilation caused by the first atomic bombs was unthinkable, but it had happened. Also, we had taken it for granted that through wars, through disasters, yet would the earth endure forever. It was clear to many of us in 1945 that this was no longer to be taken for granted. We have lived with that thought ever since, and have yet borne our children, lived our lives, done our work. The will to survive and to pass on important caring to future generations is very strong. But today we have to realize that the bombs used at Hiroshima and Nagasaki were *small* bombs, compared to today's nuclear weapons.

I ask you to think of the Holocaust in Europe, when the Nazis murdered a very great part of all the Jewish communities. That horror, surely, must never be forgotten. No amount of mourning will *ever* be enough for those millions of children, women and men whose lives were torn from them by the group of dehumanized humans who had taken power in Hitler's Germany. Are we to remember the Holocaust and the horrors of Hiroshima and Nagasaki and yet remain silent when we hear today about a "winnable" nuclear war or a "limited nuclear war"? I think not.

Our lives and the lives of all generations as yet unborn are being threatened, as never before, by the increasing possibility of a nuclear war. I believe that the question of disarmament is the most pressing practical, moral and spiritual issue of our times. I'm not talking about abstractions. I'm talking about my life and your life and my kids' lives and the lives of people everywhere. If we value our own lives, and the lives of our children and all children everywhere, if we honour both the past and the future, then we must do everything in our power to work non-violently for peace. These beliefs are not only an integral part of my social and moral stance but of my religious faith as well. Human society now possesses the terrible ability to destroy all life on earth, and our planet itself. Can anyone who has ever marvelled at the miracle of creation – who has ever borne or fathered a beloved child, who has even looked closely at a tree or a plant or a river – fail to feel concerned and indeed anguished, every single day, at this thought?

A central disagreement, of course, exists between those who think that more and yet more nuclear arms will ensure that nuclear arms will never be used, and those of us who believe that the proliferation of nuclear weapons brings us closer all the time to the actuality of nuclear war – a war that no side could possibly win; a war that would be so devastating that we cannot begin to imagine that horror. Whatever we are being told about a "limited" or a "winnable" nuclear war, the fact remains that such a war could destroy all that we, as humankind, have aspired to, have achieved. It could destroy the future, not only of the world's peoples but of all creatures that share our planet with us.

As America and Russia develop more and more nuclear arms, so the other will inevitably respond in kind. Nuclear arms have long since ceased to be a "deterrent", if indeed they were ever so, and have become by their very existence a monstrous threat. Daily, the chances are increasing for a nuclear war to break out by accident, by a failure of the intricate and not totally reliable control and warning systems on either side, or simply by human panic and a mutual mistrust between the super-powers.

Dr. Helen Caldicott, that courageous woman who has done so much in the struggle against nuclear arms, has said that both America and Russia have now enough nuclear weapons to "overkill every person on earth 16 times". Think of that. Do the world's leaders really suppose that it is all just an act on TV and that the dead would get up again and take on a different role in another TV series so they might be killed again and again? I fear greatly that many of the world's leaders have so little imagination and so little real caring that they cannot visualize at all what a nuclear holocaust would mean. Do they really think that they and their families and executive staffs would survive in deep-buried bunkers? And if, by any unlikely chance they did, what kind of a world do they think they would emerge back into? It would be a dead and a putrefying world. Dr. Helen Caldicott says, "If we look behind the headlines and understand the historical perspective, we realize that America is preparing to fight a nuclear war. Now, that should make us all distinctly uncomfortable. In fact, we should be screaming in the streets, if we really care about ourselves, our children, and if we really love this planet." With well-researched figures, Dr. Caldicott also says, "In the event of a nuclear war, we predict that within 30 days after an exchange, 90% of Americans will be dead. So will Canadians, probably Mexicans, certainly Russians, certainly Europeans, the British, and probably the Chinese."

Roger Molander, a former White House nuclear strategist for the National Security Council, in an article in *The Guardian* in April of 1982, tells of one of the many things that made him decide to give up that job. He is now Executive Director of Ground Zero, an anti-nuclear-weapons-project. He says, "The final chance event that confirmed my determination to help correct our flaws involved another military officer. It happened at a meeting in the Pentagon when a Navy Captain offered the view that in America and Europe people were getting too excited over nuclear war. He argued that people were talking as if nuclear war would be the end of the world, when in fact only 500 million people would be killed. Only 500 million. I remember repeating it to myself ... only 500 million..." Exactly. These are cold figures, statistics. It takes no time at all to say 500 million. But it all looks different, as it did to Roger Molander, if we think of each one of those people as our own children, ourselves, our parents, our friends.

It is precisely this failure of the imagination on the part of militarists and leaders that is so dangerous today, the failure to visualize what a nuclear holocaust would mean, the apparent inability to imagine the scorched and charred bodies of children ... our children or children of Russian parents or parents anywhere, and to know, by an extension of imagination that *all* children are our children. The jargon of the militarists is a distortion and a twisting of language, of our human ability to communicate. Language itself becomes the vehicle of concealment and deception. Such words as "overkill" and "megadeath" do not convey in any sense at all what would really happen – the dead, mutilated and dying people clogging the ruined cities and towns like so much unvalued discarded rubbish, the suffering humans screaming for help with no medical help available, no water, no relief at all for the unbearable pain of millions of humans except finally the dark relief of death for all. Any shelters that the few might reach would in time turn into tombs. Civil defense plans are a sham. In a nuclear war there would be nowhere to hide, and nowhere except a dead and contaminated world to emerge back into.

I profoundly believe that we must proclaim that *this must not happen*.

Yes, but what about the Russians? If we try to persuade our government to refuse cruise missile testing, aren't we playing into the hands of the bad guys? Won't the Soviet Union, as soon as they have clear superiority in nuclear arms, blow us all to hell without a second's thought? I do not think so. Isn't it necessary to have more and ever more nuclear weapons in the hands of the Americans so that we can feel *safe*? I do not think so. Let me make it clear that I hold no brief for the present Russian system of government. I hold no brief for *any* system of government that is repressive and cruel, and this includes those far-right regimes in countries such as El Salvador, to whom the USA is determinedly giving so much military aid. The USA and Russia, the two superpowers, must, I believe, co-exist in this world, even if there are some terrible things wrong in *both* systems, and *there are*. Russia suffered horribly in World War II, whereas war has not been fought on American soil since the Civil War. I cannot believe that the Russian leaders are all that anxious to begin another war in which the Soviet Union would be, if not totally annihilated, then certainly decimated beyond any hope of recovery. George Kennan, formerly U.S. ambassador to Russia, who has been awarded both the Pulitzer Prize and the Albert Einstein Peace Prize, and who is a distinguished diplomat, academic and writer, says in his book "The Nuclear Delusion", "Aren't we then ... being unrealistic in the amount of attention we devote to protecting ourselves from the Russians who, God knows, are not ten feet tall, who have all sorts of troubles of their own, who can't run an agricultural system that really works, who can't adequately house their population, who are rapidly losing their prestige and leadership in the world Communist movement, and have to reckon with China on their long frontier in the East? Isn't it grotesque to spend so much of our energy on opposing such a Russia in order to save a West which is honeycombed with bewilderment and a profound sense of internal decay?"

Quite frankly, I can't believe that Russia any longer has hopes of a world revolution. I can believe, though, that the Russian people, the ordinary people who love their children just as much as I love mine, are frightened, just as I am frightened, just as a very large proportion of the American people are frightened and are expressing that fear and outrage. The American people are indeed our cousins, and a very great many of them, young and old, are saying virtually the same things as I am saying here.

No American president has as yet declared himself willing to embrace a policy of "no first strike" in terms of nuclear weapons. President Reagan recently made the statement that America must reduce Marxism-Leninism "to the ash heap of history". If he proposed to do this by making his country such a true and fine example of social justice, of caring for the poor, of equal rights for women, of peace-making on the international scene, and of a refusal to support corrupt and violent regimes in, say, Central and South America, so that people the world over would look to America, as indeed once they did, as the home of the free, then I would say – *Great.* But I do not think that is what he had in mind. The President also, not long ago, addressed a group of fundamentalist Christians and told them that good and evil exist in the world and that the good must utterly destroy the evil. By evil, he was not referring to organized crime in his own land, or unemployment or poverty in the richest nation in the world. He was talking about

America as wearing the white cowboy hat (to use a metaphor from his Hollywood days) and Russia wearing the black one. Good guys and bad guys. George Kennan says, "I do not have, and have never had, any sympathy for the ideology of the Soviet leadership. I know that this is a regime with which it is not possible for us to have a fully satisfactory relationship. I know that there are many important matters on which no collaboration between us is possible, just as there are other matters on which we can collaborate. There are a number of Soviet habits and practises that I deeply deplore..." He goes on to say, "All this being said, I must ... say that I find the view of the Soviet Union that prevails today in large portions of our governmental and journalistic establishments so extreme, so subjective, so far removed from what any sober scrutiny of external reality would reveal, that it is not only ineffective but dangerous as a guide to political action." He concludes this portion of an essay written in 1981 by saying, "And we shall not be able to turn these things around as they should be turned, in the plane of military and nuclear rivalry, until we learn to correct these childish distortions ... until we correct our tendency to see in the Soviet Union only a mirror in which we look for the reflection of our own virtue – until we consent to see there another great people, one of the world's greatest, in all its complexity and variety, embracing the good with the bad, a people whose life, whose views, whose habits, whose fears and aspirations, whose successes and failures, are the products, just as ours are the products, not of any inherent iniquity but of the relentless discipline of history, tradition and national experience. Above all, we must learn to see the behavior of the leadership of that country as partly the reflection of our own treatment of it. If we insist of demonizing these Soviet leaders ... on viewing them as total and incorrigible enemies, consumed only with their fear or hatred of us and dedicated to nothing other than our destruction – that, in the end, is the way we shall assuredly have them, if for no other reason than that our view of them allows for nothing else, either for them or for us." In a moving essay written in 1982, entitled "A Christian's View of the Arms Race", Kennan also says, "... utterly unacceptable, from the Christian viewpoint as I see it, is the holding of innocent people hostage to the policies of their government, and the readiness, or the threat to punish them as a means of punishing their government."

Our Prime Minister recently asked the NDP leader, Ed Broadbent, who was seeking to have the whole issue of the Cruise missile testing debated in the Commons, if he, Broadbent, had written to Soviet leader Andropov to tell *him* to stop testing, too. This snide remark was, of course, beside the point. Our federal government, at the present time talking out of both sides of its collective mouth, says that on the one hand the actual testing of the Cruise hasn't yet been agreed upon and on the other hand Canada must honour its commitment to NATO. According to Pauline Jewett, NDP defense critic, who has done much research on this matter, Canada's commitment to NATO does *not* include the necessity of our allowing *America* – America, not NATO – to test nuclear weapons here. My point is that Canada could have ... and must have, in my view ... considerable impact as a mediator in nuclear arm talks, as a non-nuclear nation, as a country that might conceivably be helpful in lowering the present climate of hysteria between the two superpowers, and in bringing about world disarmament.

This is why I think we must keep on trying to make our government hear us. Why would I write to Andropov or Reagan? I don't have a vote or a voice in those countries. I have both vote and voice here, though.

I believe that our land should be declared a nuclear-weapons-free zone, with absolutely no testing of nuclear arms or production of parts for those arms allowed in our country. I think that Canada could do a great deal to bring about a gradual and verifiable reduction of nuclear arms by both sides, monitored by neutral countries such as the Scandinavian countries, and to bring about a freeze on the production and testing of nuclear weapons. Canada could be a strong influence for a "no-first-strike" agreement among nations, for multilateral disarmament and for world peace.

Canada is not powerless nor are we insignificant in a world sense. Yet our present government appears to be quite willing to allow the Cruise missile to be tested over our land, in Alberta. The Cruise missile, an American nuclear weapon, was not designed as a deterrent weapon – it was designed as a "first strike weapon". Its presence in the nuclear arsenal will not be verifiable, thus making any kind of nuclear-weapons control virtually impossible. The Litton plant in Ontario is producing, with the aid of millions of *our* tax dollars, guidance systems for the Cruise missile. Canada has sold nuclear reactors to such repressive regimes as Argentina, and is delivering fuel for those reactors, despite the fact that our government is aware that nuclear weapons could soon be within Argentina's capability. These are only a few of the many examples of Canada's complicity in the nuclear arms race.

Do we care so little about our children? Do we honour life so little that we will not speak out? I believe we do care, passionately and profoundly. Indeed, one thing that gives me hope is that so many of our churches and synagogues, so many people of all faiths, of all professions and trades, of all ages, are speaking out against the arms race and the descent into total madness. *Physicians For Social Responsibility,* active in this country as well as America and elsewhere, are telling us what human damage would be done, and how impossible any thought of medical aid would be in a nuclear war. Inter-church groups such as *Project Ploughshares* are making strong representations to our government, as are labour unions, academics and indeed and perhaps most importantly, women and men everywhere, in every walk of life. This is true in so very many places in the world today. When I speak of lobbying our own government, that is because we must begin where we are. But we join our voices with those everywhere who believe as we do.

The money spent on arms, including nuclear arms, continues to mount. Recently I read that $550 billion dollars are being spent, world-wide, yearly, on arms. An even more recent estimate puts it at $600 billion dollars. That sum is so great we cannot really comprehend it. But we *can* comprehend that for the cost of *one* Trident nuclear submarine, malaria could be wiped out from the world. Think of that for one minute. I think of the people in the world who are suffering from thirst, from starvation, from preventable diseases, from ceaseless fighting and the brutality of oppressive regimes. I think, too, of the growing number of unemployed people in our own land. I think of the Reagan program in America – more and yet more money spent on nuclear arms; less and less spent on social programs and help to the poor and the disabled.

I have to speak about how I feel as a writer. I don't like calling myself "an artist", but I guess I am, and would join with my tribal sisters and brothers in many ways. I believe that as a writer ...

an artist, if you will ... I have a responsibility, a moral responsibility, to work against the nuclear arms race, to work for a recognition on the part of governments and military leaders that nuclear weapons must never be used and must systematically be reduced. Throughout human history, artists have affirmed and celebrated life. Whether we work in words, in music, in painting, in film, in bronze or stone or whatever our medium may be, the artist affirms the value of life itself and of our only home, the planet Earth. Art mirrors and ponders the pain and joy of our experience as human beings. In many parts of the world, and over many centuries, artists have risked and even given their own lives to portray the society around them as they perceived it, and to speak out against injustices. Since the most ancient times, artists have passed on to succeeding generations the tales, the histories, the songs, the sagas, the skills of their trade. Can we conceive of a world in which there would be no succeeding generations? A world in which all the powerful works of the human imagination would be destroyed, would never again be seen or listened to or experienced? We must conceive that this is now a possibility, and one not too far in our uncertain future, either. We must not, as artists, or so I feel, stand by and passively allow this to happen. The death of the individual is the end which we will all one day meet, but in the knowledge that our children and their children will live, that *someone's* children will go on, that the great works of humankind will endure in art, in recorded history, in medicine, in the sciences and philosophies and technologies that our species has developed with devotion and a sense of vocation throughout the ages. The individual is the leaf on the tree. The leaves fall but the tree endures. New leaves are born. This concept has been the mainstay of our species from time immemorial. Now the tree itself is threatened. All art is a product of the human imagination. It is, deeply, an honouring of the past, a perception of the present in one way or another, and a looking towards the future. Whatever the medium of any particular artist, art is a reaching out, an attempt to communicate those things which most concern us seriously in our sojourn here on earth. Artists, the real ones, the committed ones, have always sought, sometimes in ways prophetic and beyond their own times, to clarify and proclaim and enhance life, not to obscure and demean and destroy it. Even the so-called literature of despair is not really that at all. Despair is total silence, total withdrawal. Art by its very nature of necessary expression, is an act of faith, an acknowledgement of the profound mystery at the core of life.

As a writer, therefore, I feel I have a responsibility. Not to write pamphlets; not to write didactic fiction. That would be, in many ways, a betrayal of how I feel about my work. But my responsibility seems to me to be to write as truthfully as I can, about human individuals and their dilemmas, to honour them as living, suffering and sometimes joyful people. My responsibility also must extend into my life as a citizen of my own land and ultimately of the world.

I do not claim to have done this well. There are no personal victories in those areas. The individual, here, becomes part of a community and only as a part of that community can one person ever be effective and true to herself or himself. There has to be the resolve not to give up, and to join with all others who believe that life itself is more important than our own individual lives, important though these certainly are.

Dr. Helen Caldicott speaks of "psychic numbing", the temptation to shut out from our minds and hearts all the terrifying things in our world. To think that the problems may just possibly go away if we ignore them. To feel that we are totally helpless, and so ... why bother trying to do anything? What Dr. Caldicott calls "psychic numbing" I would call "despair", and although I would take issue with the early Church Fathers on many things, I would agree that despair is rightly placed as one of the deadly sins. The problems of our world will not go away if we ignore them. It is not all happening on TV. It is happening on our earth, and we, humankind, are the custodians of that earth. We cannot afford passivity. We must take on responsibility for our lives and our world and we must be prepared to make our government listen to and hear us. Our aim must be no less than human and caring justice, and peace ... *for all people that on earth do dwell.*

So, if this were indeed my Final Hour, these would be my words to you. I would not claim to pass on any secret of life, for there is none, or any wisdom except the passionate plea of caring. In your dedication to your own life's work, whatever it may be, live as though you had forever, for no amount of careful and devoted doing is too great in carrying out that work to which you have set your hands. Cultivate in your work and your life the art of patience, and come to terms with your inevitable human limitations, while striving also to extend the boundaries of your understanding, your knowledge and your compassion. These words are easily said; they are not easily lived. Learn from those who are older than you are; learn from your contemporaries; and never cease to learn from children. Try to feel, in your heart's core, the reality of others. This is the most painful thing in the world, probably, and the most necessary. In times of personal adversity, know that you are not alone. Know that although in the eternal scheme of things you are small, you are also unique and irreplaceable, as are all your fellow humans everywhere in the world. Know that your commitment is above all to life itself. Your own life and work and friendships and loves will come to an end, because one day you will die, and whatever happens after that, or if anything happens at all, it will not be on this earth. But life and work and friendship and love will go on, in others, your inheritors. The struggle for peace and for social justice will go on – provided that our earth survives and that caring humans still live. It is up to you, now, to do all that you can, and that means a commitment, as this perilous moment in our human history, to ensure that life itself *will* go on.

In closing, I want to quote one verse from that mighty book ... more like a vast library ... that Dr. Northrop Frye calls "The Great Code", and which has so shaped, sometimes so ambiguously, the imagination, the art and the many facets of faith in our world. This verse is from Deuteronomy, Chapter 30.

"I have set before you life and death, blessing and cursing; therefore choose life, that both thou and thy seed may live."

Notes on Contributors

David Blewett, Professor of English at McMaster University, is the author of *Defoe's Art of Fiction* (University of Toronto Press) and the editor of Defoe's *Roxana* and Fielding's *Amelia* (Penguin Classics). He occasionally ventures into more modern fiction to teach a course on the Bloomsbury Group and to write about Canadian Fiction.

Robert D. Chambers was born in Montreal and educated at Lower Canada College, McGill University, and Oxford. After a decade of teaching at the University of Saskatchewan (Saskatoon), he joined the faculty at Trent University where he has been Chairman of the Department of English Literature and University Vice-President. He has held visiting professorships at the University of Waikato (Hamilton, New Zealand) and Duke University (Durham, North Carolina). His publications include critical studies of Ernest Buckler, Margaret Laurence, Hugh MacLennan, and Sinclair Ross. He will shortly publish a critical study of the English novel of the eighteenth century.

Marian Engel, author of several works of fiction, won the Governor-General's Award for her 1976 novel *Bear*. She was the first Chairperson of the Writers' Union of Canada (1973-74). She has been awarded posthumously the Order of Canada.

Sherrill Grace is Professor of English at the University of British Columbia. She has published widely on modern literature, especially Canadian fiction, and is the author of books on Margaret Atwood and Malcolm Lowry. She has recently completed a major study of North American Expressionism.

Evelyn J. Hinz is Professor of English at the University of Manitoba. Editor of *MOSAIC: A Journal for the Interdisciplinary Study of Literature* since 1979, she is also President of the Conference of Editors of Learned Journals. Winner of the William Riley Parker Prize for an outstanding essay published in *PMLA*, she has published numerous books and articles on a wide variety of authors and subjects, including a recent essay, "Milton, Whitman, Wolfe and Laurence: *The Stone Angel* as Elegy" (with John J. Teunissen).

Kenneth Hughes teaches English and Canadian Literature at St. John's College, University of Manitoba. He is the author of *The Life and Art of Jackson Beardy, Manitoba Art Monographs, Signs of Literature,* and numerous articles on literature, visual arts and general culture. He is currently working on two books for Talon: on visual art: *The Unbroken Body*; and on literature: *Cultural Materialism: Reading Literary Texts, Chaucer to Yeats.*

John Lennox is Director of The Robarts Centre for Canadian Studies and the Graduate Program in English at York University. He is co-author with Clara Thomas of *William Deacon: A Canadian Literary Life* (University of Toronto Press, 1982) and co-editor with Michèle Lacombe of *Dear Bill: The Correspondence of William Arthur Deacon* (forthcoming, University of Toronto Press, Fall 1988).

Patricia Morley is a teacher and a writer. At Concordia University, Montreal, she is Professor of English and Canadian Studies, and a Fellow of the Simone de Beauvoir Institute. Her numerous publications include some seven hundred book reviews, scores of articles, and eight books on Canadian and Commonwealth writers and painters. *Margaret Laurence* (Boston, 1981) and *Kurelek. A Biography* (Toronto, 1986) are her most recent books.

W.H. New is Professor of English at the University of British Columbia and editor of the critical quarterly *Canadian Literature.* He has published numerous essays on Canadian and Commonwealth writing, and his books include *Articulating West* and *Dreams of Speech and Violence: The Art of the Short Story in Canada and New Zealand.*

Michael Peterman is a Professor of English at Trent University and is the current editor of the *Journal of Canadian Studies.* He has co-edited *Susanna Moodie: Letters of a Lifetime* (1985) with Carl Ballstadt and Elizabeth Hopkins and has written *Robertson Davies* (1986) for the Twayne World Authors series.

Clara Thomas is Professor Emeritus (English), York University, and York University Libraries' Canadian Studies Research Fellow.

Christl Verduyn is Chair of the Women's Studies Program at Trent University where she is cross-appointed with French Studies. She is Book Editor for the *Journal of Canadian Studies.* She publishes in French and English on feminist writing and literary theory in Québec and English Canada and is preparing an extended study on contemporary women's writing in Canada.

Susan J. Warwick teaches Canadian and American Literature at York University.

George Woodcock was born in Winnipeg in 1912, but went to England as a child, returning to Canada in 1949. His first books of poetry and prose were published in England, where he edited NOW from 1940 to 1947. In Canada he founded *Canadian Literature* in 1959 and edited it until 1977. He has written many books of biography, history, criticism, verse, of which the best known are *Anarchism* and *The Crystal Spirit: A Study of George Orwell.* He has written much on Canadian writers and his most recent book of criticism is *Northern Spring.* His second volume of autobiography, *Beyond the Blue Mountain,* has just been published.